HANDYMAN'S HANDBOOK

The Complete Guide to Starting and Running a Successful Business

DAVID KOENIGSBERG

McGraw-Hill

New York   Chicago   San Francisco   Lisbon   London   Madrid
Mexico City   Milan   New Delhi   San Juan   Seoul
Singapore   Sydney   Toronto

The McGraw·Hill Companies

Library of Congress Cataloging-in-Publication Data

Koenigsberg, David.
    Handyman's handbook : the complete guide to starting and running a
successful business / David Koenigsberg.
        p.   cm.
    Includes index.
    ISBN 0-07-141670-6
    1. Dwellings—Maintenance and repair—Vocational guidance.   2. Dwellings—
Maintenance and repair—Miscellanea.   I. Title.

TH4815.K62   2003
690'.24—dc21   2003046340

1 2 3 4 5 6 7 8 9 0   DOC/DOC   0 9 8 7 6 5 4 3

ISBN 0-07-141670-6

*The sponsoring editor for this book was Cary Sullivan, the editing supervisor was
Stephen M. Smith, and the production supervisor was Pamela A. Pelton. It was set
in Fairfield Medium by Kim J. Sheran of McGraw-Hill Professional's Hightstown,
N.J., composition unit.*

Printed and bound by RR Donnelley.

McGraw-Hill books are available at special quantity discounts to use as premiums
and sales promotions, or for use in corporate training programs. For more information, please write to the Director of Special Sales, McGraw-Hill Professional, Two
Penn Plaza, New York, NY 10121-2298. Or contact your local bookstore.

 This book is printed on recycled, acid-free paper
containing a minimum of 50% recycled, de-inked fiber.

CONTENTS

Preface   vii

Basics

CHAPTER 1. WHAT DOES A HANDYMAN DO?   1

CHAPTER 2. GETTING STARTED: FREQUENTLY REQUESTED JOBS   4

CHAPTER 3. OTHER JOBS YOU CAN DO   8

CHAPTER 4. ACQUIRING KNOWLEDGE AND SKILLS   20

CHAPTER 5. ADAPTING YOUR CAR   31

CHAPTER 6. ITEMS TO CARRY IN YOUR CAR   35

Tools You Should Have

CHAPTER 7. BUYING TOOLS   43

CHAPTER 8. YOUR TOOLBOX   45

CHAPTER 9. ORGANIZING YOUR TOOLS   52

CHAPTER 10. CEMENT-WORK TOOLS   53

CHAPTER 11. ELECTRICAL-WORK TOOLS   56

CHAPTER 12. GARDENING AND TREE TOOLS   59

CHAPTER 13. LAYOUT AND MEASURING TOOLS   66

CHAPTER 14. PAINTING AND CAULKING TOOLS   70

CHAPTER 15. PLUMBING TOOLS   74

CHAPTER 16. PORTABLE POWER TOOLS   78

CHAPTER 17. STATIONARY POWER TOOLS   82

CHAPTER 18. OTHER USEFUL TOOLS   84

Hardware You Should Have

CHAPTER 19. BUYING HARDWARE   93

CHAPTER 20. DOOR HARDWARE   94

CHAPTER 21. ELECTRICAL-WORK HARDWARE   97

CHAPTER 22. NAILS, SCREWS, BOLTS, AND OTHER FASTENERS   104

CHAPTER 23. HANGING OBJECTS ON WALLS   110

CHAPTER 24. HOSE-REPAIR HARDWARE   114

CHAPTER 25. PLUMBING HARDWARE   116

CHAPTER 26. TELEPHONE HARDWARE   122

CHAPTER 27. OTHER USEFUL HARDWARE   125

Materials You Should Have

CHAPTER 28. CAULKING   131

CHAPTER 29. PAINTS AND PUTTY   134

CHAPTER 30. GLUES   138

CHAPTER 31. LUBRICANTS   141

CHAPTER 32. TAPES   143

CHAPTER 33. WOOD   145

CHAPTER 34. OTHER USEFUL MATERIALS   147

Equipment You Should Have

CHAPTER 35. LADDERS   151

CHAPTER 36. WORKBENCH WITH VISE   154

CHAPTER 37. OTHER USEFUL EQUIPMENT   155

Organizing and Storing Your Hardware and Materials

CHAPTER 38. BOXES   159

CHAPTER 39. SHELVES, HOOKS, RACKS, BUCKETS   165

Customer Relations

CHAPTER 40. FINDING CUSTOMERS   172

CHAPTER 41. KEEPING YOUR CUSTOMERS HAPPY   177

CHAPTER 42. HOW MUCH TO CHARGE   185

Additional Advice and Information

CHAPTER 43. BEFORE YOU GO TO THE JOB   188

CHAPTER 44. BEFORE YOU LEAVE THE JOB   191

CHAPTER 45. WORK EFFICIENTLY   194

CHAPTER 46. WORK SAFELY   201

CHAPTER 47. IMPROVISING   204

CHAPTER 48. BIG PAINT JOBS   **210**

CHAPTER 49. OLD HOUSE VERSUS NEW HOUSE   **216**

CHAPTER 50. THOUGHTS AND SUGGESTIONS   **219**

CHAPTER 51. YARD SALE AND FLEA MARKET TACTICS   **234**

CHAPTER 52. RECORD KEEPING AND FINANCES   **241**

CHAPTER 53. CLOTHING FOR THE HANDYMAN   **243**

CHAPTER 54. FOOD AND EXERCISE   **248**

CHAPTER 55. HANDYMAN MYSTERIES   **250**

Final Words   254
Index   255

PREFACE

If you enjoy working with your hands and would like to be happily and profitably self-employed for life as a professional handyman or handywoman, this book is for you. It tells you where and how to learn what you will need to know, how to acquire and store the tools and materials you will need, which jobs are the most frequently requested, how to adapt your car or truck, and how to find and keep your customers.

There are dozens of timesaving tips that will help you work better and faster. If you are already a capable handyman but have used your abilities only for projects around your own home, here is a road map to using your skills to earn a good living for as long as you wish.

I use the word "handyman" for simplicity but, of course, with the possible exception of handling heavy ladders or heavy sledge hammers, anything a male handyman can do, a woman can do just as well. So if you are female, you should not hesitate to become a handywoman if you are so inclined. The word "tradesman" refers to any carpenter, painter, plumber, drywaller, cement worker, roofer, etc.

Let my more than 25 years of experience as a handyman be your guide. If you are willing to study in order to learn what to do and practice until you learn how to do it, then nothing can prevent you from succeeding. This book will help you achieve your goals.

David Koenigsberg

ABOUT THE AUTHOR

David Koenigsberg of Roslyn, Pennsylvania, is an electrical engineer, technical writer, and professional handyman with more than 25 years' experience in the field.

WHAT DOES A HANDYMAN DO?

What a Handyman Does	1	Pros	2
Who Should Be a Handyman	1	Cons	3
Why Homeowners Need a Handyman	2		

WHAT A HANDYMAN DOES

As a handyman, you will go to someone's home or place of business to do fixing, building, or painting. Typically, you will do several small jobs at each visit. You may do electrical work or plumbing, patch a leaky roof, repair doors and windows, erect shelves, service appliances, and fix bikes, toys, and so on. You may even do some work on automobiles if you have the knowledge and inclination.

One of the most useful things you can do for a customer is to walk around the inside and outside of the house with your clipboard, a flashlight, and an ice pick to probe for rot and termite damage, and with binoculars to inspect the roof, and then make a list of things that need attention. Very few homeowners will request this service, so you should suggest it. Nowhere is it more true than with a house that an ounce of prevention is worth a pound of cure, especially if you see a place where water is starting to get in that could cause extensive and expensive damage.

WHO SHOULD BE A HANDYMAN

Do you like to work with your hands? Do you like to build and fix things? Do you like to take things apart just to see how they work? Do you like to stop and watch when you walk by a house or building being constructed? Are you fascinated by all those shiny new tools you see in the hardware store window? Would you like to be your own boss? Then perhaps you should consider being a professional handyman or handywoman.

WHY HOMEOWNERS NEED A HANDYMAN

Most things that need fixing around a house take only a few hours, or sometimes even less than an hour, to accomplish. If a home needs a new washer in the kitchen faucet, a new electrical outlet in the laundry room, and perhaps a door planed down so it will close properly, a handyman can do all three things in one visit. That saves the homeowner a lot of money compared to paying a plumber, an electrician, and a carpenter to do the work. Furthermore, the plumber, electrician, and carpenter usually are not interested in that kind of business. Many homeowners have told me they simply can't get tradesmen to come for a small job. It is understandable; a tradesman wants to have his truck, his equipment, and his helper doing big jobs where he can make much more money.

PROS

You are your own boss and have considerable control over when, where, and for whom you work. Almost every day is different; you won't get bored. There are always new challenges and you are always learning. You are always meeting new people, most of whom are very nice. There is great satisfaction in going to people's homes, doing various jobs, seeing how pleased they are, and knowing that you have made life a little better for them.

You can go into handyman work any time you feel ready. You don't have to submit any resumes or endure any job interviews. Just as you have been surfing at Malibu or hitchhiking in the Himalayas for the past 3 years, you don't have to explain to anyone. You don't need a college degree or a high school diploma. You don't even need a computer.

Unlike with many businesses, where thousands or tens of thousands of dollars are required to start up, the initial investment for a handyman, especially if you start up by doing small paint jobs, can be close to zero.

Once you have mastered your craft, you can be gainfully employed for life. There is no age limit. In good times or bad, there will always be plenty of people who own houses or apartments and who will need things fixed or built or painted. No one can fire you. No one can move your job overseas.

As you become knowledgeable about how houses are built and how they function, you can consider becoming a home inspector, which may pay better than handyman work.

When you become adept at plumbing, electrical work, and HVAC (heating, ventilating, air-conditioning) you can always find a job in the "Help

Wanted" ads. Look under "Handyman" or "Maintenance." You may get a job as a maintenance person for an apartment building. You might get one of the apartments rent-free, and sometimes with a salary in addition.

You can also buy, rehabilitate (sometimes called "renovate"), and sell houses that are run down and in need of repair. These houses are sometimes known as fixer-uppers or handyman specials. Many people make an extremely good living doing these rehabs. You must, of course, know a good deal about the housing market as well as how to do repairs to be successful. Get on friendly terms with some local realtors and they will be of great help.

CONS

You may not make as much money, especially in the beginning, as you might make at a regular 9 to 5 job, even though your hourly rate may be quite good. That is because you can expect to work only 50 to 75 percent of the time. You will have to spend time discussing jobs with the homeowners. Unlike a lawyer, you can't bill for this time. You will spend time shopping for materials; not every hardware store or home center will have what you need. You will spend time loading things into your car and driving to the customer's home. You will have to spend time reading or researching to learn how to do particular jobs. You may finish up at one place a little early but it may be too late to start at another place the same day.

There are no paid vacations, no sick leave, no medical benefits. You will have to plan for those yourself.

GETTING STARTED: FREQUENTLY REQUESTED JOBS

GETTING STARTED

Probably the easiest way to get started is to do small paint jobs for friends, neighbors, and relatives. If, in addition to painting, you can do small carpentry jobs, plumbing repairs, and electrical repairs, you are ready to begin your career as a handyperson.

At first, you should only be concerned with doing a good job and building up your list of satisfied customers and not expect to be making much money. Then, as your self-confidence and knowledge increase, you can branch out and do other jobs as well.

As you learn to do jobs more efficiently, and use more power tools to save time, your income will gradually increase.

FREQUENTLY REQUESTED JOBS

Below is a list of frequently requested jobs. The more of them you can learn to do, the more versatile you will be as a handyman and the more work you will get.

Air Conditioner   Install an air conditioner in a window. Clean or replace filters.

Assemble Kits   Assemble furniture, toys, barbecues, sheds, etc.

Batteries   Install batteries in various devices (smoke alarms, phones, flashlights, answering machines, toys).

Blacktop Driveways Do patching, crack filling, or coating of driveways.

Ceiling Fans Install ceiling fans.

Chairs and Tables Fix chairs and tables that are coming apart.

Concrete Walls or Walks Repair cracks in concrete walls or walks.

Doorbells Fix doorbells that don't work.

Doors Fix doors that don't open or close or lock properly. Plane or cut a slice off of door bottoms that are scraping the carpeting.

Drain Pipes Fix stopped-up or leaking drain pipes under sinks, bathtubs, or showers.

Drawers Fix drawers that won't open or close properly.

Drywall Repair Patch cracks or holes in drywall.

Electrical Lines Install new lines for air conditioners, microwaves, etc.

Electrical Outlets Replace defective electrical outlets. Install new electrical outlets.

Faucets Fix leaky faucets.

Furnace Filters Replace furnace filters.

Garage Doors Adjust, lubricate, or repair, garage doors.

Garbage Disposals Fix garbage disposals that are jammed or nonfunctioning.

Garden Hoses Fix leaky garden hoses.

Gates and Fences   Install or repair gates and fences.

Hooks   Install hooks in ceilings to hold hanging flower pots.

House Numbers   Install numbers on the house, porch, lawn, or mailbox.

Light Fixtures   Install light fixtures in kitchens, basements, attics, etc. Fix indoor or outdoor lights that don't work.

Light Switches   Replace defective light switches.

Painting and Caulking   Paint and caulk where required.

Pictures and Mirrors   Hang pictures and mirrors.

Roofs   Fix leaking roofs.

Showerheads   Fix or replace defective showerheads.

Sinks and Bathtubs   Caulk around sinks and bathtubs. Install shutoff valves for sinks.

Storm Windows and Screens   Fix storm windows and screens that don't work properly. Open clogged drain holes in storm windows.

Summer-Winter Changeover   Take screens down. Put storm windows up. Turn outside water off. Put hoses into storage. Clean rain gutters.

Toilets   Fix toilets that run continuously or don't flush properly. Install shutoff valves for toilets.

Trees and Bushes   Prune trees and bushes.

Vinyl Flooring or Cove Molding   Reglue or replace vinyl flooring or cove molding.

Windows   Replace broken glass. Make windows open and close properly.

Winter-Summer Changeover   Rake up the leaves left over from the previous year, pick up broken branches, take storm windows down, put screens up, turn water on, attach hoses, clean leaves and other debris out of the rain gutters, and inspect the outside of the house, especially roof, gutters, and downspouts for winter damage.

OTHER JOBS YOU CAN DO

Assembly Required	9	Lubricating Household Devices	16
Bicycles	9	Moving-Day Assistance	16
Boats	10	Noise Reduction	16
Cars	10	Organizing a Home Office	17
Exercise Equipment	11	Outdoor Play Equipment	17
Extending the Life of a Roof	11	Painting the Power Drop	17
Eyeglasses	12	Pest Control	17
Home Security	12	Preparing a House for Sale	18
Hurricanes and Tornadoes	13	Sharpening Tools	18
Insulating Pipes	14	Sheds	19
Jewelry Repair	14	Storage Systems	19
Keeping Water out of Basements	14	Telephones	19
Labeling Circuit Breakers, Fuses, and Valves	15		

When you hear the term "handyman," you usually think of someone who does small carpentry projects, plumbing repairs, electrical repairs, and other jobs to keep the house working properly. But there are also many other tasks you can do for your customers if you have the desire and knowledge. And the more tasks you can do, the more interesting, challenging, and varied your workday will be.

You can make up a printed list of items that you can usually fix, and give a copy of the list to anyone for whom you are presently working. Here are some of the possible jobs, in alphabetical order. Also included here is further information on some of the jobs in the "most requested" list.

ASSEMBLY REQUIRED

Many items are shipped as a kit of parts which the purchaser must assemble. You may be asked to do this assembling from time to time. This is not always as easy or straightforward as you might expect.

Some of the instruction sheets that come with kits are clear, accurate, and easy to follow. But many are truly dreadful. Other instructions are just plain unintelligible (attach clevis Z to gusset B as in Fig. 3A, except for models 5J through 5W; see page 11-2). Some instructions have been translated word for word from a foreign language. Some have pictures that are dark and murky and impossible to understand. Some have drawings that are so poorly done, or so reduced in size, as to be useless. Sometimes the drawings or the parts lists do not correspond to what is actually in the kit.

One woman for whom I was assembling some kits stated that if she was given a kit of parts and the assembly instructions and someone put a gun to her head and told her she had 1 hour to do the assembly, she would just say, "Go ahead and shoot."

The worst case I ever came across was a set of motorized beds that a couple had bought as kits. These beds had motors to raise the mattress behind the head or under the knees to make the bed like a recliner chair, which was very comfortable for eating or reading in bed.

After struggling with those bed kits for 2 days, these people called me. When I arrived, I found that the diagram on the front of the box was different from the diagram on the instruction sheets, and neither diagram corresponded with the parts that were in the box. In order to make those kits work properly, I had to drill some new holes in the bed frames, install longer bolts than those which were supplied, and add some heavy metal straps to hold the beds side by side as intended. Problems such as these arise when a manufacturer makes changes in the design without changing the box or the instructions or the hardware.

So there will be times when you will be better off to ignore the instructions and just study the pile of parts until you understand how they were intended to be used. And don't be too surprised if some of the fasteners are not the right size.

BICYCLES

If you have any appreciation of ingenious mechanical design, you will marvel at how bicycles have evolved to be light, strong, simple, and reliable. In most cases, when a bicycle needs repair, you can figure out what is wrong and what to do about it just by studying the problem, moving the parts, and seeing what happens (or doesn't happen). It's a lot more fun than fixing cars, where you have to crawl inside or underneath and emerge smeared with dirt and grease. There are several good books on bicycle repair, and it pays to cultivate the friendship of someone at your local bicycle shop.

BOATS

Boats often need the kind of repairs that a nonspecialist can do. If you are working on the exterior of the boat, use hardware, such as bolts, screws, brackets, and hinges that don't rust or corrode (stainless steel, solid brass, or bronze). Plated or "corrosion resistant" items are not good enough, especially if the boat is used on salt water.

Boats frequently need caulking. For most uses on a boat, silicone caulk is best. Another skill, very useful when doing boat repairs, is working with fiberglass cloth and polyester or epoxy resin. It is not difficult to learn how to do this.

CARS

Most of your customers will own a car. There are many things on a car that you can fix and customers will be very appreciative because it saves them the time of taking the car to a service station and waiting or having to go back again.

I would not attempt to work on an engine or a transmission, but here is a partial list of work on cars that anyone with some mechanical ability can do.

Antenna   Fix or replace the antenna.

Battery   Tighten or replace the hold-down clamp. Clean, tighten, or replace cables. Charge or replace the battery.

Bumpers   Tighten loose bumpers or fenders.

Doors and Windows   Fix doors or windows that won't open or close properly.

License Plates   Install new license plates.

Oil   Add oil. Also, add battery water, brake fluid, coolant, and window-washer fluid.

Roof   Paint the car roof (with rust-resistant paint to prevent further rusting or with white paint to keep the car cooler in summer).

Roof Racks   Tighten loose roof rack straps. Replace deteriorated suction cups.

Rusty Areas   Apply rust-retardant compound to rusty areas. Patch holes with sheet metal or fiberglass.

Seat Belts   Fix seat belts that don't latch or retract properly.

Spare-Tire Racks   Tighten loose tire racks. Lubricate the hold-down screw.

Tires   Rotate tires, mount snow tires, replace leaky valves.

Wipers   Fix or replace defective wipers.

EXERCISE EQUIPMENT

Many people have exercise devices in their homes. There isn't much that can go wrong with a dumbbell or a barbell, but when it comes to stationary bikes, treadmills, steppers, etc., anything that has moving parts may need servicing from time to time. Except for the electronics, if they have any, most exercise devices are easy to fix. If the electronic part of the exercise device is not working, I check for broken wires, blown fuses, loose connections, or dead batteries. If that does not locate the problem, I just tell the homeowner that I can't fix it.

EXTENDING THE LIFE OF A ROOF

Most roofs in the United States are asphalt shingle. These shingles last 15 to 25 or more years, depending on the quality of the shingle and on how much sunlight the roof is exposed to. Most homeowners don't pay any attention to their roofs until they start to leak. At that point, a complete (and expensive) new roof is often the only option.

However, if the shingles are losing the tiny granules of stone (you may see a lot of the granules in the gutters) and bare patches are starting to show, but the shingles are not yet curling or breaking, the life of that roof can be extended many years by coating the roof. It can be coated either with aluminum roof coating, which weathers to a light gray color, or it can be coated with elastomeric (rubbery) roof coating which is available in many colors. The coating can be applied with a brush or a roller. This treatment can save a homeowner the cost of a new roof.

If a homeowner asks for my opinion on roof color, I always suggest white because it reflects sunlight. This keeps the attic cooler, reduces air-conditioning costs, and extends the life of the roof.

You should also cut back any tree branches that are touching or almost touching the roof. The wind can whip these branches back and forth and cause them to tear up the shingles. Branches that overhang the roof, even if not close to it, will drop their leaves into the rain gutters and cause problems. Such branches should also be trimmed.

EYEGLASSES

I save all the old eyeglasses I come across. Sometimes I need one of the tiny screws to replace one that fell out of someone's glasses. Sometimes I can replace a broken temple (the part that goes over your ear) and the glasses are usable until the person goes to the optician. If the frame is broken, it can sometimes be repaired, at least temporarily, with Crazy Glue. Be careful not to get the glue on the lenses.

HOME SECURITY

Unfortunately, many homeowners have to be concerned about being burglarized. You can learn how to lessen the likelihood of a home falling victim to a burglar. Your local police department probably has a pamphlet on what to do. It will make suggestions, such as installing better lighting, better locks, unbreakable windows in doors where a burglar could break a small window and reach in and unlock the door from the inside; trimming bushes that could hide a burglar during a break-in; and many other useful ideas. In addition, you can install various burglar alarm systems.

Electronics stores, such as Radio Shack, and several home security companies sell these devices. You can also install a motion detector that turns on outdoor flood lights when it detects something (person or car) that is moving.

I once had several signs made up that said, "PROTECTED BY DK POLICE ALARM." I installed these signs for many of my customers, some on lawns, some on fences. Even though there was no alarm, it may have acted as a deterrent. You can now buy similar signs from companies that specialize in home security. I think they are a deterrent, they don't cost much, and they may help.

In some localities, the police department will send someone out to look at a home and give suggestions to make the home burglar resistant. There is usually no charge for this useful service.

HURRICANES AND TORNADOES

If you live where hurricanes or tornadoes are a serious threat, new houses are probably being built to be more wind resistant than those of older construction. You can retrofit some existing houses to be better prepared for the possibility of high winds. Some of the jobs that could be done are:

Battery-Operated Lights   These lights can be installed so that they go on automatically when the electric power goes out.

Hurricane Clips   These clips can be installed to reduce the chance of the roof blowing off. These are small metal devices that attach the roof to the walls of the house.

Safe Room   This room can be built in the basement, or on the first floor if there is no basement. This is a small room with very strong walls and ceiling.

Shutters   Shutters can be installed to protect windows from flying debris.

Tree Branches or Entire Trees   Branches or trees may need to be removed, especially if they have rotted areas that may cause them to fall onto the house in a strong wind.

INSULATING PIPES

This is an energy-saving procedure and very easy to do. If the home has hot water running through unheated parts of the house or garage, you slip foam plastic tubing onto the pipes or tubing. The same foam insulation is often applied to the cold water lines to prevent condensation in summer and to help prevent them from freezing in winter.

JEWELRY REPAIR

There are many instances when you can repair jewelry items such as bracelets, brooches, necklaces, rings, and watchbands. Some helpful tools to have when you do jewelry repairs are:

Epoxy Glue   Use the kind that hardens in 5 minutes.

Magnifier   Get an illuminated magnifier, the kind that is mounted on a small stand so that your hands are free.

Pliers   You will need very small needle-nose and cutting pliers.

Screwdrivers   Obtain a set of tiny screwdrivers (sometimes called watchmaker screwdrivers).

Solder   For jewelry repair, very thin rosin-core wire solder is used.

Soldering Iron   On jewelry, use a small soldering iron such as those electronics stores sell for working on printed circuit boards.

If the jewelry is really valuable, I would leave repairs to the jeweler.

KEEPING WATER OUT OF BASEMENTS

This is a very common problem and often a major problem. In many instances, you can minimize or cure this situation. Some of the things you can do to alleviate the wet basement problem are:

Cracks   Patch cracks and holes in the foundation and in the basement walls and paint the basement walls with waterproof paint.

Dirt   Pack dirt around the house, where necessary, to make sure that the ground slopes away from the house. Heavy, claylike subsoil, if you can get it, is preferable to topsoil for this job because it is less permeable to water. If you live in a rural area, dirt is readily available. If you are in an urban area, look around for construction sites and ask if you can take a few buckets of dirt. Try to get dirt that has no stones or other debris mixed in.

Gutters   Clean and repair gutters and downspouts where required.

Leaders   Add leaders to the downspouts. A leader is a nearly horizontal section of downspout attached to the bottom of the existing downspout to discharge the rainwater several feet away from the house.

Pump   Install a sump pump to pump water out of the basement.

Splash Blocks   Add these at the bottoms of the downspouts to carry water away from the house.

LABELING CIRCUIT BREAKERS, FUSES, AND VALVES

A useful task that many homeowners need done, though many are not aware of this need, is to label the circuit breakers, the fuses, and the water valves. Then, if problems arise and water or electricity has to be shut off, the homeowner, or a repairman, knows what should be done.

Circuit breaker panels usually have blank labels where you can write the function of each breaker. If you have a helper, you can turn the breakers off one by one and the helper will tell you where the power goes off. If you don't have a helper, you can plug a radio in various outlets and hear the sound stop as the power goes off. You can remove the outlet plates of the various electrical outlets throughout the house and write, on the back of each, the number of the circuit breaker that controls that outlet.

I like to label the water valves by tying a 2 × 4 manila shipping tag on or near each valve. A typical label might read: COLD WATER   2ND FLOOR. Be sure to use heavy pencil or waterproof ink, otherwise a leaky valve might wash out its own label. (I have had it happen.) Write the information on both sides of the label. Don't use cotton string to attach these tags; it tends to lose its strength and break after several years. Use synthetic string or copper wire.

LUBRICATING HOUSEHOLD DEVICES

Most homes have several motor-driven appliances. Some of these appliances have sealed motors that never need lubrication. But many appliances have motors or other moving parts that should be oiled once or twice a year. Examples are: some blowers for furnaces, oil burners, circulators, fans, humidifiers, dehumidifiers, window air conditioners, sewing machines, exercise equipment, ventilator hoods, and can openers. Most homeowners never oil anything. You can perform a useful task and extend the life of many devices with a few drops of oil. The hinges on any outside doors (house, shed, garage) should also be oiled regularly.

MOVING-DAY ASSISTANCE

You can be helpful to someone who is moving. You can disassemble beds and other furniture, pack objects in boxes, tie up the boxes, and label them. If you have a truck, or rent one, you can move some or all of the possessions. At the other end, if it is not too far away, you can reassemble everything and hang the pictures and mirrors.

NOISE REDUCTION

Unfortunately, more and more people are plagued by unwanted sounds coming through walls, floors, ceilings, and windows. The right time to address these potential problems is when the house or apartment is being built. But, in some cases, there are steps you can take to reduce the noise level. If you study books and articles on this subject, you can tell the homeowner what might be done.

It is extremely difficult to predict how much relief a particular noise-reduction job will provide. It depends on the loudness of the sound, the frequencies (low frequencies are much harder to stop than high frequencies), whether the noise is coming from inside the building or outside, the type of construction of the house (stone, brick, frame), and even on the sensitivity of the individual. Some people are driven to distraction by sounds that someone else might not even be aware of. So, if you are going to do some soundproofing, explain to the homeowner what you can do and what it will cost, but make her aware that you cannot guarantee that she will be completely satisfied with the results.

Some of the steps that can be helpful in lowering the sound level are adding insulation inside walls and adding additional layers of drywall to existing walls to reduce transmission of sound through walls and putting down thick carpeting with a thick padding underneath to reduce sound coming up through the floor. You could also add storm windows (preferably with double-strength glass) and add weather stripping around doors to reduce sounds coming in from outside. You can also buy devices that mask annoying sounds by generating soothing sounds such as white noise or ocean waves.

ORGANIZING A HOME OFFICE

Many people now work at home. They need to organize their furniture, computers, printers, monitors, copiers, fax machines, file systems, and telephones for maximum efficiency. Spend some time at stores such as Staples, Office Max, or Office Depot. Get one of their catalogs and study it. You will learn what is available and then you can buy what is needed to install and adapt what the home office requires.

OUTDOOR PLAY EQUIPMENT

You can assemble and install kits for swings, slides, and play houses for the children of the family. Be sure there are no splinters or sharp corners or edges on which a child could get hurt.

PAINTING THE POWER DROP

The "power drop" is the heavy electrical cable that runs from a high point on the house down to the electric meter. There is a similar cable running from the bottom of the meter, through a hole in the siding, and into the house. If these cables are exposed to sun for many years, and never painted, the outer jacket often deteriorates, exposing the inner insulation and allowing water to get into the cables. Sometimes, the actual copper conductors become exposed and the cables must be replaced. This is expensive and you should let an electrician do it. Do not attempt it yourself.

If the deterioration is not too severe, I put a few thick coats of paint, the same color as the house, on the cables. In severe cases, where there are holes in the jacket, I fill the holes with nonlatex caulk and then paint. In extreme cases, I wrap the cable with fiberglass tape before painting. If there is any opening around the cable where it enters the siding, it should be sealed with caulk or duct seal. These treatments stop the deterioration and keep water out of the cable. They may or may not satisfy a home inspector if the house is to be sold. In houses with underground service cables, this problem does not occur.

PEST CONTROL

You can be very helpful to many homeowners if you know something about ants, carpenter ants, honey bees, bumble bees, carpenter bees, fleas, mice, moles, raccoons, roaches, squirrels, termites, ticks, and wasps. You should learn to identify these pests, both by their appearance and by the signs they leave of their presence, and then learn the countermeasures to be used against them. If there is a wasp nest on someone's property, and it is not near a door or window, I usually suggest that the homeowner leave it alone because wasps are beneficial insects that eat caterpillars. But if the home-owner wants it removed, I do it. Similarly, I think of spiders as "good guys" because they catch flies and other undesirables. But if the homeowner wants the spiders killed, I do it. They are not an endangered species.

Recently, a customer was upset because there were ants in her kitchen closets. They were very small and there were not many of them, but she was near hysteria. She called two exterminators. One wanted $350 to get rid of the ants and the other wanted $750. I went to the hardware store and bought a set of six poison bait ant traps for $5. These traps look like tiny plastic boxes with a piece of "chocolate" inside. We put one in each cabinet where she had seen ants. In a few days the ants were gone for good.

Another woman had squirrels in her attic. They got in by walking along the power line to her roof, then climbing down the mast of the TV antenna and then gnawing through the wooden siding on the gable end. They made a terrible mess in the attic, making nests in the insulation and bringing in seeds to eat. Again, the professional exterminators wanted several hundred dollars. I put up a few sheet metal barriers to keep the squirrels out.

If the homeowner has a vegetable garden, you might have to take counter-measures against deer, rabbits, and ground hogs.

PREPARING A HOUSE FOR SALE

When a house is put up for sale, there is usually some work to be done. Some of this work is just for appearance; a nice paint job can enhance the value and get the property sold quickly. But there is often other work to be done as well.

A house may be perfectly satisfactory for the people who live in it. But, if they want to sell it to a buyer who will use a VA (Veterans Administration) or FHA (Federal Housing Administration) mortgage, the house must meet certain requirements regarding the electrical system, plumbing system, etc. You can learn what these requirements are from any realtor and do some or all of the work required to bring the house up to these standards.

SHARPENING TOOLS

I am sometimes asked to sharpen garden tools, knives, lawn mower blades, scissors, etc. With the possible exception of filing a mower blade if it isn't too dull, I take these items home and sharpen them on my bench grinder. Scissors are sharpened in a completely different way than knives. So, if you are going to sharpen scissors, be sure you know what you are doing or the scissors will be permanently ruined.

SHEDS

An outdoor shed, if there is room for it, can be used to store lawn mowers, garden tools, hoses, bicycles, oil-base paints, flammable liquids, etc. These sheds are available in kit form and are sometimes surprisingly low in price at the end of the summer season. I am sometimes asked to assemble these sheds and to install shelves, hooks, and racks to hold the various items. My experience is that the wooden sheds, though more expensive, are more durable than the sheet metal sheds. The doors on the metal sheds often seem to develop problems after a few years.

STORAGE SYSTEMS

We live in a consumer society and most people have more possessions than they have places to keep them, so they end up with big inaccessible piles of belongings. They can't see what is in those piles and they can't find what they are looking for.

In recent years, many very clever storage systems have come to market: closet organizers, shelf systems, hooks, racks, hanging baskets, and such. If you familiarize yourself with what is available, you can make big improvements in how people store their possessions. Some people make a career of just planning and installing home storage systems.

TELEPHONES

Gone are the days when homeowners depended on a specialist from the phone company to come to the house to make installations and repairs. Now it is usually a do-it-yourself job. In addition to having a basic understanding of how the phone system works, if you are installing phones at new locations, you need some knowledge of how houses are constructed so that you can determine the easiest way to run the phone wires to where they are needed. Electronics stores and home centers have books which tell you how to install telephones.

ACQUIRING KNOWLEDGE AND SKILLS

Become a Helper	20	Pamphlets	27
Books	21	Rental Center	27
Catalogs	24	Sales Clerks	27
Correspondence Courses	25	SCORE (Service Corps of Retired	
Evening Courses	25	Executives)	28
Handyman Club of America	25	Stores That Sell Appliance Parts	28
Home Centers	25	Trash and Dumpsters	28
Internet	26	TV Shows	29
Looking at Houses	26	Videos, CD's, DVD's	29
Magazines	26	Watch Jobs Being Done	29
Newspapers	27	Work at Home	29

There are many ways to acquire knowledge and skills. Here are just some of them, in alphabetical order. Use whichever ones are convenient for you.

BECOME A HELPER

Get a job as a helper to a handyman, general contractor, carpenter, electrician, painter, plumber, or builder. This is the best way to learn because you are earning while learning. Watch the "Help Wanted" ads for such job openings. But if there are none, don't take no for an answer. Go to lumber yards and home centers where you see men with trucks loading up with lumber and other items. Speak to them. Give them a card with your name and phone number. Tell them that you are looking for full- or part-time work learning about building. Tell them that you are available on short notice (like the day before) and will work for any hourly rate they wish to pay, no fringe benefits required. You could even offer to work for free for a few days; even if you aren't paid, it would probably be a useful learning experience for you.

Call builders and contractors and make the same offer. You must have your own tools and, in most cases, your own transportation. If they ask what experience you have, tell them whatever the truth happens to be. There are many tradesmen who usually work alone, but who need a helper from time to time. Always smile and be pleasant and friendly. Don't get discouraged if the first 10 people you talk to say "No." Ask them if they know anyone who might need a helper. Say "Thanks anyway," and keep trying. I know of a very successful man who says that if you have a job, you will work at it 8 hours a day, and if you don't have a job, you should spend 8 hours a day looking for one.

When you get a job, do everything possible to be as valuable an employee as you can be. Arrive early, leave late. Do things that need doing without being asked. Always do the job exactly as the employer wants it done. If you have something at home that might be useful for the job, bring it. Imagine yourself in the position of the employer and you will realize what is important to him to get the job done properly and profitably. Whatever the job is that you are working on, read about it at home. If you don't understand some aspect of the job, ask about it before you go ahead and do something wrong. The better you understand the work, the more valuable you will be to your employer. If you spare no effort to do the best possible job, you can bet that the next time that employer needs a helper, you will be the first person he will call.

Read the classified ads under "Maintenance" or "Handyman." Look for "Helper" or "Entry Level" or "Will Train" jobs. These jobs are usually for maintenance in apartment complexes, condominiums, or office buildings. When you read these ads, you will see the term "HVAC." This means heating, ventilating, and air-conditioning.

BOOKS

For almost anything you may wish to do, there is at least one book, usually several, that tells how to do it. There is no such thing as a perfect book, so you will never find a single book that tells you everything you might need to know for every possible situation. I recently looked through three books on appliance repair until I found one that gave me the information I needed to repair a certain kind of washing machine. You might have to look through several books to find the information needed to service a particular kind of toilet or kitchen faucet or to repair a certain kind of roof or floor.

Study the "how-to" books in your local library. Study the books on the book rack at the home center; it is often in some out-of-the-way corner. Your goal is to eventually acquire at least one, and preferably two or three, good books on the following subjects:

- Carpentry
- Cement work
- Drywall work
- Electrical work
- Flooring
- Hand tools
- Home inspection (recommended: *The Complete Book of Home Inspection* by Norman Becker, published by McGraw-Hill)
- Keeping basements dry
- Painting
- Plumbing
- Power tools
- Weatherproofing

In addition to books about specific subjects, don't overlook multisubject books with titles such as: *Handyman, Home Repair, Home Improvement, Do It Yourself, Fix It Yourself, Build It Yourself, New House, Old House, How It Works, How Things Work.* And keep in mind that new and useful books are published every year.

In addition, if you choose to work in the following areas, you should have books on:

- Appliance repair
- Bicycle repair
- Decks
- Gardening
- Energy conservation measures for the home
- Home security
- HVAC (heating, ventilating, and air-conditioning)
- Installing electronics
- Landscaping
- Locksmithing

- Patios
- Pest control
- Rehabilitating or renovating old houses
- Roofing
- Siding
- Telephones
- Tree work

Several companies publish sets of books that cover almost any area in which you will work. You can buy individual books or the entire set. You can contact these companies and request a list of their "how-to" books. Write to Customer Service at the following addresses or visit their websites. Some of the companies that have excellent series of "how-to" books, and the publishers of the books, are:

Better Homes & Gardens	Meredith Books, 1716 Locust Street, Des Moines, IA 50309.
Black & Decker	Creative Publishing Inc., Minnetonka, MN 55343.
Creative Homeowner Press	24 Park Way, Upper Saddle River, NJ 07458; website: www.chp-publisher.com.
Easy Home Repair (loose leaf sheets)	International Masters Publishers, 444 Liberty Avenue, Pittsburgh, PA 15222; website: easyhomerepair.com.
eBay	See website: www.ebay.com.
Handyman Club of America	12301 Whitewater Drive, Minnetonka, MN 55343.
Home Depot	Meredith Books, 1716 Locust Street, Des Moines, IA 50309.
McGraw-Hill	See website: www.books.mcgraw-hill.com.
Ortho Books	Meredith Books, 1716 Locust Street, Des Moines, IA 50309.
Popular Science	2 Park Avenue, New York, NY 10016.
Radio Shack	Tandy Corp., Fort Worth, TX 76102. Get a Radio Shack catalog and look in the index under "Books."
Reader's Digest	Reader's Digest Books, Pleasantville, NY 10570.
Sunset	For Sunset book list, write to: Leisure Arts, Inc., 5701 Ranch Drive, Little Rock, AR 72223-9633.
Taunton Press	63 South Main Street, P.O. Box 5506, Newtown, CT 06470.
Time Life	Time Life Books, Alexandria, VA.
U.S. Government Printing Office	Superintendent of Documents, Washington, DC 20402. Ask for SB 041 which lists many useful, low-cost booklets.

Most book stores have a "how-to" section. Home centers and electronics stores have books on telephones, basic electricity, electronics, etc. Libraries have a reference book called: *Subject Guide to Books In Print*. Some cities have a book store that sells nothing but "How-to" books. "How-to" books are often found at yard sales and flea markets. When you go to yard sales, ask if they have any such books.

If you have Internet access, you can find new and used books on almost any subject at Amazon.com, BarnesandNoble.com, Bookfinder.com, and other bookseller sites. There are also websites that specialize in "how-to" books. You can use Google to search for books on particular subjects

When you buy used books, look at the copyright date; it is on one of the first few pages. How old a book can be and still be useful depends on the subject matter. A good book on concrete work or carpentry or landscaping could be 30 years old and still be very useful although you must keep in mind that some newer materials and techniques will not be described in that book. But books on high-tech devices, such as telephone equipment or electronic equipment, become obsolete quite rapidly. I would try to rely on books no more than 5 or 10 years old for such devices.

When I buy a book, I take a marker pen and write the copyright year on the front cover and also on the spine of the book. That way I know, before I open the book, how old it is, and whether I should be referring to it for the job at hand. Whenever I was asked to do a job I had not done before, I would read about it the day before in whatever books I had that covered the subject.

Of course, no one could possibly remember everything in every book he has read. But you will remember that such and such a book had good information on such and such a job and, when the need arises, you can then go to that book and get the information you need.

CATALOGS

Catalogs are a useful source of information. Try to accumulate as many as you can. Especially helpful are a plumbing parts catalog and an electrical parts catalog. Ask for catalogs when you go to places that sell these parts. They are often free. When you have time, leaf through these catalogs to become familiar with what is available. Just learning the proper names for the various items is valuable in itself. Then you know what to ask for when you go to the hardware store. If you look in the back pages of magazines such as those listed in this chapter, you will see lists of free or inexpensive catalogs and instructional booklets.

CORRESPONDENCE COURSES

Look at the ads for correspondence schools in the backs of magazines. Write for information and judge whether what they have to offer may be helpful to you. Two companies that offer such courses are:

- Foley Belsaw Institute, 6301 Equitable Road, Kansas City, MO 64120
- Education Direct, 925 Oak Street, Scranton, PA 18540

EVENING COURSES

Some high schools have evening courses in home repair. These are usually at a very basic level but the instructors are often experienced tradesmen who may be helpful to you in finding work. You can also get answers to any questions you may have.

HANDYMAN CLUB OF AMERICA

This is the company that publishes *Handy* magazine. For a modest yearly cost, you get *Handy* magazine and many offers to buy various useful items, including some freebies. The address is: P.O. Box 3410, Minnetonka, MN 55343. They also sell "how-to" videos and DVDs.

HOME CENTERS

Prowl the aisles at the home center (Home Depot, Lowe's, etc.). I think of these home centers as graduate courses in fixing and building. Look at the various items for sale. Get familiar with the various hand and power tools. Even if you don't need them now, you will eventually buy and use many of them. Learn the names of the various kinds of lumber, plywood, etc. Even after 25 years of doing handyman work, I never go to a home center and wander around without coming upon some useful new tool, or hardware device, or material.

Some home centers have free demonstrations from time to time where they show how to do a particular job. Ask about these at your local home center. The big advantage of these demonstrations, as compared to watching a video, is that you can ask questions. The personnel who work at the home center are often retired tradesmen with years of experience. They can be extremely helpful in advising you about a job you are doing.

You can learn a great deal by reading the instructions on the cans, buckets, and boxes of materials (coatings, adhesives, patching materials, lubricants, etc.).

INTERNET

If you have Internet access, there are websites that give information on almost any fixing or building project. Do a search using keywords such as how to, handyman, do-it-yourself, building, fixing, home improvement, home repairs, new house, old house, rehabbing, rehabilitating, and restoring.

LOOKING AT HOUSES

When you drive around, walk around, or ride your bike, look at the houses you pass. Look at the roofs, chimneys, dormers, porches, decks, gutters, downspouts, siding, flashing, windows, etc. You will acquire an understanding of how various styles of houses are constructed. You may also see many places where repairs are needed.

MAGAZINES

There are many magazines which tell how to do building and fixing. Some magazines are devoted primarily to building beautiful objects, but more useful for the handyman is the kind of magazine that discusses how to do practical tasks. Here, in alphabetical order, is a partial list of magazines that may contain articles useful to you.

- *Handy* (12301 Whitewater Drive, Minnetonka, MN 55343)
- *Popular Mechanics* (P.O. Box 7170, Red Oak, IA 51591)
- *Popular Science* (2 Park Avenue, New York, NY 10016)
- *Popular Woodworking* (P.O. Box 5369, Harlan, IA 51593; www.pop-wood.com)
- *The Family Handyman* (P.O. Box 5232, Harlan, IA 51593)
- *Workbench* (2200 Grand Avenue, Des Moines, IA 50312; work-bench@workbenchmag.com)

When I start to read one of these magazines, I put a self-stick white label on the front cover for notes. (If there is a large light-colored area on the cover, no label is needed.) If the front cover of the magazine is so slick and glossy that you cannot write on it with a pencil or ballpoint pen, rub the area a few seconds with fine steel wool or fine sandpaper. This will scuff up the surface and make it easy to write on.

As I read, I make notes on this label to enable me to find the articles I may want to refer to at a later time. I also turn down the corner of the page where each article starts. This "dog-earing" is especially helpful in cases where there are no page numbers. (In some magazines, you may encounter

5 to 10 consecutive pages with no page numbers.) A typical label might look like this:

45	Cleaning gutters
65–71	Vinyl flooring
101	Cutting plastic
123	Ground-fault outlets

NEWSPAPERS

Many newspapers have a regular column, usually once a week, on some aspect of home maintenance. These columns are always worth reading and, in some cases, saving. Some of these columnists will answer, in their columns, letters that they consider of general interest. So, if you don't need the answer in a hurry, you could write to them and see what happens.

PAMPHLETS

Some home centers have a series of pamphlets, often a hundred or more, on almost every type of repair or construction. Get a complete set of these pamphlets; they are free, extremely well done, and very concise. Often, a careful study of the appropriate pamphlet is all you will need to tell you how to do a job you have never done before. Some typical titles are: *Drywall Repairs, Soldering Copper Tubing, Hanging Doors, Exterior Painting, Building Storage Areas.*

RENTAL CENTER

Take a look at the rental center. The tools here are the more expensive ones that you might not be able to justify buying. But, from time to time, you may want to rent one of them. The clerks at the rental center are usually very knowledgeable. Rental centers often have used power tools for sale at reasonable prices.

SALES CLERKS

The sales clerks at the hardware store, plumbing supply store, etc., can be quite helpful to you. But you should take care to be a valued customer to them, not an annoyance. Remember that, typically, your purchase is small, and they don't make much, if any, money on you.

I always try to buy at least one small item when I go to a store for advice. If I don't really need anything, I still buy something that I know I will eventually have use for. If a drawing will help explain my problem, I make a large, clear, pencil drawing before I go to the store. I try to get advice when the clerk is not busy, often midmorning or midafternoon. If I am getting advice and another customer comes up to the counter, I step back and tell the clerk to take care of the customer and I will wait to ask my questions.

Get to know these clerks by name. If you are not good at remembering names, write them down so you can address them by name the next time you come in. "Hi Bill, how are you today? I need a little advice about…" And be sure to thank them for their advice.

SCORE

Also available on the Internet is SCORE (Service Corps of Retired Executives). These kind-hearted people give free business advice by email and, in many areas, you can visit them and talk face-to-face. You might find good financial and tax advice here. The website is: www.score.org.

STORES THAT SELL APPLIANCE PARTS

If you are fortunate enough to have a store in your vicinity that sells parts for all makes of appliances, the people there can be very helpful. Often, if you tell them the make and model of an appliance and what the problem is, they can tell you what is wrong and how to fix it. And they can sell you the parts you need.

TRASH AND DUMPSTERS

You can learn a lot by studying objects that are being thrown out. Suppose you see a vacuum cleaner or a power mower in the trash. Take it home, take it apart, and study how it is constructed. The knowledge you gain that way will sooner or later prove useful.

On one occasion, I saw a very old front door in the trash. I removed the hardware, some of it solid brass, and put it in my car. The mortise lock was of a type I hadn't seen before and I kept it in the car. The next time I was at the locksmith, buying some parts, I asked the locksmith to explain to me the unusual features of this lock. A few months later, I was asked to fix an identical lock and, because of what I had learned, I knew exactly how to do it.

I have frequently learned of some new material that I didn't know existed by finding leftover pieces of it in a dumpster. Also in the dumpster, there may be empty 5-gallon buckets from various materials, for example, adhesives and coatings. These buckets are often excellent sources of information. The labels on these buckets often contain much more detailed information than you would find on a gallon can at the home center and they are easy to read because the print is not microscopically tiny. I often take one of these buckets home, read the instructions carefully, and sometimes experiment with whatever is left in the bottom of the bucket if there is enough of it.

TV SHOWS

There are several good TV shows about fixing and building houses. Some examples are:

- *Home Again*
- *Hometime*
- *Home Savvy*
- *House Detective*
- *Renovations*
- *This Old House*
- *Your New House*

Watch them when you can. In many cases, you can order videos of the shows.

VIDEOS, CD'S, DVD'S

There are "how-to" video cassettes, CDs, and DVDs on almost any build or fix subject. The video store may have a catalog which lists "how-to" videos. Handyman Club of America (see, above, under Books) sells "how-to" videos.

WATCH JOBS BEING DONE

You can learn a lot by watching others do roofing, siding, renovating, etc. I once sat in my car for half an hour while watching roofers do a job. In most cases, these workers will prove to be very friendly if you politely ask a few questions. "Hi, may I ask you a question about this roofing job?" In most cases, they will be quite willing to explain what they are doing. Once in a while, you may run into a grouch who doesn't want to tell you anything. That's his problem; don't let it bother you.

WORK AT HOME

Practice at home. Some of the jobs you can learn to do at home are drywall work, painting, caulking, sharpening drill bits and other tools, soldering copper tubing, and glass cutting. Silicone caulk and latex caulk do not behave the same when they are being applied, so you should practice until you can do a good job with each.

Study the insides of your toilet tank; flush the toilet and watch what happens. Do you understand the function of all the parts you see in there? Look at all the pipes and wires in your basement. Do you know what all of them are for? Study what is inside your breaker panel or fuse box. Look under the sink. Go outside, do you know what all the wires you see coming into the house are for? Wherever you go, notice how things are constructed.

ADAPTING YOUR CAR

Your Vehicle	31	Knots	33
Roof Rack	32	Securing the Roof Load	33
Ropes	32	Handyman with Truck	33

YOUR VEHICLE

The larger your vehicle is, the better, because then you can have more tools and materials with you at all times. You will spend less time loading and unloading objects before and after each job and you are less likely to forget something you may need. If you have a van, you are in great shape. A mini-van is fine. A station wagon is good. A car is usable but you can't carry as much. I started out doing handyman work using a VW Beetle. I removed all the seats but the driver's seat. I cut a board to fit where the rear seat had been, just to keep objects off the battery and other underseat spaces. Then, when I could afford it, I moved up to a station wagon.

Another solution, though one that is rarely used, is to have your tools and other items for your work in a trailer, and hook it to your car only when you are doing a job.

What if you don't have a car at all? I have known handymen who strapped their trusty tool boxes onto their bicycles and pedaled off to do a job. You can do the same until you can buy a used vehicle. Most lumberyards will deliver boards, and other materials to your job site. Or, your customer may be willing to transport any large or heavy items for you.

I also knew a handyman without a car who lived in an area that was under-going gentrification. When relatively wealthy people move into a badly run-down area, buy the houses, and spend a lot of money upgrading them, that is called gentrification. This man had so many major customers within a few blocks that he just walked to work each day.

ROOF RACK (Fig. 5-1)

You must have a good roof rack for carrying ladders, long boards, sheets of plywood, etc. If your vehicle doesn't have a sturdy roof rack, you should buy or build one. If your existing roof rack is toward the back of the roof, you should add a crossbar near the front of the roof. This is necessary to support ladders and long boards. Keep a red cloth or ribbon in your car and attach it to any load that extends beyond the back of your car. This is a legal requirement in some areas and a good idea anywhere.

ROPES

You should have several lengths of rope to tie objects to the roof rack. Use $1/4$-inch nylon or Dacron (polyester) rope. Twisted rope is OK, braided is better. Don't use hemp or polypropylene; the fibers tend to break and leave sharp splinters sticking out. I carry three lengths of rope that are 10 feet long, two that are 13 feet long, and one that is 25 feet long.

The long rope is used to go from the front bumper, over the roof load, and down to the back bumper. This is essential when you are carrying sheets of thin paneling or plywood, because otherwise the wind, especially air that is deflected upward from the windshield, will get under the panels and make them flop violently or even snap off. If your car bumpers are such that it is not possible to loop the rope around them, look under the car, just behind each bumper, find something sturdy at each end of the car where you can attach a small permanent loop of rope or a heavy nylon cable tie. Then tie your roof rope to those small loops. If any of your ropes show signs of wear or fraying, replace them.

You will also use your ropes to tie back bushes and tree branches so that you can get at the sides of a house to do painting or repairs.

The ends of these ropes must be treated in some way so that they will not unravel. If you know how to whip the rope ends with twine, that is fine, but time consuming. You can tape the ends with $3/4$-inch-wide black vinyl electrical tape (let about $1/4$ inch of rope extend beyond the tape so the tape is less likely to slide off. You can melt the rope ends in a flame to fuse the strands together and prevent unraveling. Done properly, this works well. I often saturate the last $1/2$ inch of the rope with epoxy glue. When it hardens, it is very permanent.

You should also color-code the rope ends so you can tell at a glance which are the 10-footers and which are 13 feet long. Any kind of paint can be used; just dip 2 or 3 inches of the rope ends into the paint, wipe off the excess, and let it dry. When these ropes are not in use, keep them neatly coiled in the car, always in the same place.

KNOTS (Fig. 5-1)

You need to know only a few simple knots for tying objects onto your car. Remember that the best knot for any job is the simplest knot that will do the job and (extremely important) is easy to untie, even if it is dark, the ropes are swollen from rain, and your fingers are numb with cold. You should know the *two half hitches,* the *clove hitch,* which is the same as the two half hitches except that the rope goes around some rigid object instead of around itself, and the *square knot.*

Another useful knot when tying things into bundles, or tying up boxes for someone who is moving, is the *bowline knot.* Practice these four knots until you can tie and untie them with your eyes closed. Encyclopedias and scout manuals usually have illustrations of how to tie knots.

SECURING THE ROOF LOAD

Until you are experienced and very sure of what you are doing, always err on the side of using more ropes than appear necessary to secure the roof load. If you go over railroad tracks or a stretch of bumpy road, pull over to the side of the road, get out, and see if the load is secure and all the ropes are still tight. You could even deliberately seek out a bumpy stretch of road as a test. You might be amazed at how clever and sneaky boards and ladders can be at finding ways to work themselves loose.

HANDYMAN WITH TRUCK

If you are really serious about working full-time as a handyman, and you want to maximize your earnings, you will eventually have a large truck in which you carry almost everything needed for almost any job. This will save a lot of time otherwise spent loading and unloading before and after each job. If you have a cell phone or a pager in your truck, you can receive calls while on a job and schedule your day more efficiently.

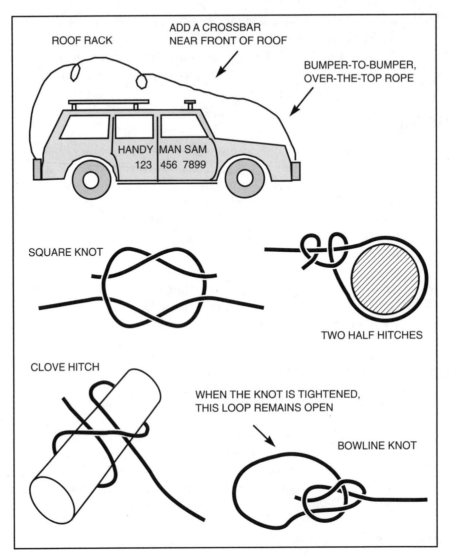

ROOF RACK

ADD A CROSSBAR
NEAR FRONT OF ROOF

BUMPER-TO-BUMPER,
OVER-THE-TOP ROPE

HANDY MAN SAM
123 456 7899

SQUARE KNOT

TWO HALF HITCHES

CLOVE HITCH

WHEN THE KNOT IS TIGHTENED,
THIS LOOP REMAINS OPEN

BOWLINE KNOT

FIGURE 5-1 Roof rack, knots.

ITEMS TO CARRY IN YOUR CAR

Bow Saw	35	Magnet	38
Broom	35	Materials to Carry in Your Car	38
Crosscut Saw	36	Rope with Pulley	40
Drop Light	36	Rugs	40
Extension Cords	36	Safety Goggles	41
Eyeglasses Band	36	Socket Wrenches	41
Flashlight	36	Sweatband	42
Hardware Items	37	Wedge	42
Knee Pads	38	Work Gloves	42
Lopping Shears	38		

In addition to your tool box, here are some items I suggest you have in your car at all times.

BOW SAW

Have a bow saw (sometimes called a *cordwood saw*) with a 21-inch blade. You might need this to cut some branches to gain access to whatever part of the house you must work on. You might even need it if you go to someone's house to do some roof repair. When you get on the roof, you may see some tree branches that are scraping the roof and causing damage. You can use your lopping shears and the bow saw to cut back those branches. The bow saw can also be used to cut boards and 2 × 4s although the cut will be rather rough and irregular.

BROOM

Keep an old broom in your car. You will need it frequently.

CROSSCUT SAW

Carry a small crosscut saw. It is useful in many carpentry projects and it does not require electricity.

DROP LIGHT

This is sometimes called a trouble light. This light is indispensable. Get one with a long cord. Be sure to buy a high-quality drop light. It should have a metal (not plastic) shield behind the bulb. It should have a swiveling hook that has enough friction so that the light stays aimed in the direction you choose. If possible, the hook should be big enough to hook over a pipe that is 2 inches in diameter. The drop light should have an on/off switch and a 3-prong outlet built into its side. Put a 3:2 adapter on the plug so that you can plug it in anywhere.

Your drop light should be rated to use a 100-watt bulb. Buy a rough service bulb, 100-watts, if you can find one. Rough service bulbs are much less likely to stop working if the drop light is accidentally dropped. Always carry an extra bulb in your car. Be careful when using your drop light around water, such as when doing plumbing work. One drop of water on the bulb when it is hot will shatter it.

EXTENSION CORDS (Fig. 6-1)

Get a 25-foot extension cord and a 50-foot extension cord and reels to keep them on. I fasten a 6-outlet power strip to the side of the reel so that, in effect, I have an extension cord with six outlets at its end. Carry a 3:2 adapter with this cord in case you have to plug it into a 2-wire outlet. Extension cords that are just coiled up by themselves, without a reel, tend to get tangled and you can waste a lot of time untangling them.

EYEGLASSES BAND

If you wear glasses and you are looking down from a window or roof, and your skin is wet with sweat, there is a strong tendency for your glasses to slide off and go crashing down onto whatever is below. An elastic band, which is fastened to the ends of the temples of your glasses, and goes around the back of your head, will prevent this disaster.

FLASHLIGHT

Carry a good bright flashlight, the kind that uses two D cells. Check it from time to time to be sure it is still working. A top-quality flashlight at a home center may cost several dollars more than a cheap one. However, pay the extra amount; it is worth it for the increased reliability.

HARDWARE ITEMS

I also carry several boxes with the following hardware items:

Angle Brackets   Have a box of assorted steel angle brackets (the kind that would form a straight metal strap if it was bent flat) with sizes from $3/4$ inch $\times$ $3/4$ inch up to 4 inches $\times$ 4 inches.

Bolts ($\frac{1}{4}$-inch)   In a compartment box keep several sizes of $1/4$-inch bolts, flathead and roundhead, with nuts and washers.

Bolts ($\frac{5}{16}$-inch)   In another compartment box keep several sizes of $5/16$-inch bolts, flathead and roundhead, with nuts and washers.

Bolts ($\frac{3}{8}$-inch)   A third compartment box should contain several sizes of $3/8$-inch bolts, flathead and roundhead, with nuts and washers. Also, carry a few very large washers, $1^1/2$-inch and 2-inch, in this box.

Drywall Screws   Carry a box containing individual boxes of every size of drywall screw from $3/4$ inch to 4 inches. Drywall screws come with fine threads and coarse threads. The coarse threads are better. They go in and out faster, they hold better in soft materials, and they are less likely to cause wood to split. In addition to the drywall screws, this box also contains a small box of flathead Phillips wood screws #6 $\times$ $1^1/2$ inches (used to attach shelf standards to a wall), and a small box of flathead Phillips wood screws #4 $\times$ $1/2$ inch used for small work such as small hinges. This box of screws is one of my most useful items. Don't be without it.

Machine Screws (6–32)   A compartment box should have several lengths of 6–32 machine screws, flathead and roundhead or binder-head, with nuts and washers.

Machine Screws (8–32)   Your compartment box should contain several sizes of 8–32 machine screws, flathead and roundhead or binder-head, with nuts and washers.

Machine Screws (10–24 and 10–32)   A compartment box should also have several sizes of 10–24 and 10–32 machine screws, flathead and roundhead or binder-head, with nuts and washers.

Nails   You will need a box containing several boxes of nails of lengths from $3/4$ inch to $3^1/2$ inches, both head nails and finish nails.

KNEE PADS OR A THICK RUBBER KNEELING PAD

These are essential when kneeling on hard surfaces, especially hard irregular surfaces. If you will be working in a particular spot only, the kneeling pad is fine. If you must continually move around, the knee pads are better.

LOPPING SHEARS

Lopping shears are similar to pruning shears, but with long handles. (See Fig. 12-1.) They are used for cutting small tree branches. It is good to have these shears with you at all times; not just when you expect to be doing tree work. The reason is that you will often have to cut away some branches to get at a cellar window or an air conditioner, make room for your ladder, or do some painting.

MAGNET

Carry a small magnet to use for determining whether something is stainless steel or solid brass or brass-plated steel. Most, but not all, stainless steels are nonmagnetic. Stainless steel kitchen knives are magnetic. Aluminum and brass are nonmagnetic. This magnet is especially useful at flea markets and yard sales. If your car has a metal dashboard, you can put this magnet onto the dashboard, ready for use.

MATERIALS TO CARRY IN YOUR CAR

In addition to all the tools and hardware items listed above, I like to have the following materials in my car:

Aluminum Sheet   I carry a roll of sheet aluminum, 12 inches wide. This is sold at roofing supply places to use for flashing and other purposes. Buy the kind that is painted white on one side and brown on the other.

CRC or WD40 Lubricant   A spray can of CRC or WD40 lubricant is very useful. These are good penetrating oils to help loosen threaded fasteners that are rusted in place. They also help retard rusting. Try not to use these compounds indoors because they have a persistent unpleasant smell.

Glue   I use 5-minute epoxy, which is created by mixing equal amounts from two tubes (epoxy and hardener). I keep these tubes in a small, sturdy, wide-mouthed plastic jar with a screw-on lid.

Paint Stirrers   A few wooden paint stirrers like the ones paint stores give you when you buy a can of paint will come in handy. I use these to stir paint, but they are also useful as shims and spacers.

Rags   You should carry a few rags for wiping objects clean. Rags are also needed when painting or caulking. The rags should be of a soft absorbent material. Old cotton underwear is perfect for this assignment. I have a plastic bag with rags and extra plastic bags inside. Both are useful when doing paint jobs.

Sandpaper   Carry a few sheets of sandpaper: 40-grit, 80-grit, and 160-grit, or something similar.

Silicone Lubricant   You should have a spray can of silicone lubricant. These cans come with a spray wand which is a length of very thin plastic tubing. Don't lose this wand because there may be times when you must have it to get the lubricant into otherwise inaccessible spots. The wand is often held onto the can with a piece of tape. Add a few rubber bands to make sure the wand does not get lost. Don't let silicone spray get in your eyes, it is very painful. Silicone spray can be used indoors because the odor is slight and it disappears quickly.

String   A roll of string is useful to tie things that do not require strong twine.

Twine   Also useful is a roll of strong twine (baling twine) used to tie up bundles of branches and to tie up cartons of belongings when someone is moving.

Vinyl Sheet   Try to carry a few pieces of sheet vinyl (some scraps from a vinyl siding job). White is the most useful color, but take whatever you can get.

Water   You will need two canteens of drinking water when working. Don't fill the canteens more than 90 percent full or they may burst if the water freezes on a cold winter night. In summer, the water may get quite hot. I found that I could get accustomed to drinking hot water and it quenches a thirst just as well as cold water.

Wood (¾ × 2)   Carry a few pieces of wood (white pine), $^3/4$ inch × 2 inches and 2 or 3 feet long.

Wood (⅜ × 1)   Also carry a few pieces of wood (white pine) $^3/8$ × 1 inch and 2 or 3 feet long.

ROPE WITH PULLEY

You will need a rope, 12 feet long, with a pulley on one end, for tying branches into bundles. See Chap. 50, Thoughts and Suggestions, and especially Fig. 50-1, for details on how to do this.

RUGS

Among the most useful items to carry in your car are two or three pieces of old carpet. Look around on trash day and you can easily find old carpeting. Try to get the kind of carpet that has a soft backing rather than a hard stiff backing. Get two or three pieces that are about 3 feet wide and 6 feet long. Carpeting is easy to cut if you use a sharp utility knife and cut from the back side. You will find many uses for these rugs. Here are some examples:

- Whenever you have expensive tools or other items in your car, cover them with rugs or rags so that people walking by cannot see what you have.
- These rugs make excellent kneeling pads to protect your knees from hard floors. Fold them so that you have several thicknesses to kneel on. You can also use them outdoors if you have to kneel on wet or muddy surfaces. They can be lifesavers if you have to sit, kneel, or lie on a fiery-hot black asphalt roof on a summer day.
- You can spread one of these rugs on the hood of your car and then put tools and other items on it as you work, making a sort of instant worktable. Objects won't roll or slide off of it and it will protect the finish of your car.
- These rugs make excellent drop cloths to catch drops of paint when you are painting something. Turn the rug upside down so that drops

of paint will not harden on the good side of the rug where they may hurt if you kneel on them. (If the homeowner has a door mat near where you are painting, turn that upside down as well.) These drop cloths are especially good if you are painting outside on a windy day where ordinary lightweight drop cloths tend to blow away.

- You may be working in someone's home where there is light-colored carpeting. You must be very careful not to leave any dirt marks on this carpeting. Spread out one or two of your rugs (but only if they are very clean) and keep your toolbox, tools, and other items on these rugs. Do the same on bare wooden floors to prevent scratching the floor. If your rugs are not very clean, carry an old, but clean, bed sheet for this purpose.

- You may be working outdoors, fixing a fence for example, where the grass or weeds are very tall. Any tools or other items you put down here tend to disappear forever. Spread out one of your rugs and keep all the tools and hardware on the rug.

- You can spread one of these rugs on the roof of your car before putting odd-shaped objects on your roof and tying them to your roof rack. This will protect the roof of your car from dents and scratches.

- If you have to move a heavy object (refrigerator, washing machine) across a smooth floor, turn one of your rugs upside down, get one end of it under the object, then pull on the rug to slide the object to wherever you want it.

- If you have to place a ladder on uneven ground, you can fold a rug to the necessary thickness and place it under one leg of the ladder. A solid object is better for this purpose, but the rug will do if necessary.

- If you are carrying a piece of window glass or other fragile item in your car, you can wrap it in a rug to protect it from objects that might slide or fall on it while you are driving.

SAFETY GOGGLES

Keep your safety goggles in a bag or container in the glove compartment so they won't get dirty or scratched.

SOCKET WRENCHES

Carry a box of socket wrenches, 3/8-inch drive, socket sizes from 5/16 inch to 1 inch and metric sockets from 5 millimeters to 19 millimeters. You can omit the metric sockets when you are first starting out. Deep sockets are more expensive than the standard sizes, but they are also more useful because they can be put over longer bolts and still reach the nut that you want to turn.

SWEATBAND

See Chap. 53, Clothing for the Handyman.

WEDGE

Carry a wooden wedge, cut from a piece of 2 × 4, 12 inches long and 2 inches thick at the thick end, used for placing under one leg of a ladder to compensate for uneven ground.

WORK GLOVES

See Chap. 53, Clothing for the Handyman.

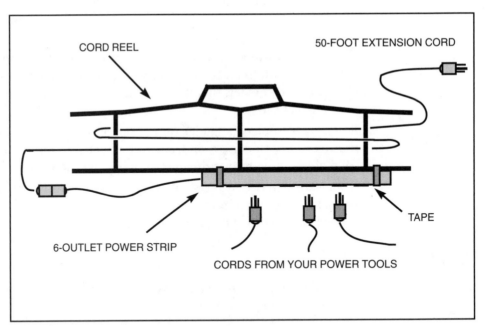

FIGURE 6-1 Cord and reel.

BUYING TOOLS

You will need lots of tools and, when you are starting out, that means a major expense. But you don't have to buy them all at once. Start out with the list of tools that I describe for my tool box, then add to that as needed.

Don't buy cheap tools. They just will not do the job. Cheap screwdrivers will bend or break when you try to turn a stubborn screw. Cheap chisels will not stay sharp. Cheap cutting pliers will get dents in their jaws instead of cutting properly. At first, it will seem hard to tell good from bad but, after awhile, you will learn to recognize a good tool or an inferior one in a few minutes.

Go to a home supply center or a large hardware store and look at the tools. See how they feel in your hand. If they have moving parts, do they move smoothly? See how much, or how little, attention to detail you see in the construction of the tool and its handle. Pick up a claw hammer. Look at the tapered slot in the claw that is used to pull nails. Are the inside edges of the slot sharp so that the hammer can grip a nail along the shank of the nail as well as just below the head of the nail? Does the slot taper to a sharp point so that the hammer can grip even very small nails? If so, you are looking at a good hammer.

Price is usually a good indicator of quality. The more expensive tools are almost always better quality than the low-priced ones, although I would not go overboard and use price as the only criterion. A hammer with the head painted black will drive nails just as well as a more expensive hammer with a chrome-plated head. There are some brand names on a tool that are an assurance of quality, but many good-quality tools have unfamiliar names or no names at all.

Always test out tools to be sure you know how to use them and to be sure that they are working properly before you take them to a job. I once bought lopping shears of a reputable manufacture and when I took them to a job, I found them to be defective. The cutting jaws were not ground properly. The store replaced the shears, but I lost a lot of time.

Try to buy good tools cheaply. See the section on yard sales and flea markets. If you are working for an elderly homeowner, ask if she has any tools that she might be willing to sell. A widow will sometimes sell her late husband's tools that she has no use for. Places that repair or rent power tools sometimes have good used tools for sale. If you know a retired plumber, carpenter, electrician, etc., ask if he has any tools to sell.

Don't overlook your local dollar store as a source for tools, hardware, and materials of all kinds. You may find some amazing bargains there.

If I have an opportunity to buy a top-quality tool at an extremely low price, I usually buy it even if I already have one or more of them. What do I do with those extra tools? I sometimes make up a kit of basic tools to give as a gift to a child who has reached an age where he (or she) wants to start building things. One of these basic tool kits also makes a fine gift for a couple who are buying their first home. Another use is for friends or neighbors who want to borrow a tool. And, of course, it is nice to have a backup inventory of good tools in case one of mine gets lost or broken.

YOUR TOOLBOX

Bottom Compartment	**45**
Top Tool Tray	**46**

You must have a big sturdy toolbox to carry your frequently needed tools. If your toolbox is new and shiny, you might consider painting it some dark ugly color to make it unattractive to thieves. If the tool box is in your car where it can be seen, cover it with a rug or an old rag.

My toolbox is 21 inches long (53 centimeters), 9 inches wide (23 centimeters), and 8 inches deep (20 centimeters). It has two levels, a large bottom compartment, and a shallow tray on top. Here is what I carry in my toolbox. Many years of experience have taught me that these are the most useful items to have with me.

BOTTOM COMPARTMENT

This is what I carry in the bottom compartment of my toolbox.

Box Wrenches (Fig. 8-1)   I carry four sizes: $3/8$–$7/16$, $1/2$–$9/16$, $5/8$–$11/16$, and $3/4$–$25/32$.

Chalk Line   This is used to snap straight lines on flat surfaces.

Cold Chisel   My chisel is $1/2$ inch wide and 10 inches long.

Electric Drill   My drill has a $3/8$-inch keyless chuck and is variable speed and reversible.

Hacksaw   Mine is a fine-tooth hacksaw with an extra blade. By fine tooth, I mean 24 or more teeth per inch. A fine-tooth blade can be used to cut thick or thin sheet steel or tubing, although it will not cut thick steel as quickly as a coarse-tooth (18 teeth per inch) blade. But a coarse-tooth blade will not cut thin sheet steel or tubing without sticking and jamming and sometimes losing some teeth. By thin, I mean $1/16$ inch or less.

Half-Round File   This file has coarse teeth and is 10 or 12 inches long.

Pipe Wrench   I like a 10-inch wrench.

Plane   I carry a block plane. This is a small plane that you use with one hand.

Pliers   I use large channel-lock pliers.

Square   Mine in an 8-inch square.

Tin Snips   I use large tin snips.

TOP TOOL TRAY

In the top tool tray I have the following items.

Adapter   I carry a 3:2 electrical adapter used to plug a 3-wire plug into a 2-wire outlet.

Adjustable End Wrenches   I have 4-inch, 6-inch, and 10-inch wrenches. See Fig. 8-1.

Allen Wrenches   These are sometimes called hex key wrenches. I have a set from $5/64$ inch to $1/4$ inch.

Carpenters Pencil   This is a wide flat pencil with soft lead, used for marking boards, and other material.

Center Punch   This is a punch with a sharp point. It is used to strike a surface, usually a metal surface, to make a small indentation to start a drill.

Chalk   Include a piece of blue chalk and a piece of white chalk: The blue chalk is used on white or light surfaces, the white chalk is used everywhere else.

China-Marking Pencil   This is a red pencil (sometimes called a grease pencil).

Compass   I carry a small compass for drawing circles and transferring outlines.

Countersink   This should be $1/2$ inch or more in diameter, with a $1/4$-inch or $3/8$-inch shaft, suitable for cutting metal, not just wood.

Cube Tap   The cube tap is sometimes called an octopus outlet. It is an electrical device. You plug it into an outlet and then you can plug three devices into it. (Do not use for devices that draw heavy current.)

Drill Bits (High-Speed)   I carry a set of high-speed steel drill bits from $1/16$ inch to $3/8$ inch in diameter. Note the emphasis on "high speed." You can also buy carbon-steel drill bits. They cost less but they get dull quickly, especially if used for drilling steel. Learning to correctly sharpen drill bits takes a lot of practice, but it is absolutely essential that all your drill bits be sharp at all times. Practice on old large bits until you can get it right every time. If you just cannot get the hang of it, you can buy devices ("Drill Doctor," etc.) that can be used to sharpen drill bits. They work well, but are expensive.

Drill Bits (Large-Diameter)   I have large-diameter drill bits. These are $1/2$-inch-diameter, $5/8$-inch-diameter, and $3/4$-inch-diameter drill bits with $3/8$-inch-diameter shanks so they will fit into the chuck of the electric drill.

Drill Bits (Long)   I carry long drill bits that are $1/4$-inch and $1/2$-inch in diameter. These bits should be at least 6 inches long and even longer than that is still better.

Duct Seal   A small container of duct seal, a nonhardening substance used to seal holes, is useful. It has a consistency like modeling clay.

Electrical Tester   This has a small neon bulb and two leads about 6 inches long. It is used to test for the presence of electricity.

Electrician's Tape   This is a small roll of black vinyl tape.

Hammer   A claw hammer is an essential tool for your toolbox.

Heat-Proof Grease   I carry a small container of plumber's heat-proof grease (or silicone grease).

Hose Washers   These are used on garden hoses and washing machine hoses.

Ice Pick   The ice pick is used to make holes in wood for starting screws and to probe for rot or termite damage and to probe interior walls to locate the studs. Still another use of the ice pick is to dig hardened paint out of a Phillips-head screw so that the screw can be turned. This may be essential if you have to remove a storm window that has been painted and the screws that hold it on are filled up with paint.

Line Level   You hang a line level on the middle of a string to make sure the string is level.

Lubricating Oil   A small can of light household oil should be included. Be sure the cap fits tightly or in summertime the oil will leak out and make a mess in your toolbox.

Measuring Tape (10 Feet Long)   You should have a 10-foot-long measuring tape in your toolbox.

Measuring Tape (20 or 25 Feet Long)   A 20- or 25-foot-long measuring tape is a must for certain jobs.

Nail Set   This is a punch with a small tip; it is used to drive a nail head below the surface.

Outlet Tester   You plug this into a 3-wire outlet. It has tiny lights to show whether the outlet is properly wired and properly grounded.

Paint Can Openers   A paint can opener looks like a bottle opener. It has a blade like a screwdriver blade which is bent upward. Carry two of these. They are small and inexpensive and on occasion you may need to use both at once.

Phillips Bits   I include a #1 bit that is 1 inch long. This is for small screws. I also include #2 bits that are 1 inch long, 2 inches long, and 4 inches long.

Pliers (Diagonal)   I carry diagonal cutting pliers.

Pliers (Long-Nose)   I also carry long-nose pliers.

Pliers (Standard)   Standard pliers are essential.

Putty Knife   This is similar to a spatula. Among its many uses are pressing patching compounds into cracks and holes, prying up moldings, and loosening windows that have been painted shut.

Round File   This is sometimes called a rat-tail file. It is $1/4$ inch in diameter and is 6 or 8 inches long.

Scissors   I find scissors that are 10 inches long useful.

Screw-In Outlet   This is used to replace a bulb in a fixture so that you can plug in your drill or trouble light.

Screwdriver (Ratchet)   I carry a ratchet screwdriver with removable bits: two slot bits and two Phillips bits #1 and #2. For additional drive bits that can be used with this screwdriver, see Chap. 18, Other Useful Tools, and see Fig. 18-2.

Screwdrivers (Slot and Phillips)   You will need several sizes of slot and Phillips screwdrivers, including short stubby screwdrivers and offset screwdrivers for tight places.

Sharpening Stone   I use a stone that is 4 inches long. This is used to sharpen the plane blade, the wood chisel, the utility-knife blade, and your pocketknife blade.

Stud Finder   An electronic stud finder is essential.

Teflon Tape   This tape is used for sealing threaded pipe fittings.

Torpedo Level   The torpedo level is used to establish horizontal and vertical for small jobs. It is not as accurate as larger levels.

Utility Knives (Fig. 8-1)   I carry two utility knives: one with a standard cutting blade, including extra blades, and one with two special blades, a blade for cutting rugs and a blade for scoring plastics such as Plexiglas. Scoring means cutting a shallow groove to prepare for either bending or snapping off.

Wire Nuts   A few nuts of small and medium sizes should be included.

Wire Strippers   Wire strippers are needed for #10 wire to #16 wire.

Wood Chisel   Carry a $5/8$-inch- or $3/4$-inch-wide chisel.

This is indeed a lot, and it is rather heavy: 38 pounds (17 kilograms). If you cannot handle this much weight, use a separate box for the heavy items.

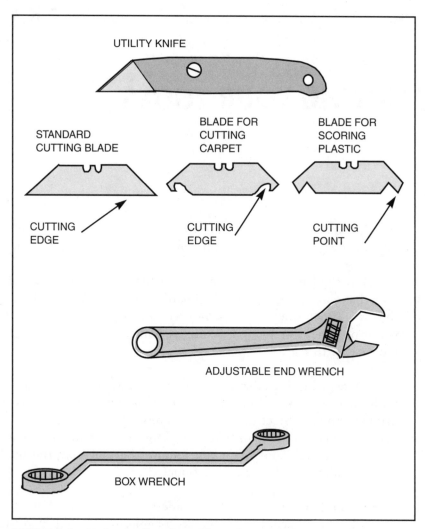

UTILITY KNIFE

STANDARD
CUTTING BLADE

BLADE FOR
CUTTING
CARPET

BLADE FOR
SCORING
PLASTIC

CUTTING
EDGE

CUTTING
EDGE

CUTTING
POINT

ADJUSTABLE END WRENCH

BOX WRENCH

FIGURE 8-1 Utility knife, adjustable end wrench, box wrench.

ORGANIZING YOUR TOOLS

You should be able to see all your frequently used tools at a glance, so you can take what you need (or think you might possibly need) and be on your way.

Probably the best way to organize your tools is on pegboard. The larger the area that you can cover with pegboard, the better. Get the kind of pegboard that is 1/4 inch thick and has $^{1}/_{4}$-inch holes spaced 1 inch apart. If you buy white pegboard, or paint it white, it will make the area brighter and the tools easier to see.

There are many varieties of pegboard hooks. Some are ideal for holding tools such as screwdrivers, others for hammers, shears, rolls of tape, etc. Study them and select the ones that are best for your needs. Try to buy the pegboard hooks that snap tightly into the holes. Some hooks are loose and floppy in the hole and when you remove the tool from the hook, the hook tends to fall out and land on the floor.

Some people like magnetic tool holders. They are convenient to use but I don't like them because they tend to magnetize the tools and the tools then tend to accumulate gritty iron filings.

Keep the tools you use most often at chest or eye level. Group the tools: all the screwdrivers together, all the pliers together, etc. If you have a workbench with drawers, you can keep the less frequently needed tools in the drawers.

Big tools, such as gardening tools, are best hung up wherever you can find space. Hang them high with the handles downward; that leaves more room at floor level.

CEMENT-WORK TOOLS

Brick Chisel	53	Small Triangular Trowel	54
Cold Chisel	53	Smoothing Trowel	54
Edge-Rounding Trowel	53	Spray Bottle	54
Line-Making Trowel	53	Syringe	54
Plastic Mixing Tub	54	Wire Brush	55
Pointing Trowel	54		

The following tools are useful when you do cement work.

BRICK CHISEL

This is a wide chisel used for cutting bricks to length. Don't buy one at retail until needed.

COLD CHISEL

If you have to trim flagstones to size, you can use a heavy cold chisel and a heavy (3-pound) hammer. Don't buy until needed.

EDGE-ROUNDING TROWEL

You might want this when repairing a curb or concrete steps. Don't buy it until it is needed.

LINE-MAKING TROWEL

This trowel makes a groove about $1/2$ inch deep and $1/4$ inch wide in concrete after it has been poured but before it hardens. It is used for sidewalks. Don't buy this until it is needed.

PLASTIC MIXING TUB

If you are mixing up a small batch of cement, 2 quarts or less, you can use a 5-gallon bucket. But for larger batches, a plastic mixing tub, because it is wide and shallow, is much easier to use. Don't buy this until it is needed.

POINTING TROWEL

Pointing refers to placing (or replacing) cement mix or mortar mix in the spaces between bricks or stones in a wall. The pointing trowel is used for this purpose. It is just a strip of steel, usually about $5/8$ inch wide, with two bends in it. Don't buy this until you need it. There is also a tool called a hawk which is used to hold the mix when you are pointing. You can make your own hawk out of a 12-inch by 12-inch piece of plywood with a cylindrical handle fastened perpendicularly in the center of the plywood.

SMALL TRIANGULAR TROWEL (Fig. 10-1)

This is the basic tool for small cement jobs. It can also be used with roofing cement. You must have one. Buy one with a blade that is 6 or 7 inches long.

SMOOTHING TROWEL

This is a rectangular steel trowel, used for smoothing concrete. They come in all sizes, one that is about 4 inches by 12 inches is a useful size for most jobs. If a rougher surface is desired, for nonslip purposes, a wooden trowel, called a float, is used. Don't buy a smoothing trowel or a float at retail until needed.

SPRAY BOTTLE

Save a bottle from window cleaner or other detergent. It is the ideal device for dampening surfaces prior to applying patching cement. In some cases, you might want to add some bonding agent to the water in the bottle. In this case, be sure to rinse the bottle and spray mechanism thoroughly after use.

SYRINGE (Fig. 10-1)

A syringe, sometimes called a turkey baster, consists of a rubber bulb and a plastic or metal tube. You can use it to direct puffs of air into a hole or crack to clean out the loose debris before you fill the hole with cement. It is also useful for blowing debris out of corners of window sills after scraping and sanding and prior to painting.

WIRE BRUSH (Fig. 10-1)

If you are using patching cement, you will get better adhesion if you first wire-brush the surface even if it appears perfectly clean. See the write-up in Chap. 34, "Other Useful Materials."

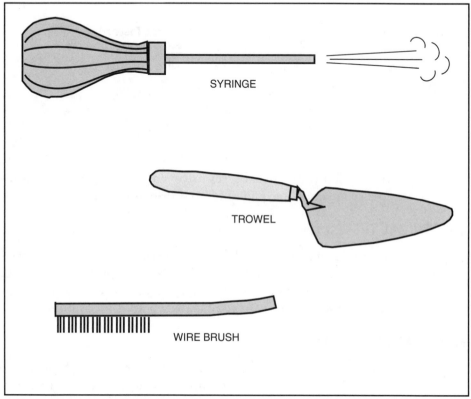

FIGURE 10-1   Syringe, trowel, wire brush.

ELECTRICAL-WORK TOOLS

Electrical Tester	56	Outlet Tester	57
Fish Wire	56	Stud Finder	57
Long Drill Bits	56	Wire Stripper	57
Multitester	57		

In addition to the usual screwdrivers and pliers, there are a few specialized tools you should have in order to do electrical work.

ELECTRICAL TESTER (Fig. 11-1)

This is a small neon bulb with two wire leads, used to test for the presence of voltage. It lights up if there is approximately 75 or more volts present. It will not work on cars where the voltage is only 12 volts. You should have one in your toolbox. Keep another at home.

FISH WIRE (Fig. 11-1)

Fish wire is a long, coiled, flat wire that you push through a hole in a wall or ceiling. You then attach a phone wire, or electrical wire, to the end of the fish wire and pull it back through the hole. Fish wires come in various lengths. For residential work, the 50-foot length is sufficient.

LONG DRILL BITS

You should have a few long drill bits for wood and for masonry. When you are running electrical wires, phone wires, or TV cables through walls or ceilings, you may need very long drill bits, 18 inches long or more. A $1/4$-inch hole is usually big enough for phone wires, and a $3/8$-inch or $1/2$-inch hole is usually big enough for electrical wires. Armored cable (BX) may require a larger hole. You can either buy long drill bits or use a bit extender (usually about 18 inches long), that holds shorter drill bits. On rare occasions, you might have to use two bit extenders, this is most likely to occur in an old house.

MULTITESTER (Fig. 11-2)

This is sometimes called a multimeter, or a volt-ohm-milliammeter, or a VOM. It is used to measure voltage, resistance, and current. It is extremely useful when you are trying to fix any electrical device. You can buy an inexpensive VOM at electronics stores. If you have not used one before, you should spend some time reading the instructions and experimenting with it to become familiar with what it can do.

OUTLET TESTER (Fig. 11-1)

This 3-pronged device indicates whether an outlet is wired correctly or incorrectly. Carry it in your toolbox.

STUD FINDER (Fig. 11-2)

This clever and inexpensive electronic device finds where the studs are. It works well on drywall walls, but not very well on plaster-and-lath walls.

WIRE STRIPPER (Fig. 11-1)

The wire stripper is like a small, thin, flat pair of pliers. It has two sharpened V-shaped notches that cut through the insulation on a wire. You then slide the cut piece of insulation off the end of the wire. It takes some practice to be able to cut through the insulation without cutting into the copper wire. It is a good idea to practice using the wire stripper on various sizes of solid and stranded wire. If you have to remove more than about $1/2$ inch of insulation, it may be easier to do it in two operations.

Some wire strippers have a series of different-sized holes, one for each gauge of wire. If you do telephone installations, you may need a special wire stripper designed to strip extremely thin wires.

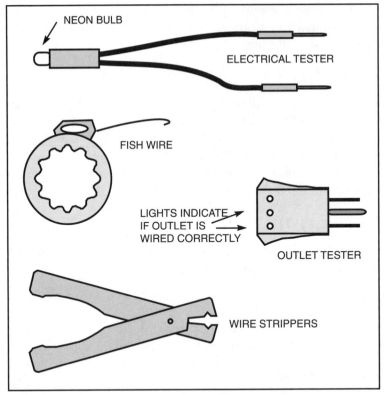

FIGURE 11-1 Electrical tester, fish wire, outlet tester, wire strippers.

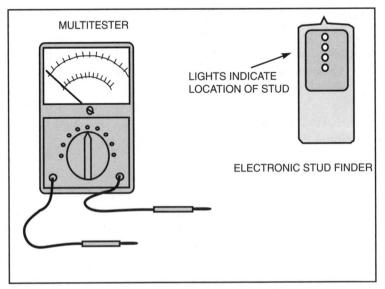

FIGURE 11-2 Multitester, electronic stud finder.

GARDENING AND TREE TOOLS

Axe	59	Hole Digger	61
Bow Saws	59	Lopping Shears	61
Digging Bar	60	Pick	61
Dirt Rake	60	Pole Pruner	61
Grass Rake	60	Pruning Shears	62
Hand Trowel	60	Shovel	62
Hatchet	60	Sickle	62
Hedge Shears	60	Spading Fork	62
Hedge Trimmer	60	Paint Garden Tools White	62
Hoe	61		

Here, listed in alphabetical order, are the most useful tools for gardening and tree work.

AXE

An axe is not often needed because chain saws are so much better for cutting trees. You may occasionally use an axe to cut a tree when a chain saw is not available. You might find one useful to chop the roots of a bush you are pulling out of the ground. Another occasional use of the axe is to split firewood. If the axe is stuck in a piece of wood you are trying to split, don't hammer on the axe head; that will ruin the axe. Wiggle the axe free or use wedges and a sledge hammer to free it instead. Always wear your safety goggles when using an axe.

BOW SAWS (Fig. 12-1)

Other useful tools for tree work are bow saws, sometimes called cordwood saws. Buy one with a 21-inch blade and one with a 30-inch blade. Be sure you buy good-quality blades with some "set" to them. "Set" refers to the alternate teeth being bent outward from the blade in opposite directions. You can sight along the teeth to see the set. If the blade does not have enough set, it will stick and jam, especially in wet sappy wood.

DIGGING BAR (Fig. 12-1)

A digging bar is a long heavy steel bar with a chisel-like blade at the end. If you are installing wooden fence posts, you will dig holes for them with a hole digger. But if you run into a root or a rock while digging, you may need a digging bar to cut the root or break up the rock for removal.

DIRT RAKE (Fig. 12-2)

The dirt rake is used to smooth out an area of dirt or sand, either for gardening purposes, or before laying sod, or before laying flagstones or paver bricks, or before pouring concrete.

GRASS RAKE (Fig. 12-2)

The grass rake has springy "fingers" made of metal or bamboo. It is used to rake up leaves or grass trimmings. I like a big wide grass rake with a long handle. One clever design is adjustable in width; you can open it wide for large areas and close it up to get in between bushes.

HAND TROWEL

You must have a hand trowel for digging small planting holes. If the trowel has a white or yellow handle, it will be more visible and you are less likely to lose it.

HATCHET

A hatchet is not essential, but it is useful for cutting twigs off branches that you are bundling. It is the perfect tool for chopping vines that are growing on trees or walls.

HEDGE SHEARS

These are large, hand-operated shears. They are fine for trimming a bush or a small hedge.

HEDGE TRIMMER

For trimming large hedges, you must have an electric hedge trimmer. Buy a good-quality trimmer with a long cutting bar. I made a wooden handle, 6 feet long, that I attach to my hedge trimmer so that I can trim hedges many feet thick. It also enables me to trim tall bushes and small evergreen trees.

HOE

A hoe is useful for gardening work, such as loosening hard dirt and scraping away weeds that are starting to grow. It is also perfect for mixing cement in a big plastic tub.

HOLE DIGGER (Fig. 12-1)

Metal fence posts can usually be driven into the ground with a sledge hammer. But if you are installing wooden fence posts, you must have a hole digger. I like the kind that resembles two narrow shovels facing each other. I paint the handles of my hole digger white, then I paint black bands on them every 6 inches so I can tell how deep the hole is.

LOPPING SHEARS (Fig. 12-1)

Lopping shears are like heavy pruning shears with long handles. You use both hands to operate them. I keep my lopping shears in my car because they are so often needed to provide access for jobs that are not related to tree work.

PICK (Fig. 12-3)

Although you won't need it very often, the pick is a useful tool. The pick you buy should have one pointed end and the other end, which is sometimes called a mattock, should be about 4 inches wide. You can use a pick to dig planting holes in hard ground or to remove rocks that are in the way of whatever you are doing. The mattock end is the perfect tool for cutting tree roots that are running along the surface of the ground. I have also used my pick for chopping ice or hard-packed snow to liberate someone's car from a driveway. With the advent of global warming, that may no longer be necessary.

POLE PRUNER (Fig. 12-3)

If you are going to do any tree work, you will need a pole pruner. A pole pruner is a telescoping tube which can extend to about 12 feet. It has a saw on the end and also a cutting blade that you activate by pulling on a rope. The cutting blade can cut branches up to about 1 inch in diameter. The saw can cut through branches up to about 4 inches in diameter. Using a pole pruner can be quite demanding on the arm and shoulder muscles.

When you buy a pole pruner, spend enough to get a strong sturdy one, the cheap ones simply will not do the job. I recommend an aluminum pole pruner, rather than fiberglass, because they cost less and are lighter and therefore easier to handle. But they do conduct electricity, so never use one near electric wires.

PRUNING SHEARS

These are the small shears that you hold in one hand. They can cut twigs up to about $3/8$-inch in diameter.

SHOVEL (Fig. 12-2)

I am often asked to transplant bushes or small trees. I find the most useful shovel to be one with a long handle with a D-shaped handgrip and a very narrow blade. The blade should be about 6 inches wide and 8 or 10 inches long. Ideally, it should have a rounded or pointed end to make it easier to push into the ground.

SICKLE (Fig. 12-3)

A sickle is a curved cutting blade, about a foot long, with a wooden handle. It is useful for cutting weeds near a pole or fence where the mower cannot reach.

SPADING FORK (Fig. 12-2)

A spading fork is a big digging fork with four prongs. Many people call it a pitch fork, although that is a different tool. The spading fork is good for loosening soil preparatory to planting. It is also good for removing sod to prepare for a flower bed and for turning over the material in a compost pile.

PAINT GARDEN TOOLS WHITE

I like to paint the handles of garden tools (rakes, shovels) white. That makes them easier to see if you are working while night is falling or if leaves are falling or blowing around.

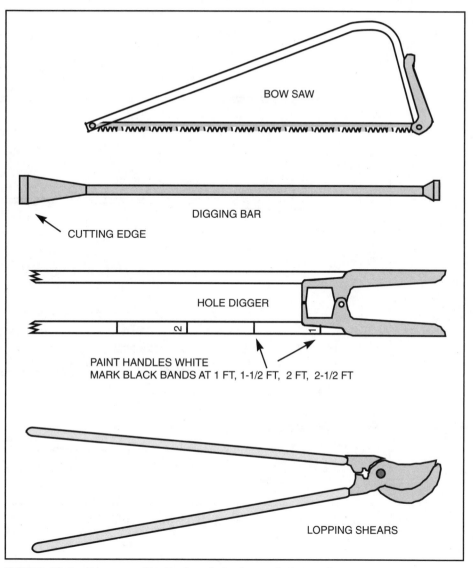

FIGURE 12-1 Bow saw, digging bar, hole digger, lopping shears.

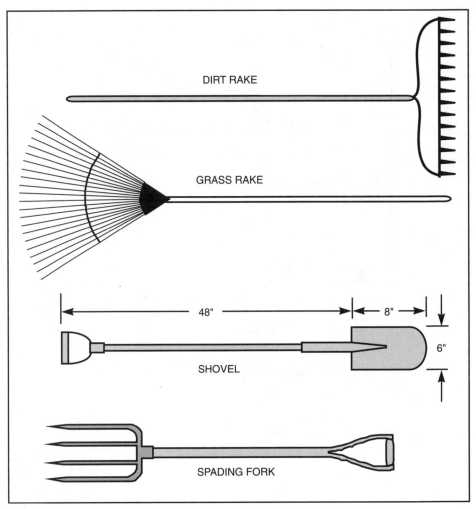

FIGURE 12-2 Dirt rake, grass rake, shovel, spading fork.

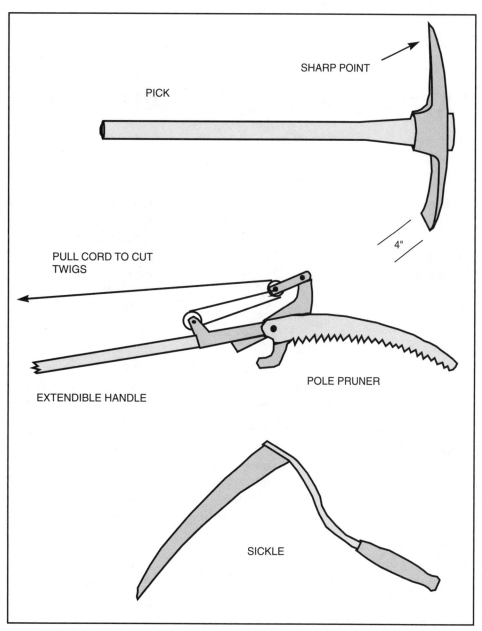

SHARP POINT

PICK

4"

PULL CORD TO CUT TWIGS

POLE PRUNER

EXTENDIBLE HANDLE

SICKLE

FIGURE 12-3 Pick, pole pruner, sickle.

LAYOUT AND MEASURING TOOLS

Bevel Gauge	66	Protractor (for Measuring Angles)	67
Compass	66	Speed Square	67
Dividers	66	Steel Measuring Tape	67
Drill Gauge	67	Straightedge	67
Drywall Square	67	Triangles: 45-Degree and	
Framing Square	67	30-60-90–Degree	68
Outside Calipers	67	Try Square	68

Layout refers to marking something, usually wood or sheet metal, preparatory to cutting, bending, or drilling. The following tools will take care of most of your layout and measuring needs.

BEVEL GAUGE (Fig. 13-1)

A bevel gauge is like a small square, but the angle of the square is adjustable. It is usually used to transfer an angle from an existing structure to something you are making that must fit that structure.

COMPASS

The compass has one pointed leg and a pencil on the other leg. It is used to draw small circles and to scribe outlines from an edge to a surface.

DIVIDERS (10- OR 12-INCH; Fig. 13-2)

A divider is used to scribe arcs or circles. It can also be used to transfer dimensions from one place to another and to step off equal distances along a line or an arc. For drawing large circles, you can attach a short pencil to one leg.

DRILL GAUGE (Fig. 13-2)

A drill gauge is a flat piece of steel or plastic with holes in it ranging from $1/16$ inch to $1/2$ inch. It is used to determine the size of a drill bit by seeing which hole it fits into.

DRYWALL SQUARE (Fig. 13-3)

This is a large square whose long arm is 4 feet long. In addition to its intended use for drywall work, it is also helpful for laying out patterns on plywood, paneling, and flooring.

FRAMING SQUARE (Fig. 13-3)

If you are building or fixing something small, you can use the try square that you carry in your toolbox. For larger jobs, a framing square is much more accurate. A framing square is about 16 inches by 24 inches.

OUTSIDE CALIPERS (10-INCH; Fig. 13-1)

These calipers are used to determine the diameter of cylindrical objects such as dowels and pipes.

PROTRACTOR (Fig. 13-2)

This is used for measuring angles.

SPEED SQUARE (Fig. 13-3)

This square has graduations on it which make laying out angles for rafters and other members easy.

STEEL MEASURING TAPE

This should be 12 feet long or longer.

STRAIGHTEDGE

This should be 48 inches long and marked in inches. Some straightedges come as two 48-inch sections that can be connected to make 96 inches. The straightedge can be clamped to a sheet of plywood and used as a saw guide.

TRIANGLES (Fig. 13-1)

These are made of transparent plastic. Use 45-degree and 30-60-90–degree triangles in 10-inch or 12-inch sizes.

TRY SQUARE

This is a versatile tool for small work. For larger work, the framing square is more accurate.

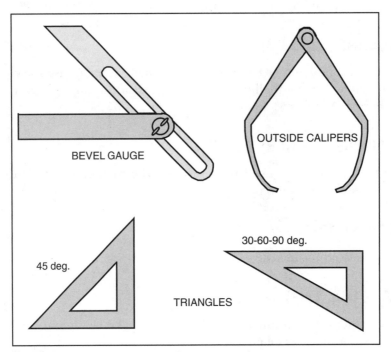

BEVEL GAUGE

OUTSIDE CALIPERS

45 deg.

30-60-90 deg.

TRIANGLES

FIGURE 13-1 Bevel gauge, calipers, triangles.

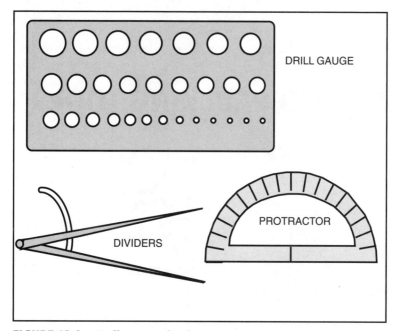

FIGURE 13-2 Drill gauge, dividers, protractor.

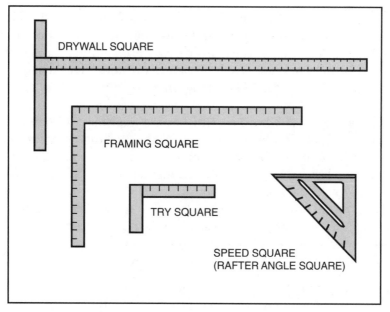

FIGURE 13-3 Drywall square, framing square, try square, speed square.

PAINTING AND CAULKING TOOLS

Brushes	70	Paint Tray	72
Caulking Gun	70	Roller	72
Drop Cloths	71	Roller Covers	72
Extension Handles	71	Scraper	72
Paint Brush Extender	71	Wire Brush	72
Paint Can Opener	71		

BRUSHES

You should have paint brushes of all sizes from $^1/_2$ inch wide to 4 inches wide. There is also a large round brush called a pound brush. It holds a lot of paint and is a great time saver if you are painting railings, fences, ornamental iron work, or other intricate surfaces. The disadvantage of the pound brush is that it takes a long time to clean after use.

Buy only top-quality brushes. Brushes are available with natural bristle, nylon bristle, and polyester bristle. The natural bristle brush is not the best for water-based paint because the bristles tend to soften after a half hour or more of use. The nylon bristles are fine for everything except shellac; the alcohol in the shellac will soften the bristles. In both cases, the bristles will recover their springiness after the brush is cleaned and allowed to dry. The polyester brushes seem to work well with any paint. Learn how to clean brushes properly and they will last for years. Some brushes have longer handles than others. All other things being equal, I prefer the longer handles; they will extend your reach.

CAULKING GUN (Fig. 14-1)

You must have at least one, preferably two, caulking guns. There are two common types of caulking guns. In one type, the rod that pushes the caulk out of the cartridge is perfectly round. The other kind has a push rod with notches in it for the trigger mechanism to engage. The gun with the notched rod is far superior. Don't buy the kind with the round rod. After some use, the rod gets chewed up and rough and becomes very difficult to use.

Why would you want more than one caulking gun? There may be times when you will use two kinds of caulk alternately on the same job. Also, there may be times when you will want to have two caulk cartridges in use, one on which the spout is cut near the tip to lay down a very narrow bead of caulk and the other cut to a larger opening to lay down a wide bead of caulk.

DROP CLOTHS

Ask friends to save their old bed sheets for you to use as drop cloths. They will catch paint spatters but not spills or big gobs of paint. So, if those are possible, spread plastic under the sheets. You can buy inexpensive plastic drop cloths. They are fine for draping over furniture but if you use them on a floor, any drops of paint will tend to stay wet for awhile and you must be careful not to step on them and track paint onto a floor or rug.

EXTENSION HANDLES

You must have a few extension handles of various lengths for your roller. These handles will allow you to paint ceilings and high walls without using a ladder. You can buy telescoping handles that extend up to 16 feet or more. The extension handle has a threaded end that screws into the roller handle.

PAINT BRUSH EXTENDER (Fig. 14-2)

A useful device to have when you are painting from a ladder is a paint brush extender. You can buy or improvise this device. You can make one as follows: Take a broom handle and cut the end at 45 degrees. Drill a small perpendicular hole, all the way through, in the face of this cut and put a small bolt through the hole so it extends an inch beyond the cut face. You can now mount a paint brush on this bolt and hold it in place with a wing nut. This will greatly increase the area you can reach before you have to move the ladder. You can also buy or adapt a paint scraper to use with an extension pole.

PAINT CAN OPENER

This tool does a better job of opening paint cans than the usual screwdriver.

PAINT TRAY

You will need a paint tray to hold the paint that you apply to the roller. Some of these trays are made of a nonstick plastic that allows you to easily peel off dried paint, but the metal trays are fine.

ROLLER

For most jobs, the 9-inch roller is best. You might occasionally use a 7-inch roller for smaller areas and you might use a very thin roller for painting behind radiators or toilet tanks. There are also huge rollers (18-inch) that you might use when coating a flat roof. Most rollers use a $1/4$-inch-diameter steel rod for the bent part that goes from the handle to the part that turns. They are OK for most tasks, but the roller that uses a $5/16$-inch rod is better when used with a long extension handle because it flexes less.

ROLLER COVERS

The roller cover is the cylinder that slides onto the roller. It holds the paint and rolls it onto the wall. Roller covers come with nap (the fuzzy covering) of various lengths. The short nap gives the smoothest coating but it is only suitable for smooth flat surfaces. Longer naps hold more paint and are used for rough or irregular surfaces.

SCRAPER (Fig. 14-2)

There are many styles of paint scraper. I find that the triangular scraper is most useful. These scrapers can get dull rapidly if you are scraping paint on metal or masonry surfaces. I sometimes take 3 or 4 scrapers with me when I have to do extensive scraping on such surfaces. Use your bench grinder to keep your scrapers sharp.

WIRE BRUSH

The wire brush is useful for brushing rust or loose paint off a surface to prepare for painting. (See Fig. 10-1.) Also, an individual wire from this brush may be just right for opening up the hole in the tip of a can of spray paint.

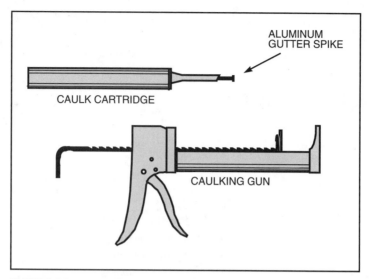

FIGURE 14-1 Caulk cartridge, caulking gun.

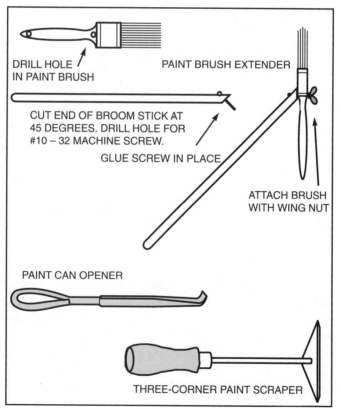

FIGURE 14-2 Paint brush extender, paint can opener, three-corner paint scraper.

PLUMBING TOOLS

Basin Wrench	74	Plunger	75
Closet Auger	74	Propane Torch	75
Drain Augers	74	Seat Wrenches	76
Handle Puller	75	Spud Wrench	76
Pipe-Threading Tools	75	Stem Wrenches	76
Pipe Wrenches	75	Tubing Cutter	76

Here, listed alphabetically, are the most useful tools for plumbing work.

BASIN WRENCH (Fig. 15-1)

The basin wrench is a cleverly designed tool that is used to get up behind washbasins or sinks to tighten or loosen the water supply lines.

CLOSET AUGER

An auger is a coiled wire that resembles a long spring. A closet auger is a specially shaped auger used for unclogging toilets.

DRAIN AUGERS

Drain augers (sometimes called *snakes*) are used to dislodge whatever may be clogging up a drain. They look like spiral-wound steel springs. You feed them down the drain and turn them to loosen whatever is in there. They come in various lengths. The shorter ones are easier to handle, but the longer ones are sometimes needed when the obstruction is far from the drain opening. If you have one drain auger that is 10 feet long and another that is 25 feet long, they will take care of most clogged drains.

HANDLE PULLER (Fig. 15-2)

When you have to replace the washer on a water valve or faucet, the first thing you must do is to remove the handle. In 9 out of 10 cases, this is fairly easy to do. But, occasionally, you will encounter a handle that has corroded onto the valve stem so tightly that you cannot get it off with penetrating oil and pliers or by tapping with a hammer. In that case, you need a handle puller. The handle puller is an inexpensive tool that has two arms that hook under the handle and a long screw that you tighten to pull the handle off. You will very rarely need a handle puller, but it is small and inexpensive, so it is a good idea to have one "just in case." When you encounter a difficult-to-remove handle, you should put a little grease on the valve stem before you replace the handle so it will be easy to remove the next time.

PIPE-THREADING TOOLS

There was a time when every plumber had to have pipe-threading tools to cut threads on the ends of galvanized iron pipes. Fortunately, those days are gone because copper tubing has replaced iron pipe. However, on rare occasions, when working in an old house, you might need to have a piece of pipe threaded. Most plumbing supply places and some hardware stores can do this for you. It doesn't pay to buy your own pipe-threading equipment unless you need it frequently and live a long way from a store that can thread pipes for you or you come across such equipment being offered for sale at a very low price. It is heavy and bulky, so don't buy it unless you have a place to keep it.

PIPE WRENCHES (Fig. 15-2)

I suggest that you have three pipe wrenches: 6-inch, 10-inch, and 12-inch.

PLUNGER

This is the tried and true "plumber's helper." You always try this tool first and if it does not open up a clogged drain, you then start with the drain augers.

PROPANE TORCH

A propane torch is indispensable when you do copper tubing work. You may also use it on rare occasions to thaw a frozen water pipe, or to soften hardened putty or old paint before scraping. I have a box labeled "TORCH." In this box I have my propane torch, an extra container of propane, a spark igniter for lighting the torch, wire solder (be sure to use nonlead solder on water-supply tubing), two sizes of wire brush for cleaning inside $^1/_2$-inch and $3/4$-inch tubing prior to soldering, a small roll of open-weave abrasive cloth to clean the outside of tubing (you can use ordinary sandpaper instead), a small can of soldering flux, and a tubing cutter. When I have to do a plumbing job with copper tubing, I have everything I need in this box except any copper tubing and fittings that might be required.

If you use a propane torch near anything that can burn, use sheet metal shields, or some bricks, or a few pieces of asbestos shingle, to shield the combustible material from the flame. If you don't have any sheet metal with you, you can usually find a big tomato juice can in the trash, remove the ends with a can opener, and cut it as needed.

SEAT WRENCHES (Fig. 15-1)

The seat is the part of the faucet that the washer bears down against to shut off the flow of water. The seats are usually removable and sometimes have to be replaced when they develop small openings that allow the water to leak past the washer. There are two styles of seat wrench; both look like a rod bent at a right angle. One style has smoothly tapered arms, one hexagonal and one square. The other style has arms with discrete steps on its arms to fit various sizes of seats. It is a good idea to have one of each kind of seat wrench, then you are prepared for almost any faucet.

SPUD WRENCH (Fig. 15-1)

A spud wrench is an adjustable-end wrench which is used to turn the large nuts that are used with sink and washstand drain fittings. You may not need a spud wrench if you have large channel-lock pliers.

STEM WRENCHES (Fig. 15-1)

These are double-ended sockets that look like a piece of steel tubing formed into a hexagonal shape at each end. There are some plumbing jobs, especially on some bathtubs, that you simply cannot do unless you have the right size sockets. They are not expensive. I have a set that goes from $3/4$ inch to $1^1/4$ inches.

TUBING CUTTER (Fig. 15-2)

You can use a fine-tooth hacksaw to cut tubing, but the tubing cutter does a faster, cleaner job.

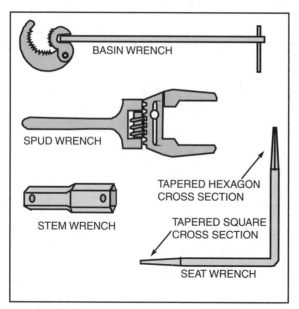

FIGURE 15-1 Basin wrench, spud wrench, stem wrench, seat wrench.

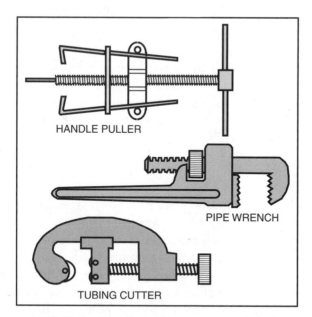

FIGURE 15-2 Handle puller, pipe wrench, tubing cutter.

PORTABLE POWER TOOLS

Chain Saw	78	Bits for Electric Drills	79
Circular Saw	78	Hammer Drill	80
Cordless Drill	79	Reciprocating Saw	80
Drywall-Screw Gun	79	Router	80
Electric Drills	79	Saber Saw	81

Here, in alphabetical order, are the most useful portable power tools.

CHAIN SAW (Fig. 16-1)

I use a 16-inch electric chain saw. If you expect to be doing tree work at a distance from an electric outlet, you might buy a gas-powered chain saw. Be very respectful of chain saws; make sure you know what you are doing, observe all the safety precautions, and make sure your saw is in perfect working condition.

CIRCULAR SAW (Fig. 16-1)

A circular saw is the indispensable work horse for carpentry. Buy one with a carbide-tipped, general-purpose blade. You need only one circular saw; you can change the blade for special purposes. I have three other circular saws in addition to the one with the general-purpose blade. This saves the time required to change blades. One saw has a very-fine-toothed blade for making clean smooth cuts in paneling but it does not work well in anything thicker than $1/4$ inch. One saw has a 32-tooth blade for making clean cuts in plywood. And one saw has an old, used, general-purpose carbide blade that I use for dirty lumber and boards that may have hidden nails lurking within, and for making cuts in asphalt-shingled roofs (as for installing skylights or ridge vents).

CORDLESS DRILL (Fig. 16-1)

A cordless drill is a time-saver, especially if you are working on a ladder or if electricity is not readily available. Buy one which is rated at least 9.6 volts (more is better) and has a keyless chuck. Keep it charged so it is ready whenever you need it and so that the battery won't go permanently dead. Try not to leave your cordless drill in your closed up car on hot summer days. That might shorten the life of the battery.

DRYWALL-SCREW GUN

This tool resembles an ordinary electric drill, but it has a special front end designed to drive drywall screws. If you do a lot of drywall work, this tool is indispensable. If you only do occasional small drywall jobs, you can use the drywall-screw bit described under Bits for Electric Drills, below.

ELECTRIC DRILLS (Fig. 16-1)

I have several electric drills in addition to the one in my tool box. I buy one whenever I see one at a low price at a yard sale. Why so many? Sometimes I do a job where I have to drill two sizes of hole, one for the shank of a screw and the other as a pilot hole for the threaded part of the screw. Then I may need another drill with a countersink bit to countersink the hole. Finally, I may need a Phillips bit to drive a screw into the hole. So I have several drills, all plugged into the power strip at the end of my extension cord, each with a different bit, and I use one after the other, without having to stop to change bits. Also useful for this situation is a drill with a quick-change chuck where you just pop in one bit after another as needed, but you must have special bits with hexagonal shanks.

Although electric drills are very durable devices, they do sometimes fail, and it is usually better to buy a new one or a good used one than to fix an old one. All of my drills are $3/8$ inch (chuck size) except for one big brute with a $1/2$-inch chuck. If you have to drill a large hole ($3/4$ inch or larger) through a thick wooden post and the post is pressure-treated wood and soaking wet, you will need this kind of horsepower to do the job.

BITS FOR ELECTRIC DRILLS

The following items are used with your electric drill.

Drywall-Screw Bit   This bit is like a Phillips screwdriver bit but it has a stop ring to allow the drywall screw to be driven to the correct depth, but no farther. (See Fig. 18-2.) If you have a drywall-screw gun, you won't need this bit.

Hole Cutters   When they are needed, you might buy some hole cutters, especially the sizes needed for installing locks in doors.

Spade Bits   You should also have a set of spade bits from $1/2$ inch to $1^1/2$ inch. These bits are used for drilling large holes in wood.

Twist Bits   You should have a complete set of standard-length, high-speed steel drill bits (often called *twist bits*) from $1/16$ inch to $3/8$ inch. It is a good idea to also have the following five sizes: $7/16$ inch, $1/2$ inch, $9/16$ inch, $5/8$ inch, and $3/4$ inch. The drill bits that are over $3/8$ inch in diameter should have $3/8$-inch shanks so they will fit into the chuck of your electric drill. And, as mentioned elsewhere, you should have some very long drill bits and some carbide-tipped masonry bits.

HAMMER DRILL (Fig. 16-1)

A hammer drill is similar to an electric drill, but it also hammers the drill bit into the work as the bit is turning. It makes quick work of drilling holes in cinder block, and in most (but not all) stone and concrete. It can also be used to drill holes in tiles, as for mounting bathroom fixtures. You will need a set of carbide-tipped drill bits, sizes $3/16$ inch to $5/8$ inch. If you can get a few very long carbide-tipped drill bits (12 inches long or longer), you will find them useful if you have to run a phone or electric line through the foundation wall of a house.

RECIPROCATING SAW (Fig. 16-1)

This is a handheld saw with a blade that goes back and forth, something like an electric knife. It is often called a *Sawzall*, although that is just a brand name, or a *recip*. It is used much less frequently than the circular saw but there are times when nothing else will do the job. It can be used for cutting metal as well as wood. It is useful for demolition work and for cutting holes in walls and roofs.

ROUTER

I have a router but I rarely have need for it. If you do a lot of cabinet work, you will use a router. I suggest that you not buy a router until you have a job that requires it, unless you come across a good used one at a very low price.

SABER SAW

The saber saw is used to make straight or curved cuts in wood or metal. You need not have a saber saw when you start out, but eventually you will find it helpful to have one. You should have a variety of blades, some for wood, some for metal, some with coarse teeth, and some with fine teeth.

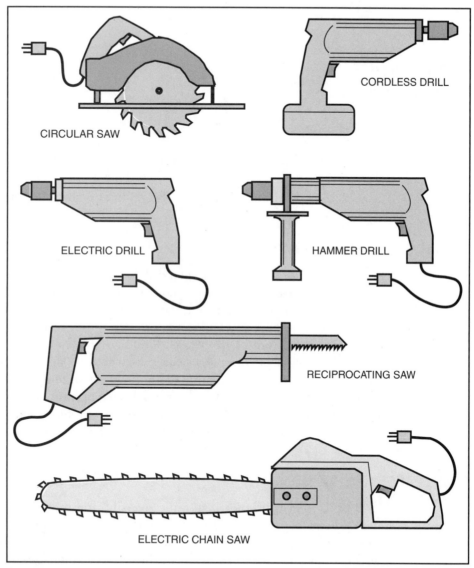

FIGURE 16-1 Portable power tools.

STATIONARY POWER TOOLS

Bench Grinder	82
Drill Press	82
Table Saw	83

The most useful stationary power tools are, in alphabetical order:

BENCH GRINDER (Fig. 17-1)

The bench grinder is used to sharpen drill bits, hand tools, garden tools, lawn mower blades, scissors, and other tools. Bench grinders are not very expensive. However, when you start out, you can get by with a medium-grit grinding wheel mounted on an electric motor, with a tool rest (which could be a wooden block) in front of the wheel. Grinding creates a lot of heat, so you should also have a jar of water nearby in which to dip tools that you are grinding to keep them from getting too hot. Excessive temperature can ruin a good tool. If you see the steel tool turning brown or blue or purple as you are grinding, it is too hot. Never grind aluminum or brass or wood, they will clog up the grinding wheel. Always wear safety goggles when grinding.

DRILL PRESS (Fig. 17-1)

A drill press can drill holes faster, more easily, and more accurately than a handheld electric drill. I use mine so much that I would feel lost without it. You don't need one when you are starting out but, if you can afford one, a drill press will pay for itself in time saved. Buy a good one. My drill press is fastened down to my work bench. If you have room for it, a stand-alone drill press that stands on the floor can handle bigger work. It also costs more.

TABLE SAW (Fig. 17-1)

A table saw is like a table with a circular saw blade sticking up through a slit in the table. The saw stays put and you push the wood through it. A 10-inch (diameter of the blade) table saw is big enough for almost any job. A table saw is a very useful device to have but it requires a lot of floor space all around it so that you can handle long boards and big sheets of plywood. I put wheels on two legs of my table saw so I can wheel it outside when I have to work with large pieces. A radial-arm saw is more versatile than a table saw, but it costs more.

You can buy a metal stand, made of angle iron, for your table saw. A better way, if you have the inclination, is to build a two-drawer stand for the saw. One drawer catches the sawdust, the other holds extra blades, sanding disks, and other items for use with the saw.

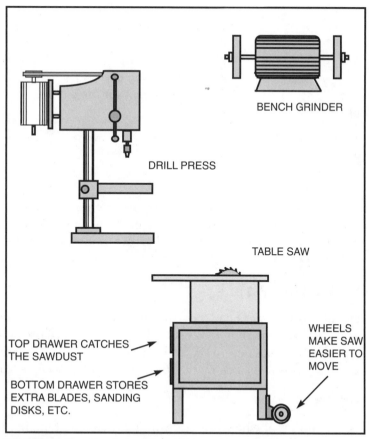

BENCH GRINDER

DRILL PRESS

TABLE SAW

TOP DRAWER CATCHES
THE SAWDUST

WHEELS
MAKE SAW
EASIER TO
MOVE

BOTTOM DRAWER STORES
EXTRA BLADES, SANDING
DISKS, ETC.

FIGURE 17-1 Bench grinder, drill press, table saw.

OTHER USEFUL TOOLS

Ball Peen Hammer	84	Metal Punch	87
Bolt Cutter	84	Sledge Hammer	88
Box Wrenches	85	Small Pry Bar	88
Brace and Auger Bits	85	Splitting Wedges	88
C-Clamps	85	Staple Gun	88
Carbide Hacksaw Blade	85	Taps and Dies	88
Come-Along	86	3-Foot Level	89
Drive Bits	86	Tile Cutter	89
Drywall Tools	86	Vise Grip Pliers	89
Files	87	Wood Rasp	89
Framing Square	87	Wrecking Bar	89
Glass Cutter	87	Marking Your Tools	89
Gutter-Cleaning Tool	87		

In addition to the tools described in previous chapters, you will eventually need most of the following tools. You need not have them when you start out, but if you can acquire them at bargain prices, do so. Otherwise, buy them when needed.

BALL PEEN HAMMER (Fig. 18-1)

One end of this hammer head looks like an ordinary hammer, the other end is rounded, like half a marble. It is useful for those few occasions when you are using rivets other than pop rivets. You can often buy one of these hammers at low cost at a yard sale or flea market because not many people want them.

BOLT CUTTER (Fig. 18-1)

This is a helpful tool when you are working with wire fencing. It makes cutting heavy wire effortless. Bolt cutters come in all sizes. You only need the small or medium size. If you buy used bolt cutters, make sure the jaws are sharp and that they meet perfectly.

BOX WRENCHES

These are very useful wrenches. (See Fig. 8-1.) They completely encircle the nut or bolt that you are turning so they cannot slip off or damage the nut or bolt (or your knuckles). In addition to the three sizes that I recommend for your toolbox, it is well to also have the following two sizes at home:

- $^{13}/_{16}$–$^{7}/_{8}$ inch
- $^{15}/_{16}$–1 inch

Box wrenches are especially useful when you are working on cars, bicycles, or mowers.

BRACE AND AUGER BITS

The brace and bit were used to drill holes for thousands of years before electricity was discovered. They are still useful on occasion. For example, you may have to drill some 1-inch-diameter holes in a wooden fence where electricity is not available. Most cordless drills don't have the power to drill holes that large but, with a brace and bit, it is easy. When the need arises, buy a brace and some auger bits from $^{1}/_{2}$ inch to 1 inch in diameter.

C-CLAMPS (Fig. 18-1)

These are clamps shaped like the letter "C." They have a threaded rod that you turn to tighten the clamp. Their most common use is when gluing two pieces of wood together. The clamps hold the wood while the glue sets. You will find many other uses for them; for example, you can attach two of them to a heavy sheet of plywood to serve as carrying handles. I like to have two or more C-clamps of each size from 1 inch to 5 inches. If you spray the threads of the C-clamp with silicone spray, the clamps will be easier to open and close.

CARBIDE HACKSAW BLADE

On extremely rare occasions, you may have to cut steel that is too hard for an ordinary hacksaw blade. An example might be when someone has a padlock that must be removed and he doesn't have the key. You can buy a hacksaw blade which has tungsten carbide grit embedded in the cutting edge. Don't buy it until you need it. The carbide blade can also be used to cut a glass bottle in half, although no one has ever asked me to do that.

COME-ALONG

Also known as a fence puller, this is a ratcheting device, sometimes with pulleys, that enables you to pull something with several hundred pounds of force. It is used when installing chain-link fencing. You might also use it to pull a bush out of the ground. If you see a come-along at a low price at a yard sale, buy it. Otherwise, don't buy one until you need it.

DRIVE BITS (Fig. 18-2)

In addition to the slot-head bits and the Phillips-head bits that are suggested to carry in your tool box, there are six other types of drive bits that are shown in Fig. 18-2. The most frequently needed ones are at the top of the drawing and the least frequently needed are at the bottom.

All of these bits can be used in a ratchet screwdriver that has removable tips. They can also be used with a $1/4$-inch ratchet wrench that has a $1/4$-inch hex socket attached. And they can be used with an electric drill.

Phillips-Head Drive Bits   Buy three sizes: #1, #2, and #3.

Slotted-Head Drive Bits   These are for driving the standard slotted-head screws. Some of these bits have a plastic sleeve that keeps the bit from sliding out of the slot in the screw head.

Drywall-Screw Drive Bit   There is only one size.

Nut-Driver Bits   Buy a set that goes from $3/16$ to $7/16$ inch. If you have the same size sockets for a $1/4$-inch drive socket wrench, you may not need these nut drivers.

Allen-Head Drive Bits   If you have a set of Allen wrenches, you may not need these bits.

Torx Bits, Robertson (Square Recess) Bits, Clutch Bits   If you work only on houses, you may never need these bits. But you may need them if you work on cars, household appliances, stereos, and office equipment.

DRYWALL TOOLS

In addition to the drywall square mentioned in Chap. 13, Layout and Measuring Tools, you should have a few taping knives of various widths and a drywall saw, the kind that has a sharp point at the end. You can push this saw through the drywall and then cut out whatever opening is required.

FILES

In addition to the files in your toolbox, you should have a few others at home:

Flat or Half-Round File   This should be a coarse-tooth file, 12 inches long.

Round File (Coarse-Tooth)   This file should also have coarse teeth, be $3/8$ inch or $1/2$ inch in diameter and 10 or 12 inches long.

Round File (Small)   This file should be $1/8$ inch or $3/16$ inch in diameter; any length is fine. It is used to shape or enlarge small holes in metal.

Triangular File   This file should be $3/8$ inch across the flat and 8 or 10 inches long.

FRAMING SQUARE

If you are building or fixing something small, you can use the try square that you carry in your tool box. (See Fig. 13-3.) For larger jobs, a framing square is much more accurate. A framing square is about 16 inches by 24 inches.

GLASS CUTTER

Buy a good-quality glass cutter and practice using it at home until you are good at cutting glass. This skill can be a big time-saver if you have to replace a window and you don't know the exact size that is needed. You can take a piece of glass that you know is oversized and cut it to size at the job site.

GUTTER-CLEANING TOOL (Fig. 18-3)

If you find yourself cleaning gutters frequently, you can easily make a tool to speed up this work. See the instructions in Fig. 18-3.

METAL PUNCH (Fig. 18-4)

This is a punch similar to those used to punch holes in paper, but much heavier. It is designed to punch holes in sheet metal. It will punch holes in soft sheet aluminum up to about $1/8$ inch thick, or in mild steel up to about $1/16$ inch thick. It will also punch holes in vinyl siding, leather belts, etc. It comes with several punch bits ranging in diameter from about $3/32$ inch to about $5/16$ inch. It is not essential to have one of these punches, but it comes in handy often enough so that it will eventually pay for itself in time saved.

SLEDGE HAMMER

You will need a sledge hammer for driving fence posts into the ground. You may also use it for breaking up concrete or for driving steel wedges to split firewood. Sledge hammers come in many weights, from 8 pounds to 16 pounds or more. The heavier the hammer, the more effective it will be in driving fence posts. But don't buy a sledge hammer heavier than you can handle.

SMALL PRY BAR (Fig. 18-4)

This is a small flat steel bar, perhaps 10 inches long. It is bent slightly at one end and turned up 90 degrees at the other end. It is useful for removing nails and wooden trim, and for prying up rugs, flooring, and windows that are stuck shut.

SPLITTING WEDGES

These are heavy steel wedges that you use in conjunction with a sledge hammer to split firewood. In most cases, it is cheaper for the homeowner to buy split firewood rather than pay you to split it. I like to split firewood, but it's hard work, and I would not suggest that you do it unless you enjoy it.

STAPLE GUN (Fig. 18-5)

You will find many uses for a staple gun. Buy a good quality staple gun and all the sizes of staples to go with it, from $1/4$ inch to $9/16$ inch. Buy the "chisel point" staples. I like the staple guns that can be set at either of two force levels, but this is not essential. If you do a lot of insulation work, you should have a hammer tacker which is like a staple gun that you swing like a hammer instead of squeezing like a pistol.

TAPS AND DIES

Taps are used to cut threads inside a hole. Dies are used to cut threads on a rod. You will almost never need to do either of those operations. However, you may occasionally need a tap or a die to clean up existing damaged threads. If you come across some low-cost, second-hand taps and dies, the following sizes are the ones you may occasionally find useful:

Taps and dies: 8–32, 10–32, 10–24, $1/4$–20
Dies only: $5/16$–18, $3/8$–18, $1/2$–13

Don't buy at retail until needed.

3-FOOT LEVEL

For many purposes, the small torpedo level in your toolbox will suffice. But for more accuracy on larger jobs, you should have a 3-foot or 4-foot level. The aluminum levels work fine and usually cost less than the wooden ones.

TILE CUTTER

If you work with ceramic tiles, such as those used on bathroom walls and on some floors, you should have a tile cutter. It's a device with a sharp point that runs on rails to scratch a straight line on a tile and then break the tile along the line. You should also have a tile "nipper" which is like a pair of pliers that is used to nibble away at a tile to make curved cuts.

VISE GRIP PLIERS

Vise grips, as they are called, are very useful. A vise grip can hold a nut, which would otherwise be out of reach, while you turn the bolt. It can also hold a round bar to turn it or to stop it from turning.

WOOD RASP

A wood rasp is like a file with very coarse teeth. It is not essential to have a wood rasp, but it is occasionally useful when you have to shape a piece of wood and it doesn't matter if the wood is left with a rough surface. Shaping a wooden handle to fit a hammer head would be one example. It can also be used to enlarge a hole in a wooden door if the existing hole is too small for the lock you are installing. If you buy a wood rasp, buy a big, half-round one. Don't use it on metal; that will ruin it.

WRECKING BAR (Fig. 18-4)

This is a heavy steel bar, perhaps 24 or 30 inches long, with one end curved. It is used for prying apart boards that are nailed together and for pulling out big nails. You won't need the wrecking bar very often, but it is good to have one, especially if you are repairing wooden decks or fences.

MARKING YOUR TOOLS

You might want to get a small can of paint of an unusual color, or perhaps a bottle of nail polish, and put a wide band of it on each of your tools. That way, you will not accidentally take someone else's tool that happens to be the same as one of yours and they will not take one of your tools. This could happen when you are working at a home where the owner has a lot of tools, or you might be working in the same room as another tradesman who has a tool just like one of yours. You can also use an engraving tool to permanently mark your tools. That will prove ownership if the tool is stolen and recovered.

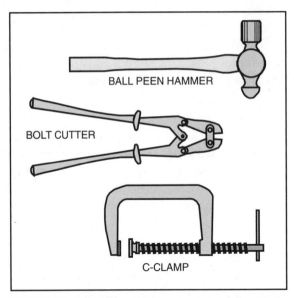

FIGURE 18-1   Ball peen hammer, bolt cutter, C-clamp.

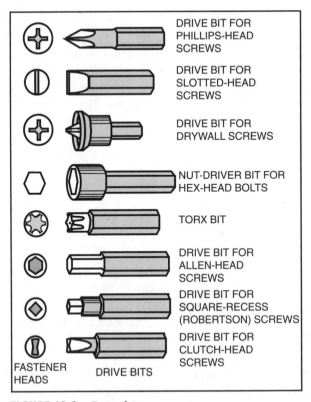

FIGURE 18-2   Drive bits.

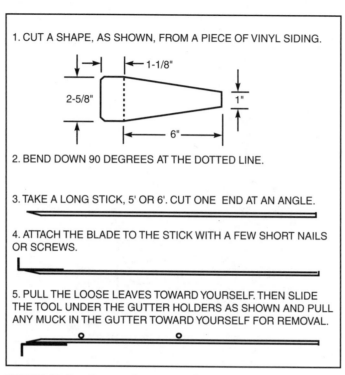

1. CUT A SHAPE, AS SHOWN, FROM A PIECE OF VINYL SIDING.

1-1/8"

2-5/8"

1"

6"

2. BEND DOWN 90 DEGREES AT THE DOTTED LINE.

3. TAKE A LONG STICK, 5' OR 6'. CUT ONE END AT AN ANGLE.

4. ATTACH THE BLADE TO THE STICK WITH A FEW SHORT NAILS OR SCREWS.

5. PULL THE LOOSE LEAVES TOWARD YOURSELF. THEN SLIDE THE TOOL UNDER THE GUTTER HOLDERS AS SHOWN AND PULL ANY MUCK IN THE GUTTER TOWARD YOURSELF FOR REMOVAL.

FIGURE 18-3 Gutter-cleaning tool.

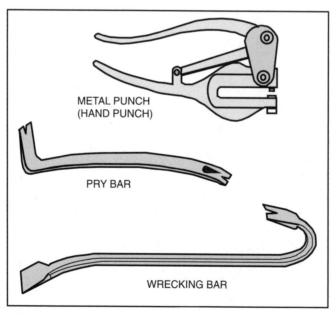

METAL PUNCH
(HAND PUNCH)

PRY BAR

WRECKING BAR

FIGURE 18-4 Metal punch, pry bar, wrecking bar.

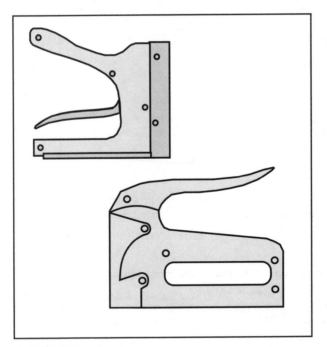

FIGURE 18-5 Staple guns.

BUYING HARDWARE

The next few chapters contain long lists of hardware items you should have at home. And they are only partial lists. You might wonder whether it really makes sense to have so much. After all, there are hardware stores where you can buy whatever you need. The answer is yes, it does make sense because of the time it saves. You can easily lose an hour or two of valuable time just shopping around for items you could have had at home. If something is small and inexpensive, and there is a good chance that it will be needed sooner or later, and (very important) you can store it in such a way that you can find it immediately when you need it, it pays to have it.

Always buy good-quality hardware. Whether it is a faucet for the kitchen sink or a lock set for the front door, always pay enough to get a quality item that will look good and work well for many years. Price is usually a good indicator of quality, but ask around to learn which brands are long lasting and reliable.

When you buy hardware, you are more likely to get the good-quality items you want at the home center or the large hardware store than at the little mom and pop store that sells pots and pans and other items for the housewife. Look for men with pickup trucks and heavy work shoes buying supplies early in the morning, and you are probably in the right place.

When buying an item, perhaps something for plumbing work or electrical work, it is a good idea to know the proper name of the object you are buying. You will get what you need much faster if you ask for a "J-bend" instead of "that curvy thing under the sink." If you have catalogs, you can find the correct name for the item you need.

DOOR HARDWARE

Door Scope	94	Lock Cylinders with Keys	95
Doorstops (Swinging)	94	Locksets	95
Doorstops (3 Inches Long)	95	Rollers	95
Doorstops (Hinge)	95	Safety Chains	96
Doorbell	95	Storm Door Closers	96
Garage Door Hardware	95	Storm Door Latches	96
Jimmy-Proof Lock	95	Turnbuckles	96
Knockers	95		

A handyman is frequently asked to fix doors that have one sort of problem or another. In order to do this, you must have a good understanding of how doors are installed, from the rough framing to the installation of a prehung or non-prehung door. You should know how the various types of interior and exterior locks work. In most cases, a problem with a door can be fixed by working with what is there. But sometimes you will have to buy new locksets. If you have a local locksmith shop, the people there can be very helpful.

There are so many varieties of locks and other door hardware that it is not practical to attempt to have spare parts for all of them. But there are some things worth having on hand.

DOOR SCOPE

This is like a little telescope that lets a person inside see who is outside.

DOORSTOPS (SWINGING)

These doorstops swing down from the door to the floor. Don't buy at retail until needed.

DOORSTOPS (3 INCHES LONG)

These are like a tightly wound spring with a plastic bumper on one end and a screw on the other. They screw into the baseboard and stop the door from opening so wide that the door knob bangs into the wall. You should buy several 3-inch-long doorstops and, if you can find them, a few that are 4 inches long.

DOORSTOPS (HINGE)

These doorstops mount on the hinge pins. Buy two or three of these.

DOORBELL

When a doorbell stops working, the most likely cause is a defective push button. Sometimes you can scrape the contacts clean, sometimes the button must be replaced. Then check out the wiring and the bell or chime. The occasional, but least likely, cause of the problem, is the transformer. I like to have on hand a few push buttons, one of which is an illuminated push button, an extra chime, and a 16-volt transformer.

GARAGE DOOR HARDWARE

Garage door hardware consists of rollers, latch, hinge, handle, and lock. Don't buy these at retail until they are needed.

JIMMY-PROOF LOCK (Fig. 20-1)

These are very strong and secure locks, used for exterior doors.

KNOCKERS (RARELY NEEDED)

Don't buy these at retail until they are needed.

LOCK CYLINDERS WITH KEYS

Don't buy lock cylinders until they are needed.

LOCKSETS

You will need one or two locksets for interior doors.

ROLLERS

Keep a few sets of adjustable rollers for closet sliding doors on hand.

SAFETY CHAINS

This is the kind that allows the door to open a few inches without letting anyone come in.

STORM DOOR CLOSERS (Fig. 20-1)

These closers are cylinders with springs inside. They often need replacing after several years of use. Occasionally you can rejuvenate one of these by removing the speed-adjustment screw and squirting some oil inside.

In some cases, the stop "washer" that slides along the closer rod, and is intended to hold the door open, doesn't do its job. Sometimes this can be remedied by bending that washer, using large channel-lock pliers, so that the bent tab on the washer is at a right angle to the rest of the washer. Buy only good-quality closers, and have a few on hand. Some newer storm doors use two closers.

STORM DOOR LATCHES

These come in various styles. Ask at your hardware store which style is most widely used and have one spare on hand.

TURNBUCKLES

You might need a turnbuckle that has rods to pull sagging doors back into square. (See Fig. 27-2.) Don't buy these until they are needed.

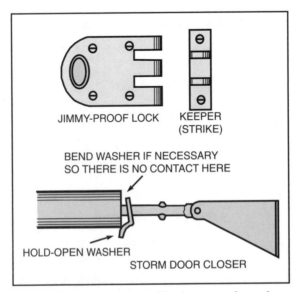

FIGURE 20-1 Jimmy-proof lock, storm door closer.

ELECTRICAL-WORK HARDWARE

Batteries	97	Fluorescent Tubes	101
Bulb Receptacles	98	Light Bulbs	101
Circuit Breakers and Fuses	98	Outdoor Electrical Fixtures	102
Dimmers	98	Power Strips	102
Doorbell and Push Button	99	Six-Way Outlets	103
Electrical Boxes	99	Surface-Mount Electrical Hardware	103
Electrical Cable	100	Switches	103
Electrical Outlets	100	Wire Nuts	103
Extension Cords	100		

BATTERIES

Strictly speaking, a battery consists of two or more cells connected together in one package. So, in the list below, only the 9-volt battery should be called a battery, the others are cells. However, cells are often called batteries.

I am often asked to fix devices that use cells or batteries. Sometimes the metal parts in the equipment that make contact with the cells or batteries get corroded and need cleaning (use fine sandpaper). More often, the equipment just needs new cells or batteries. I like to keep a few of each of the following common sizes on hand. It saves a lot of time when I have to fix someone's smoke alarm, flashlight, answering machine, or toys that require batteries.

- D cells
- C cells
- A cells
- AA cells
- AAA cells
- 9-volt batteries

I always buy alkaline batteries for my customers, even though they cost more, because they last longer. When I buy batteries, I mark the date of purchase on each battery. This is not necessary if the battery has an expiration date on it. I store my batteries in the refrigerator where they have a longer shelf life.

BULB RECEPTACLES

Bulb receptacles are white plastic or porcelain devices that fasten to an electrical box, usually on the ceiling. You then screw a light bulb into the receptacle. Some receptacles have a built-in outlet so you can plug something into them and some have a pull chain so you can turn the light on or off. They are not expensive and it is well to have a few of each style on hand.

CIRCUIT BREAKERS AND FUSES

The purpose of circuit breakers and fuses is to turn off the electricity when a circuit is drawing too much of it, whether because of a short circuit or being overloaded. Circuit breakers come in several styles, but one style is the most common. Ask at your hardware store which style is most common in your area. I like to have on hand a few of each of the following sizes of *breakers*.

- 15 amps
- 20 amps
- 30 amps

Many older houses use fuses instead of circuit breakers, so it is good to have the most commonly used sizes on hand. Buy only the time-delay fuses (sometimes called slo-blo). I like to have on hand the following sizes of time-delay *fuses*.

- 15 amps
- 20 amps
- 25 amps
- 30 amps

DIMMERS

Dimmers are used to adjust the brightness of incandescent lights. They can also be used to adjust the speed of fans, such as window fans. In most cases, dimmers cannot be used with fluorescent lights, although there are some special fluorescent lights which can be dimmed. You should be aware that dimmers sometimes cause a lot of noise and static on AM radio stations. They may also interfere with TV reception. I find that the knobs on dimmers frequently break, so if you are replacing a dimmer and the knob is OK, keep the knob.

DOORBELL AND PUSH BUTTON

It's a good idea to have an extra doorbell, or chime, or buzzer to use when determining why someone's doorbell isn't working. You should also have an extra push button or two in case that is what needs replacing. See Chap. 20, Door Hardware.

ELECTRICAL BOXES

Electrical boxes are made of steel or plastic. They go on a wall or in a wall and they contain outlets, switches, or dimmers. Most of the original boxes in a new house are plastic. Most boxes intended for installation in an existing house are steel. It is well to have a variety of steel boxes on hand.

Handy Box   Handy boxes are used very frequently. They are rectangular boxes with rounded corners. They are mounted *on* the wall, rather than *in* the wall. Handy boxes are frequently used in basements and garages. You can put a switch or an outlet in a handy box.

Octagon Box   There are also octagonal boxes that are surface mounted. They are roomier inside than the handy box and are better if you have several wires and connections inside the box. They can also hold two duplex outlets so that you can plug four things into the box.

Pancake Box   If you are installing a box for a ceiling fixture at a spot on the ceiling where there happens to be a joist, you can use a pancake box, which is only $1/2$ inch deep.

Switch Box   The "switch box," a rectangular steel box, is used for the majority of cases when you are installing a switch or an outlet. You cut a rectangular hole for it in the wall and it is held in place with Madison bars or with hardware that comes with the box.

If you are installing a dimmer, which is usually much larger than a switch, you can use a deep box if there is room in the wall to accommodate it. That will leave more room for the various wires that may be in the box. If the space between the two sides of the wall is small, you may have to use a shallow box.

Whenever I install a switch or an outlet in a steel box, I always wrap the switch or outlet with two turns of electrical tape so that the connection screws are covered. I do this before pushing the switch or outlet back into the box. This prevents accidental short circuits if the switch or outlet touches the side of the box or a ground wire.

Cover Plates for Boxes   For all of the above electrical boxes, you should have several cover plates that are designed to hold duplex outlets, a few cover plates designed to hold switches, and one or two blank covers. The blank covers have no holes in them. They are used to "blank off" a box that is no longer in use.

ELECTRICAL CABLE

The most widely used electrical cable is 14–2 with ground. It is used for all indoor circuits that do not carry more than 15 amperes of current. Also widely used is 12–2 cable which can carry up to 20 amperes. You should have some of each on hand, and buy other types of cable when needed.

ELECTRICAL OUTLETS

These come in brown and ivory. Unless the homeowner wants brown, I always use the ivory outlets. It is much easier to see where the holes in the outlet are, especially if you are plugging something in when the light is dim or the outlet is behind a sofa. If the store where you are buying outlets has two kinds of outlet, buy the heavier, more expensive variety. Most outlets are rated at 15 amperes. Use a 20-ampere outlet if the electrical line and the circuit breaker are rated for 20 amperes. If you are installing a new outlet outdoors or in a room with a concrete floor, such as a basement or garage, or within 5 feet of water (sink, bathtub, etc.), the code now requires the use of a GFCI (ground fault circuit interrupt) outlet. On rare occasions, you might want to install a surface-mount outlet.

EXTENSION CORDS

In addition to the long extension cords that you employ when working at some distance from a house, it is well to have some extension cords to give to customers for use inside a house. Here is what I like to have on hand.

2-Wire Extension Cords   I have 2-wire extension cords that are 6 feet long and 9 or 12 feet long, and in both white and brown.

3-Wire Extension Cords   These are for computers and other appliances that must be grounded. I keep two of these: one that is 6 feet long and another that is 9 or 12 feet long.

3-Wire Heavy-Duty Extension Cords   These are for air conditioners, etc. Two of these, one 6 feet long and one 9 feet long should be sufficient.

Another useful cord is the type that has a switch somewhere along its length. This switch is used to turn on whatever device the cord is being used with.

There are also cords that have an outlet on the back of the plug and a switch at the end of the cord. You plug such a cord into the wall, then you plug an appliance such as a lamp or a TV into the outlet on the back of the plug. The switch at the end of the cord is then used to turn the appliance on or off.

FLUORESCENT TUBES

I like to have on hand cool-white 40-watt, 30-watt, 20-watt, and 15-watt fluorescent tubes, and starters for those sizes (for older fixtures). There are other sizes of fluorescent tubes, but they are expensive and rarely used, and I would not buy them until needed.

Compact fluorescent bulbs (they screw in like an ordinary bulb) are becoming more popular and less expensive, so I like to have a few of each of the popular sizes on hand.

Fluorescent fixtures also have a component called a ballast. I wouldn't replace a defective ballast. It is usually better to just buy a new fixture.

Books that tell how to service fluorescent lights usually have tables of symptoms. If you compare the problem with those tables, you can usually tell whether you need a new tube, starter, or ballast.

LIGHT BULBS

I find it helpful to have a wide variety of bulbs on hand. I am often asked to fix or install a lighting fixture. Sometimes the only fix needed is a new bulb. The homeowner may not have any bulbs for the new fixture. Having the right bulb can save a trip to the store. If you are looking at an electrical parts catalog, bulbs may be called "lamps." I like to have on hand the following light bulbs:

25-Watt, 40-Watt, 60-Watt, 100-Watt, 150-Watt Bulbs   This makes a good selection of light bulbs.

40-Watt Appliance Bulb   This is a small bulb suitable for ovens and refrigerators.

Indoor Floodlights (75-Watt, 150-watt)   Some newer floodlight bulbs can be used indoors or outdoors.

Long-Life Bulbs   At the electrical supply store or the home center, you can buy long-life bulbs. These bulbs cost more than ordinary light bulbs but they last many times as long as a standard bulb. It makes sense to use them in situations where the bulb is hard to get at to replace. Examples might be where a heavy ladder is required or where an elderly person cannot reach. Buy several long-life bulbs of various wattages. The compact fluorescent bulbs have an even longer life and they use less energy, but they won't always fit in every fixture.

Night-Light Bulbs   These are small-base bulbs in various wattages (3-watt, 7-watt, etc.).

Outdoor Floodlights   Use 75-watt or 150-watt lights.

Rough-Service Bulbs   These are for use in your drop light. Use a 100-watt bulb if available, otherwise use a 75-watt bulb.

Small-Base 60-Watt Bulbs   These bulbs are used in chandeliers and other lighting fixtures.

OUTDOOR ELECTRICAL FIXTURES

I am often asked to install outdoor electrical outlets or floodlights. I like to have on hand the necessary outdoor boxes and waterproof connectors, outlets, bulb holders, and a special sunlight-resistant electrical cable.

POWER STRIPS

Power strips are useful devices. You plug the power strip into a properly grounded outlet and the power strip either lies on the floor or desktop or is mounted on the wall. You can then plug six devices into the power strip. Most power strips have a small circuit breaker built in. Don't buy cheap power strips; pay a little more and get a good one. You can usually tell by the weight—the heavier, the better.

If the power strip is to be used with computer equipment, the recommended type is the kind that has two surge suppressors built in, one for the computer and one for the modem. These suppressors provide protection against voltage spikes, possibly caused by lightning, that may come down the power line or the telephone line.

SIX-WAY OUTLETS

These outlets plug into and screw onto a standard duplex outlet. They then provide six places to plug devices into. These devices are useful for clocks, lamps, and TVs, but they should not be used for appliances that draw a lot of current such as air conditioners, irons, etc.

SURFACE-MOUNT ELECTRICAL HARDWARE

If you are installing new wiring, there may be situations where it is difficult or impossible to run the wires inside the wall. An example would be a masonry basement wall. In such situations, you can use surface-mount components, such as those made by Wiremold. This is a more expensive solution than just running armored cable around, but it looks nicer, which may be important to the customer. You should familiarize yourself with these components, but there is no need to buy them until they are needed.

SWITCHES

The commonly used switch is usually called a toggle switch. You should always have on hand an assortment of switches. I like to have several single-pole switches and a few 3-way switches. The 3-way switch is for installations where a light can be turned on and off from two different locations; for example, the top and bottom of a flight of stairs. Replacing a 3-way switch can be tricky, so make a note of what is connected to what before you disconnect an old three-way switch. Pay particular attention to which wire is connected to the screw on the switch which is darker in color than the other two. This is the critical wire, the other two wires can be connected to either of the two remaining screws. Switches usually come with brown or ivory handles. I use ivory unless the customer wants brown.

WIRE NUTS

These are sometimes called solderless connectors. You should have several of every size, from the tiny ones that are used inside some electric clocks and other small electric appliances to the large sizes that can be used to connect several size-12 or size-10 copper wires. When you use a wire nut to connect wires, hold the wire nut and pull on each wire individually to make sure it is secure in the wire nut.

NAILS, SCREWS, BOLTS, AND OTHER FASTENERS

Buying Fasteners	104	**Washers**	106
Bolts	104	**Nails**	106
Small Bolts (Machine Screws)	105	**Rivets**	107
Carriage Bolts	105	**Pop Rivets**	107
Metric Bolts	106	**Screws**	107
Nuts	106	**Tacks**	109

You will need dozens of different types and sizes of fasteners. Here is information on those you will find most useful.

BUYING FASTENERS

Whenever you buy fasteners (nails, screws, bolts, washers, etc.) always try to buy zinc-plated (sometimes called galvanized) fasteners. The plated fasteners resist rusting and the cost difference is negligible. The exceptions are the drywall screws which come only with a black finish. But you can buy deck screws for outdoor use. Deck screws are similar to drywall screws but they do have a plated finish.

BOLTS

For any given diameter of bolt, there are coarse threads and fine (sometimes called SAE) threads. Examples would be $1/4$–20 bolts which have a diameter of $1/4$ inch and have 20 threads per inch, these are the coarse threads, and $1/4$–28 bolts which have 28 threads per inch, these are the fine threads. For bolts that are $1/4$-inch in diameter or larger, the coarse threads are best for most purposes. The fine threads are used on cars because they are more resistant to coming loose from vibration. The bolts I would suggest having on hand are:

1/4–20 Bolts   I keep both roundhead and flathead bolts on hand in several lengths from $3/4$ inch to 3 inches.

5/16–18 Bolts   I have flathead bolts in several lengths from 1 inch to 3 inches.

SMALL BOLTS (MACHINE SCREWS)

Small bolts are usually called machine screws. They come in various diameters, various lengths, and various head styles. The smaller diameters are referred to in numbers rather than fractions of an inch. A 10–24 machine screw has a diameter of $3/16$ inch and has 24 threads per inch, and an 8–32 machine screw has a diameter of approximately $5/32$ inch and has 32 threads per inch. You should practice looking at various machine screws and bolts until you can tell, just by looking, the diameter and the number of threads per inch. Below is a list of the machine screws I would want to have on hand at all times.

4–40 × 1/2-Inch Binder Head Machine Screws   These machine screws are used for repair of small items.

6–32 Machine Screws   I have both roundhead and flathead screws in several lengths from $3/8$ inch to 2 inches.

8–32 Machine Screws   Both roundhead and flathead screws in this size and in several lengths from $3/8$ inch to 2 inches come in handy.

10–24 Machine Screws   I keep both roundhead and flathead 10–24 screws in several lengths from $3/4$ inch to 2 inches.

10–32 Machine Screws   I like to have both roundhead and flathead 10–32 screws in several lengths from $3/4$ inch to 2 inches.

CARRIAGE BOLTS

A carriage bolt has a large rounded head and a short square section of the shank just below the head. The square section fits tightly in a hole and stops the bolt from turning when the nut is tightened.

Carriage bolts are useful when you are working on outdoor wooden structures such as decks, stairs, furniture, or play equipment. The following sizes of carriage bolts will prove useful.

¼-Inch-Diameter Carriage Bolts

I like to have ¼-inch bolts that are 2 inches, 3 inches, and 4 inches long.

5/16-Inch-Diameter Carriage Bolts

I also have 5/16-inch bolts that are 2 inches, 3 inches, and 4 inches long.

3/8-Inch-Diameter Carriage Bolts

This size carriage bolt 3 inches and 4 inches long is sufficient.

METRIC BOLTS

Bolts with metric threads are becoming more widely used in the United States, so from time to time you may need some of them. The sizes of metric bolts are designated in millimeters of diameter. They are used on some cars and on some foreign-made items such as bicycles, toys, and appliances. If you have to match a thread on something you are fixing, and none of your fasteners seem to fit, although some of them *almost* fit, chances are you need a metric nut or bolt. Metric nuts and bolts are often more readily available in auto supply stores than at your local hardware store.

NUTS

For all of the machine screws and bolts listed here, you should also have nuts. Hex nuts are preferable because it is easier to turn them with socket wrenches, but square nuts are all right.

WASHERS

For all of the above bolts and machine screws, you should have flat washers of two sizes. One size washer should be the standard size that is intended for that diameter of bolt. The other size washer should have the same size hole in the center but should be about twice the diameter of the standard washer. These large-diameter washers are sometimes called *fender washers*. You will find them to be very useful, especially when you are bolting together pieces of wood or pieces of sheet metal.

NAILS

You should have a wide assortment of nails. Buy plated nails. I suggest the following:

Aluminum Nails

I like to have 1-inch and 2-inch aluminum nails on hand.

Finish Nails   These are nails with a very small head. Buy several sizes from $3/4$ inch to 3 inches. (Small finish nails are sometimes called *brads*.)

Head Nails   You will need several sizes from $3/4$ inch to $3 1/2$ inches. (Small head nails are sometimes called *wire nails*.)

Roofing Nails   These are made of galvanized steel and I like to have these in 1-inch and $1 1/2$-inch lengths.

RIVETS

A rivet is like a short bolt with no threads. You put it through matching holes in pieces to be joined, then you hammer the end of the rivet with a ball peen hammer until it spreads out and holds the two pieces together. You can improvise rivets, on the rare occasions when you need them, by cutting a steel or aluminum nail or bolt to the proper length.

POP RIVETS (Fig. 22-1)

Pop rivets are very convenient. Their big advantage is that they can be used in situations where you only have access to one side of the hole that the rivet goes into. This is sometimes called "blind riveting." Another advantage is that they take only a few seconds to install. Pop rivets are useful when you are repairing automobile bodies and when you are working on gutters and downspouts.

It is worth having a pop-riveting tool (Fig. 22-1) and an assortment of rivets to go with it. The pop rivets come in steel and aluminum. The steel rivets are stronger, but the aluminum rivets don't rust. The rivets come in various diameters and in various grip lengths. The grip length refers to the combined thickness of the two objects you are fastening together. If you are riveting together something $1/16$ inch thick and something $1/8$ inch thick, you want to use rivets that have a grip length of $3/16$ inch.

SCREWS

Listed alphabetically below are the most frequently needed screws.

Deck Screws   Deck screws are similar to drywall screws, but they are zinc plated (galvanized) and are intended for outdoor use. I like to have $1 1/2$-inch, 2-inch, $2 1/2$-inch, and 3-inch deck screws.

Drywall Screws   I like to have a complete inventory of drywall screws; all lengths from $3/4$ inch to 4 inches. The $3/4$-inch drywall screws are sometimes hard to find; you can use $3/4$-inch flathead sheet metal screws instead. The 4-inch drywall screws are hard to find and rarely needed, but it is well to have them on hand for those few special cases. Drywall screws are made with fine threads and coarse threads. I prefer the coarse threads; it takes less time to install or remove them and they are less likely to cause the wood to split.

If you must use drywall screws on outdoor construction, it is a good idea to put a dab of oil-base paint on each screw head. If you don't do this, within a year or two you will see an unsightly rust spot at each screw head.

Lag Screws Lag screws, sometimes called *lag bolts,* are like thick wood screws, but they have a square or hex head and you use a wrench to turn them instead of a screwdriver. They are often used on outdoor construction projects. I like to have several lag screws in 2-inch, 3-inch, and 4-inch lengths.

Sheet Metal Screws Sheet metal screws are similar to wood screws except that the threads go all the way up to the head of the screw instead of having a smooth shank as on the wood screws. I find the sheet metal screws to be more versatile than the wood screws. I recommend having several sizes of sheet metal screws, both flathead and binder head, in lengths up to 2 inches. A binder-head screw is somewhat like a roundhead screw but it is wider and flatter. I always buy Phillips-head screws whenever possible. They can be installed and removed more quickly than the slotted-head screws.

Wood Screws I rarely need round-head wood screws, especially when I have the binder-head sheet metal screws available in the smaller sizes. I do like to have on hand flathead wood screws in 2-inch, $2^1/2$-inch, 3-inch, $3^1/2$-inch, and 4-inch lengths. Again, buy the Phillips-head screws.

Be sure to have some #6 $\times$ $1^3/4$-inch flathead screws; they are used to attach wall standards to the wall; the standards hold the shelf brackets which hold the shelves. You should also have some tiny flathead or ovalhead screws (#4 $\times$ $3/8$-inch, and #4 $\times$ $1/2$-inch). These tiny screws are used in the hinges on some kitchen cabinets.

For most work on a boat and for most outdoor jobs at the seashore, it is best to use brass, bronze, or stainless steel screws, bolts, etc.

TACKS

I suggest that you have two boxes of aluminum tacks, $3/8$ inch long, and $1/2$ inch long. These tacks will be useful if you are replacing screening in a wooden screen door or window screen, or if you are covering a rotted window sill with sheet aluminum.

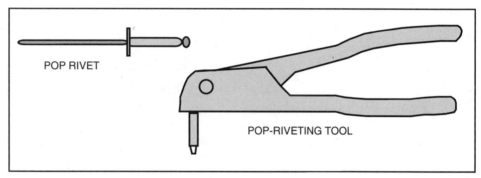

POP RIVET

POP-RIVETING TOOL

FIGURE 22-1   Pop rivets, pop-riveting tool.

HANGING OBJECTS ON WALLS

Hollow Walls   110   Screw-in Hooks   112
Solid Walls   111   Picture Hangers   112
Screw Eyes   112   Other Devices   113

You will frequently be asked to hang objects on walls. The hardware you use to do this will depend on whether the object is heavy or light and on what kind of wall you are hanging it.

HOLLOW WALLS

If you are dealing with a hollow wall, try to put the screws you are using into the studs. (The studs are the vertical 2 × 4s inside the wall.) The easiest way to find the studs is with an electronic stud finder, but you can often find the studs in a drywall wall by tapping lightly with the handle end of a screwdriver and listening carefully to the sound. The hollow sound is between the studs, the solid sound is where the studs are. Another way to find the studs is to push a sharp ice pick through the drywall where you think a stud may be. If you don't hit a stud, move to the right or left and try again until you find it. If you do this probing just above the baseboard, the holes it leaves will be less conspicuous.

If you are in an old house, the walls may be plaster on lath, and it will be harder to find the studs (lath is thin horizontal strips of wood, about 2 inches wide, spaced about $1/2$ inch apart, and nailed to the studs). The stud finder may not work and the tapping-sound procedure may not work either. If the object to be hung is not extremely heavy, you can put the screws you are using into the lath. When you drill a pilot hole for the screw you will be using, make sure it brings out some wood chips, not just plaster dust, in which case you have drilled between the lath strips.

If you must find a stud in a lath wall, you can try drilling a tiny hole to the right or left of an electrical switch or outlet or measuring 16 inches from a corner, or drilling a series of tiny holes just above the baseboard. When you find a stud, the others should be 16 inches center to center from it.

Moly Bolts (Fig. 23-1)   If the wall is drywall, and you cannot put the screws where the studs are, you can use hollow-wall anchors. The most common hollow-wall anchor is the "Moly" bolt. You drill a hole in the wall and insert the Moly bolt. Then you tighten the screw until the Moly bolt flattens out behind the drywall and holds itself in place. You then remove the screw and put it through whatever you are hanging and back into the Moly bolt. Moly bolts vary in diameter and in the "grip length," which is the thickness of the wall they can be used on. Wall thicknesses can be as little as $3/16$ inch (for paneling), up to $1^1/4$ inches, but most drywall you will encounter will be either $1/2$ inch thick or $5/8$ inch thick. You should have Moly bolts of several diameters and several grip lengths.

Once in place, the Moly bolt cannot be removed. If it is no longer needed and you want the wall to look as it did before, you can hammer the Moly bolt in a short distance, fill the hole with spackle, and paint if necessary.

Toggle Bolts (Fig. 23-1)   Another type of hollow-wall anchor is the toggle bolt, sometimes called a butterfly bolt. It has two wings that open up behind the wall after you have pushed it through a hole you made in the wall. It requires a much bigger hole than a Moly bolt but it can hold more weight. Toggle bolts are used to hold the ceiling hooks that are used for hanging flower pots. They are also used for "swagging" a chain and electric cord across a ceiling to a ceiling light. It is good to have a few of these ceiling hooks on hand.

SOLID WALLS

For solid walls, such as cinder block, brick, concrete, and stone, you can sometimes hammer a cut nail or a masonry nail directly into the wall. A better way is to drill a hole in the wall, put a plastic masonry shield (Fig. 23-1) into the hole and then use a screw or a screw hook to attach the object to the masonry shield. The three sizes of shields that will be sufficient for almost all jobs are $3/16$ inch, $1/4$ inch, and $5/16$ inch in diameter. The easiest way to drill the holes for the shields is with a hammer drill with a masonry bit. If electricity is not available, you can use a star drill and a heavy hammer.

SCREW EYES (Fig. 23-1)

You can put a horizontal row of screw eyes on a wall to hang up screw-drivers, pliers, etc. Screw eyes are sometimes used in conjunction with hooks to hold screen doors closed. If you need a screw-in hook and have only a screw eye, you can force the eye open to make it into a hook. Large screw eyes are sometimes used as gate hinges.

SCREW-IN HOOKS (Fig. 23-1)

These are metal hooks in the shape of a question mark. You can screw them into a stud in a stud wall or into a masonry shield in a solid wall. It is well to have several of the various sizes of screw-in hooks. The very small ones are used to hang up cups in kitchens. The very large ones can be screwed into the wall or ceiling of a garage to hang up bicycles. You will find many uses for the in-between sizes as well, for example, to hold an outdoor clothesline.

PICTURE HANGERS (Fig. 23-1)

I am often asked to hang pictures or mirrors on walls. I like to have on hand an assortment of picture-hanging hooks. They resemble a twisted metal strap and have a nail that goes into the wall at a sharp downward angle. I have several of each size from the tiny ones intended to hold 2 pounds or less to the big ones rated at 100 pounds. If the picture weighs more than the rating of the biggest hook you have, you can use two hooks set in the wall an inch or two apart.

It is also good to have some of the stranded steel wire that is used to hang pictures, some for light pictures and some for heavy pictures, and some of the little metal tabs that fasten to the back of the picture frame that you attach the wire to. If you don't have any of this stranded wire, you can use monofilament or braided nylon fishing line. Be sure to use line that is rated at several times the weight of the picture; I would use 100-pound line to hang a 25-pound picture. If you don't have 100-pound line, you can use lighter line doubled up or tripled up.

The homeowner may specify the exact location of the picture as you hold it up against the wall. You can then place a light chalk mark, or a small piece of masking tape, on the wall to indicate where one corner of the picture should be. However, it can be difficult to know exactly where to put the hook. In most cases, the easiest way is to simply put the hook where you guess it should be. Then put the picture on the hook and see where it hangs. If it is an inch too low and half an inch to the right of where you want it, simply remove the hook and place it an inch higher and half an inch to the left. Patch the original hole with spackle, if necessary.

OTHER DEVICES

In addition to those described above, there are many other devices for hanging objects on walls and new ones seem to be coming out all the time, so try to be aware of what is available. Picking the right hardware can save time and make a hard job easy.

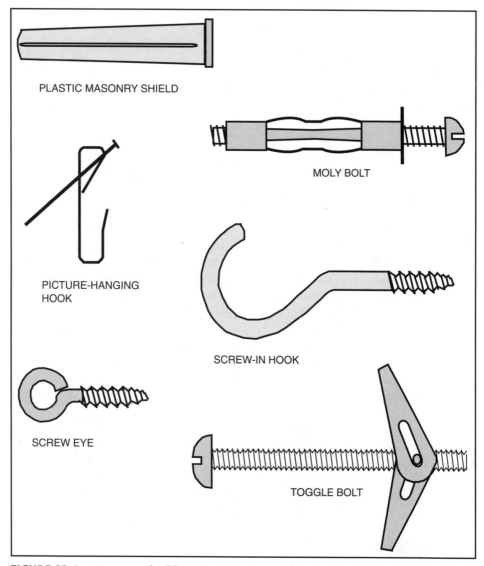

FIGURE 23-1 Masonry shield, Moly bolt, picture-hanging hook, screw eye, screw-in hook, toggle bolt.

HOSE-REPAIR HARDWARE

Hose-Repair Fittings   114
Hose Washers   114
Hose Hanger   114

HOSE-REPAIR FITTINGS (Fig. 24-1)

In warm weather, garden hose repair is a frequently requested job. I like to have some of the plastic fittings that are used to make a new female end on the hose, some to make a new male end, and some that are used to rejoin the two pieces of hose when I have cut out a leaky section. These hose repair fittings come in two sizes, one size is for hoses whose inside diameter is $5/8$ inch to $3/4$ inch. The smaller size is for hoses with $1/2$-inch inside diameter. The larger-size hose is more common, so buy more fittings for larger hoses than for thinner hoses. I also like to have a few hose nozzles to replace defective ones.

HOSE WASHERS

At each end of the hose, there are hose washers made of rubber or soft plastic. These washers sometimes need replacing. They become compressed and lose their elasticity and then the connection leaks. On rare occasions, I have to use two washers together to get a tight seal. These washers are inexpensive and are frequently needed for garden hoses and washing machine hoses, so buy a dozen of them.

HOSE HANGER

I also like to have a hose hanger. This is a metal or plastic device. You fasten it to the wall of a house or garage and loop the hose over it instead of letting the hose lie on the ground in a big jumble.

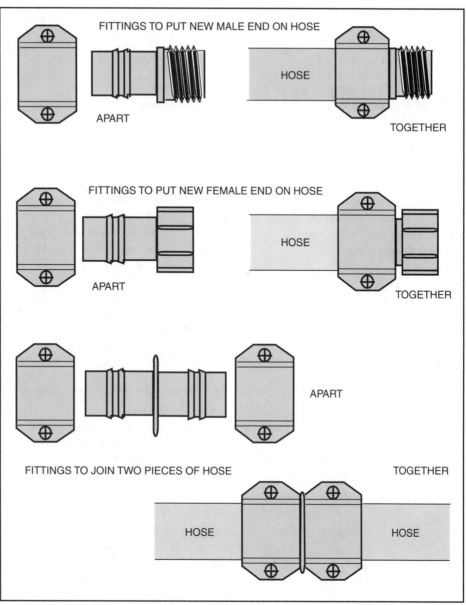

FIGURE 24-1 Hose-repair hardware.

PLUMBING HARDWARE

Aerators 116
Copper Tubing and Fittings 117
Faucet Washers 117
Flexible Supply Hoses 117
Showerheads 117

Sink Hardware 117
Toilet Hardware 118
Valves for ½-Inch Copper Tubing 119
Valves for Toilet Shutoff 120
Valve Seats 120

AERATORS

Most faucets have aerators. This is the little device that screws into (or onto) the spout. It mixes air with the water so the flow is soft and bubbly instead of irregular and splashy. Aerators frequently need replacing. Sometimes you can just unscrew them and remove the accumulated dirt. But frequently the aerator has corroded to the point where it must be replaced. There is no standardization of aerators, so it is a good idea to have three or four of the most commonly used sizes on hand. Ask your plumbing store clerk which sizes are most popular. It is also a good idea to have a few adapters that are used to make an aerator fit a particular faucet. If you put Teflon tape or a small dab of grease or vaseline on the threads of an aerator, it will be less likely to leak at the threads and it will be easier to remove if necessary.

When you buy an aerator, it usually comes with a flow restricter. This looks like a metal washer with a small hole in the middle. It restricts the flow to conserve water but it can be removed to increase the flow. In most homes with good water pressure, the restricter can be left in place. But, in some homes with low water pressure, the homeowner might want it removed.

COPPER TUBING AND FITTINGS (Fig. 25-1)

You should have some $^1/2$-inch-diameter copper tubing and a variety of fittings for $^1/2$-inch tubing. Here is a starter list with the suggested number to buy:

- **Copper tubing ($^1/2$-inch)** A few pieces a foot or more long.
- **Standard couplings** Buy four.
- **Slip couplings** Buy four.
- **Ells** Buy two.
- **Tees** Buy two.

FAUCET WASHERS

You should have an assortment of faucet washers (I like the kind that is called tapered or "pig nose") in all sizes from 00 to $^1/2$. Be sure to buy washers made by a reputable manufacturer. There are many cheap faucet washers on the market that do not last very long. You should also have an assortment of the small brass screws that hold the washers in place.

FLEXIBLE SUPPLY HOSES

Flexible Hoses for Sink Use hoses with stainless steel braid to connect the water supply to a sink. Buy two that are about 10 inches long and two that are about 16 inches long.

Flexible Hoses for Toilet Again, use hoses with stainless steel braid to connect the water supply to a toilet. Buy one about 6 inches long and one about 10 inches long.

SHOWERHEADS

Showerheads also come with flow restricters. Again, leave them in unless the homeowner wants more flow. It's a good idea to have an extra showerhead or two in your inventory. They sometimes do need replacing.

SINK HARDWARE

Leaks in the drainpipes below kitchen and bathroom sinks are quite common, so you should have some of the most common replacement parts ready to use. Kitchen sinks use $1^1/2$-inch-diameter drainpipes and bathroom sinks (often called lavatories), usually use $1^1/4$-inch-diameter pipes. These drainpipe fittings are available in plastic or metal. I think the plastic ones are easier to use, but the metal ones are fine provided you don't buy the ultracheap ones that are made of very thin metal.

You should have the following components in both the $1\frac{1}{4}$-inch and $1\frac{1}{2}$-inch sizes.

Couplings   Buy one of each size.

J Bends   Buy one of each size.

Tail Pieces   Buy one of each size.

Traps   Buy two of each size.

Washers   Because new drainpipe washers are often the only things needed to cure many drainpipe leaks, you should buy at least six washers of each size ($1\frac{1}{4}$ inches and $1\frac{1}{2}$ inches).

TOILET HARDWARE

Toilet repair is a frequently requested job. You should study the mechanisms inside various toilet tanks until you understand how the most common ones work. You should have on hand a few of the following items:

Fill Valves   Buy a few fill valves, sometimes called refill valves. I like Fluidmaster valves best. These valves, and similar ones from other manufacturers, consist of a cylindrical plastic float that slides up and down on a square plastic bar. They are easy to install, are easy to adjust for proper water level, and usually work reliably for several years.

If a time comes when the Fluidmaster valve does not shut the water off completely and the water level in the tank continues to rise until water runs into the overflow tube, it is time to install a new seal in the valve.

Extra Seals   These are needed for Fluidmaster fill valves. This is the only part that ever needs replacing.

Flush Handles   This is the little handle you push downward to flush the toilet. If the handle does not move freely and easily, it may just need a few drops of oil, usually best applied from inside the tank. If this does not help, or if the handle is broken, install a new handle. Don't buy the cheapest one; it may look fine but may corrode and not last very long.

Be aware that the nut that holds the flush handle in place usually has a left-hand thread. Do not use excessive force on this nut or the tank may crack. If the nut is hard to turn, use a penetrating lubricant such as WD-40, CRC, or Liquid Wrench.

Flush Valves   The flush valve is the device that allows the water in the toilet tank to run into the toilet bowl when the flush handle is pushed. Some toilets use a tank ball, which resembles a black rubber ball that moves up and down at the end of a vertical brass wire. Some toilets use a flapper valve, which is hinged at one end. It opens to allow the water to pass, then it closes again. The flapper valve is usually more reliable.

When a customer reports hearing a sound of running water for several seconds, then silence for many minutes or hours, then a repeat of the sound, it means the flush valve is leaking and must be replaced. You can check for a leaking flush valve by putting some coloring matter, or a bit of dark latex paint, in the tank. If the flush valve leaks, you will see dark water slowly seeping into the bowl.

Float Rods and Floats   Many toilets, especially older ones, use a float, which is a plastic ball about the size of a grapefruit. It is connected to the fill valve by a metal float rod. The float moves up and down with the water level in the tank, and, when it moves up high enough, causes the water to be turned off. In order to get the proper water level in the tank, the float rod must be bent, up or down, by hand. This is a trial-and-error process.

Toilet-Seat Bolts   Newer toilet seats are usually held in place with plastic nuts and bolts. Unlike older toilet seat fasteners, made of metal, these plastic fasteners do not corrode. However, they sometimes break, especially if a heavy person sits down suddenly and moves a bit from side to side. So it is well to have a few spare plastic nuts and bolts on hand.

If you are replacing an old toilet seat, the metal nuts that hold it on may be very difficult to remove due to corrosion or rust. Use a penetrating lubricant and the correct size of socket wrench. Avoid excessive force or you may crack the toilet. In extreme cases, fortunately very rare, you may have to use a hacksaw blade to remove the old nuts. Whenever I work in someone's bathroom, I always check the toilet seat to see if it is loose, and, if it is, I tighten the bolts.

VALVES FOR ½-INCH COPPER TUBING

Compression Valves   Buy two with red handles and two with blue handles.

Stop and Waste Valves Buy one with a red handle and one with a blue handle.

Ball Valves Buy two.

The usual kind of valve, which requires many turns of the handle to turn it on or off, is sometimes called a compression valve. I suggest buying four of these valves for $1/2$-inch copper tubing; two with red handles (to indicate hot water) and two with blue handles for cold water. The valves are the same, only the handles are different.

There are also "stop and waste" valves. These are the same as the compression valve but they have an additional small brass cap on the side which can be used to drain water out of any parts of the system that are higher than the valve itself.

Another type of valve, called a ball valve, requires only a 90-degree swing of the long handle to turn it on or off. The ball valve costs more, but it is easier to use, especially for elderly people or people with arthritis. I show both types of valve to the homeowner and ask him which he prefers. Before you buy a ball valve, make sure it is not to be installed in such tight quarters that there will not be enough room to swing the handle.

VALVES FOR TOILET SHUTOFF

You may occasionally have to replace the shutoff valve under a toilet. These valves come in so many variations that it is probably best to wait until you need one and then buy it.

VALVE SEATS

If you do a lot of faucet repairs, you should have an assortment of valve seats. They look like small brass rings. The valve seat is the part of the faucet that the washer bears against to shut off the flow of water. In most cases, when you are asked to fix a faucet that is dripping from the spout, a new washer is what is needed. But, occasionally, the problem lies with the valve seat. How do you know if the valve seat is defective? Look at it, using a flashlight. If you see a crack or a small opening in the rim of the seat, the seat should be replaced. If you can't see the seat, try to run your little finger around the rim of the seat. It should be perfectly smooth. If you feel a rough spot, the seat is defective. Another clue to a defective seat is if the part of the washer that bears against the seat looks rough and torn up. You can buy a plastic compartment box with an assortment of seats at the plumbing supply store.

There are tools for resurfacing valve seats, but they don't always work, so it is better to replace the seat if you can. Some faucets don't have removable seats, so the resurfacing tool is the only remedy other than replacing the faucet.

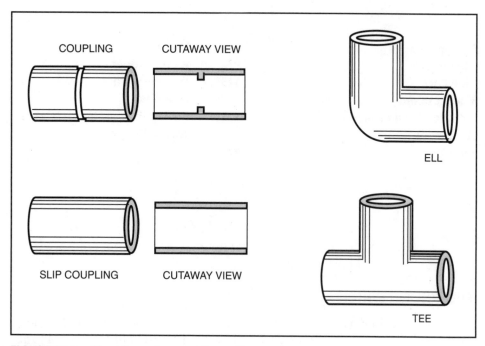

FIGURE 25-1   Coupling, slip coupling, ell, tee.

TELEPHONE HARDWARE

Telephone Wire	122	Line Tester	123
Phone Jacks	122	Wire Stripper	123
Line Cord	123	One-Piece Phone	124
Handset Cord	123	Final Test	124
Adapter, 4-Pin to Modular	123	Buying Phones and Hardware	124
Adapter, 2:1	123	Wiring Diagram	124
Coupler	123		

Fixing or installing a telephone is a common request. Here is what you should have on hand:

TELEPHONE WIRE

When you install a new jack, you will connect it to the phone system using telephone wire. This cord is usually round, about $3/16$ inch in diameter, and it usually contains four thin wires, red, green, black, and yellow. You may have to drill holes to run this cord through walls or floors and you may also staple it to baseboards. There are special staplers for this use.

PHONE JACKS

The jack is a female connector that is installed in a wall or on the base-board. You run wires to these jacks from existing jacks or (preferred) from the "bridge" device which is near where the phone wire comes into the house. The phone then plugs into the jack. The jacks come in many styles. You should have a few of the most common ones. Ask at the home center or electronics store which jacks are the most widely used.

LINE CORD

This cord runs from the wall jack to the type of phone that sits on a table or desk. It is not used with wall-mounted phones. It usually has a modular plug on each end. It could be a coiled cord but is usually a flat cord. The flat cord is better if it has to be run under a rug. White and ivory are the most common colors for line cords for kitchen phones.

HANDSET CORD

Sometimes called *modular handset cord*. This coiled cord runs from the telephone itself to the handset (the part you hold in your hand). It has narrower plugs than the modular plugs used to connect the phone to the wall jack and it can be used only from the telephone to the handset. These handset cords come in all colors.

ADAPTER, 4-PIN TO MODULAR

Old houses often have the old 4-pin jacks, about the size of an ice cube, that were used with 4-pin phone plugs. The adapter converts these old outlets to the newer modular style. The modular plugs are usually clear plastic and are about the size of the tip of a little finger.

ADAPTER, 2:1

You plug this adapter into a phone jack or a coupler and you can then plug two phones into the adapter. You should have several of these on hand. There are also 3:1 adapters, but they are rarely needed.

COUPLER

The coupler is a small rectangular device that can be used when the cord intended to run from a phone to a wall jack isn't long enough. It has a female connector at each end. You plug the phone cord into the coupler, then run another cord from the coupler to the jack.

LINE TESTER

This is a small inexpensive device that you plug into a jack. If the green light lights, the jack and the wiring to the jack are OK. If the red light comes on, the wires to the jack are reversed.

WIRE STRIPPER

The wire stripper that you use for electrical work may not work on the very thin wires used for phones so you may have to buy a stripper made for phone work. They are not expensive.

ONE-PIECE PHONE

You will use this to test a new or existing phone jack. If you get the dial tone, in most cases the jack is OK. But, to be certain, you should use a line tester to be sure the polarity is correct.

FINAL TEST

If you have just installed a new phone, it is a good idea to call someone and have them call you back so you can be sure the ringer, the outgoing voice, and the incoming voice are all working properly.

BUYING PHONES AND HARDWARE

Phones in good working condition are often available at yard sales. Some people sell their phones simply because they are redecorating and they want new phones of a different color. If the seller plugs in the phone, and you hear the dial tone, the phone is usually OK. However, to be sure, you should call someone and have them call you back. Inexpensive telephone hardware is often available at your local dollar store.

WIRING DIAGRAM (Fig. 26-1)

This diagram shows the names of the cords that connect the various components of the residential phone system. There may or may not be a device called an entrance bridge between the interface and the wall jacks. The bridge is used to connect two or more phones in parallel.

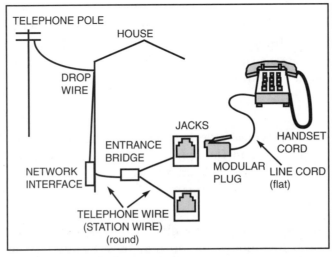

FIGURE 26-1 Telephone system.

OTHER USEFUL HARDWARE

Angle Iron and Aluminum Angle	125	Knobs	127
Barrel Bolts	125	Lamp Parts	128
Bicycle Parts	126	Magnetic Latches	128
Cabinet Latches	126	Padlocks	128
Cable Ties	126	Pulleys	128
Casters	127	Roof, Gutter, and Downspout Repair	128
Eyebolts	127	Springs	128
Fence Hardware	127	Standards and Brackets for Shelving	129
Handles	127	Staples	129
Hasps	127	Turnbuckles	129
Hinges	127	Window Locks	129
Hose Clamps	127		

Here is an alphabetical list of other hardware items that you will find uses for.

ANGLE IRON AND ALUMINUM ANGLE

Various sizes of angle irons and aluminum angles have many uses when building or fixing all sorts of things. I like to accumulate many sizes and lengths of these. Some of the useful sizes are:

- $1/2$-inch $\times$ $1/2$-inch angle   Any length.
- $3/4$-inch $\times$ $3/4$-inch angle   Any length.
- 1-inch $\times$ 1-inch angle   Any length.
- $1\,1/2$-inch $\times$ $1\,1/2$-inch angle   Any length.

BARREL BOLTS (Fig. 27-1)

Small barrel bolts are used for windows, large barrel bolts are used for doors. I often install barrel bolts on rarely used doors and windows to make a home more burglar resistant. It is good to have an assortment of barrel bolts on hand.

BICYCLE PARTS

If you do occasional bicycle repair, it is well to have on hand a few of the following parts:

- Brake parts for coaster brakes and hand brakes
- Cables
- Chains and master links for chains
- Gear levers
- Handbrakes
- Handle grips
- Inner tubes (and valves and valve caps)
- Kickstands
- Locks
- Pedals (left-foot and right-foot)
- Pumps
- Reflectors
- Rim liners
- Seats
- Spokes (and a spoke wrench)

CABINET LATCHES

There are many different devices used to hold cabinet doors shut. I like to have a variety of them on hand. I get some of them from cabinets being discarded. If they are not in perfect condition, they will at least do the job until a new one can be procured. In some cases, a used latch is the only option when the original latch is no longer being manufactured.

CABLE TIES (Fig. 27-1)

These are useful and inexpensive devices made of nylon strap. They come in all sizes, from 2 inches long to 3 feet or more. You wrap the tie around whatever objects you want to hold together, put the tapered end of the tie through the thick end, and pull to tighten. The cable tie will remain tight until you cut it off. Cable ties were originally intended to hold bundles of electrical wires together but they are useful for nonelectrical applications as well. If you have several sizes of these ties, you will find many uses for them. Some newer styles of cable ties can be opened and reused.

CASTERS

If I see an office chair or other furniture with casters being discarded, and the casters are good quality and in good condition, I take the casters and often find uses for them.

EYEBOLTS

Eyebolts are not needed very often. They are used for swings and as hinges on some gates. Don't buy these at retail until they are needed.

FENCE HARDWARE

If I come across them at yard sales, I like to accumulate latches, hinges, fittings, fence posts, and other hardware for wooden fences and chain-link fences. I would not buy them at retail until they are needed.

HANDLES

In my "HANDLES" box, I have drawer pull handles of various styles, garage door handles, pot handles, handles for files, etc.

HASPS (Fig. 27-2)

Hasps are used in conjunction with padlocks for doors on sheds and garages. I would not buy hasps at retail until they are needed.

HINGES

I would not buy any hinges at the hardware store until I needed them. But hinges are often available at yard sales at low cost, so I accumulate a variety of sizes and styles.

HOSE CLAMPS (Fig. 27-2)

One type of hose clamp consists of a stainless steel strap with angled slots to engage a screw that you turn to tighten the clamp. It is good to have an assortment of these clamps. They are useful on cars, washing machines, and other equipment.

KNOBS

I have a box labeled "KNOBS." In it are dozens of knobs of all sizes, shapes, and colors. There are knobs for radios, TVs, electronic equipment, lamps, washing machines, stoves, dimmers, toasters, drawer pulls, pot lids, etc.

I get many of these knobs from items that people are discarding. If I am fixing something that has a broken or missing knob, even if I don't have an exact matching knob, I can at least make the device usable. Then the homeowner can buy the exact replacement knob, if desired.

LAMP PARTS

If you see old lamps being discarded, save the metal parts such as harps, finials, and threaded tubing. They may prove useful when you have to repair a lamp.

MAGNETIC LATCHES

These are used on cabinet doors and closet doors. If you have a few on hand, you are sure to find uses for them.

PADLOCKS

Buy a few good-quality padlocks of various sizes. Don't buy padlocks that have a flat key that looks like it was stamped out of sheet metal. Such locks are very easy to pick.

PULLEYS

I like to have an assortment of various sizes and styles of pulley. Small pulleys are useful for ladders, clotheslines, and flagpoles. Big pulleys are useful for tree work.

ROOF, GUTTER, AND DOWNSPOUT REPAIR

Gutters and downspouts are often in need of attention. It is well to have a few of the various devices that are used to attach gutters to roofs and fascia and a few of the devices that are used to hold downspouts in place. Also desirable: a length of rectangular white aluminum, or vinyl, downspout and a few elbows for use with it.

SPRINGS

In my "SPRINGS" box, I have dozens of assorted springs, but the ones I am most likely to need are:

Patio Furniture Springs   These are used under the pad on patio furniture. These springs tend to rust out and break if the furniture is exposed to rain for several years.

Storm Door Springs   These are compression springs that absorb the shock when the wind suddenly whips the door open. They are used with an attached chain.

Window Balance Springs
These are used in some newer windows which do not use sash weights.

STANDARDS AND BRACKETS FOR SHELVING

Standards are the channel-shaped lengths of steel or aluminum that are attached to the wall in a vertical direction. They have slots every inch to hold the shelf brackets. I like to have on hand some standards that are 4 or 5 feet long and some brackets that are 8 inches, 10 inches, and 12 inches long. The advantage of the standard-and-bracket shelf system is that it is very easy to change the spacing between the shelves. Try to buy the steel standards and brackets, they are much stronger than the aluminum ones.

STAPLES

In addition to the staples for use in your staple gun, it is good to have several other kinds of staples for other uses.

BX Staples
These steel staples are used for fastening BX armored cable to studs or joists.

Fence Staples
These are used to attach wire fencing to wooden fence posts.

Insulated Staples
Used for fastening an electrical cord to the baseboard or other interior wood trim.

Romex Staples
These are plastic staples that come with two nails and are used to attach Romex-type cable to studs or joists.

Telephone Cable Staples
These staples either nail on or stick on and are used to attach telephone cables and cable TV cables.

TURNBUCKLES (Fig. 27-2)

Turnbuckles come in all sizes. The most useful turnbuckles are the ones that come with two threaded rods and are used to pull sagging doors, storm doors, and screen doors back into square. Also useful are the large turnbuckles that are used in conjunction with heavy wire to fix sagging gates and garage doors.

WINDOW LOCKS

I like to have on hand a few window locks for double-hung windows. These are sometimes referred to as *clamshell* locks.

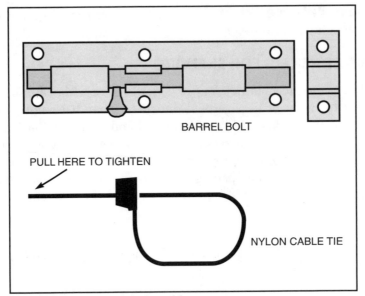

FIGURE 27-1 Barrel, bolt, cable tie.

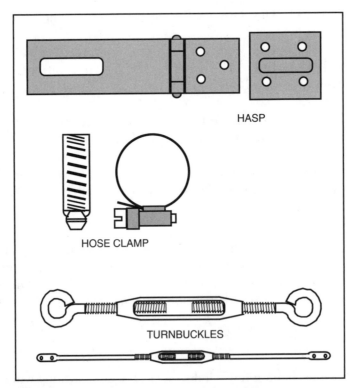

FIGURE 27-2 Hasp, hose clamp, turnbuckles.

CAULKING

Latex Caulk (Siliconized Latex, White)	131	Butyl Caulk, Gutter Seal Caulk	132
Silicone Caulk (Clear)	131	Polyseamseal, Phenoseal, Polyurethane	132
Silicone Caulk (White)	132	Sealing the Caulk Cartridge	133
Silicone Caulk (Black)	132		

Caulking compounds, also referred to as *caulking* or simply *caulk*, come in many varieties. Their main use is to fill cracks and holes to keep water out. When I come across a new kind of caulk, I usually buy one tube to see how it performs. Here is some useful information about caulking.

LATEX CAULK (SILICONIZED LATEX, WHITE)

This is the most widely used caulk. It is latex caulk with a small amount of silicone in it. It is inexpensive and very easy to use because it flows easily, you can smooth it easily with a fingertip, and any excesses clean up with a damp cloth. It is fine for many purposes, but when exposed to full sun, it will sometimes shrink, dry out, harden, and crack in a few years. When you buy latex caulk, price is a good indicator of quality. Buy the best. It will keep for years if unopened and protected from freezing. Buy at least two or three tubes of latex caulk. You will use it on almost every exterior paint job.

SILICONE CAULK (CLEAR)

Clear silicone caulk is useful where you don't want the caulk to be noticeable. It can be used to seal a crack in a roof of any color. It is widely used to seal shower enclosures. Silicone caulk is also a good adhesive. Mirror men use it to attach mirrors to walls and doors. You can use it to glue a loose shingle in place, attach house numbers, etc. It is ideal to reattach a loose floor tile or wall tile, provided the surfaces are dry.

Silicone is the most expensive caulk, but it is also the most durable. I have seen silicone caulk on a roof where it was exposed to full sun for 20 years and it was as flexible as the day it was applied. It has a shorter shelf life than other caulks, which means it will become unusable if it sits around for a few years. If it has been opened and partially used, it will usually harden and become useless in a few months.

Before you take silicone caulk to a job, try a small amount to be sure it comes out of the cartridge and starts to harden in 10 minutes or less. If it does not have a strong vinegar-like odor and does not start to get hard and rubbery in 10 minutes, it may never harden, and you will have to remove any that you have applied and start again with a fresh cartridge. More frequently, silicone caulk will go bad by simply hardening in the tube.

I like to keep one tube of clear silicone caulk on hand. When I buy silicone caulk, I mark the date of purchase on the cartridge. When I take a cartridge from the shelf and it is more than a year old, I know that it may not be usable.

SILICONE CAULK (WHITE)

This caulk is also available in almond and other colors. It is the only caulk to use for bathrooms and kitchens; any others will crack or turn black with mildew. Most silicone caulks cannot be painted. (You can paint them, but the paint will peel.)

SILICONE CAULK (BLACK)

This caulk is used for cracks in blacktop driveways and cracks in black roofs. There are less expensive black caulks for these purposes but they are not as long lasting as silicone.

BUTYL CAULK, GUTTER SEAL CAULK

Butyl caulk and gutter seal caulk stay soft and stretchy. They are good for sealing gutters, roof and chimney flashing, and cracks between masonry walls and sidewalks. I like to have brown, gray, and white gutter seal caulk or butyl caulk on hand. Don't use butyl caulk where appearance is important because it tends to accumulate dirt.

POLYSEAMSEAL, PHENOSEAL, POLYURETHANE

Polyseamseal and Phenoseal are brand names. Polyurethane is a generic type of caulk. These caulks cost more than latex caulk, but they shrink less and are more durable, even when exposed to full sun. They can be used instead of putty when installing window glass, which saves a lot of time, and they can be painted.

SEALING THE CAULK CARTRIDGE

When you use only part of the caulk in a cartridge, you want to be able to keep the rest in a usable condition for as long as possible. The plastic caps that come with the caulk are usually not useful because they no longer fit on the spout after you cut the spout at an angle. Buy some aluminum gutter spikes. These are the big aluminum nails that are used to attach gutters to houses. They come in two diameters. I prefer the thicker ones which are about $1/4$-inch in diameter and 7 inches long. Some are round and some are square. I push one of these spikes into the nozzle of the caulk cartridge as far as it will go. (See Fig. 14-2.) When I am ready to use that caulk again, I use pliers to pull the spike out. This usually keeps caulks usable for several months. Don't use unplated steel nails with latex caulks; they will rust and discolor the caulk. If you use a fingertip to smooth the caulking, always wet the finger first, so the caulk will not stick to your skin.

PAINTS AND PUTTY

Gallons	135
Spray Paints	135
Putty	136

After many years of handyman work, I have accumulated more than 70 gallon cans of paint. Some are nearly full, some nearly empty. Most are latex (water base), some are oil base. Some are primers, most are finish coat. Some are high gloss, some are flat (no gloss), most are semigloss or satin gloss (satin gloss is halfway between semigloss and flat). Some are interior paints, some are exterior. I have almost every imaginable color. I rarely buy quarts; it is not cost-effective.

I also have about 20 cans of spray paint. These spray paints dry in minutes and are fine for small jobs. They can be used for interior or exterior work. After using a can of spray paint, it is a good idea to turn the can upside down and spray until clear gas is coming out of the nozzle. If you don't do this, the nozzle tends to clog up with paint and become unusable.

It is not a good idea to use interior paints for exterior surfaces. They do not hold up well to the weather and they tend to get mildew, especially if they are not in a dry sunny location. Similarly, it is not a good idea to use exterior paints inside because they sometimes contain toxic mercury antimildew compounds. Some paints are labeled INTERIOR/EXTERIOR. They can be used in either location.

If I were just starting out, there are only a few kinds of paint I would want to have on hand because they are so frequently needed. I would buy the others when required. Here is what I would want to have:

GALLONS

- Interior semigloss or satin gloss, white, latex
- Exterior semigloss or satin gloss, white, latex
- Exterior primer for wood, oil base
- Antirust primer for metal, oil base

SPRAY PAINTS

These paints are suitable for interior or exterior use.

- Gloss white
- Gloss black
- Flat black

Never buy cheap paint, it won't cover well, it is less washable, and it is less durable. If a manufacturer has two or more brands, always buy the top of the line. Most of the cost of a paint job is usually labor, so saving a little on the material doesn't make sense.

Similarly, always buy the best-quality paint brushes. A highest-quality (and highest-price, of course) paint brush is almost like a living thing in your hand. It seems to know what you want to do. If you do a lot of painting along edges, for example, where a wall meets the ceiling or where the window frame meets the glass (this is sometimes referred to as *cutting in*), only a top-quality brush will do a good job. It will rapidly pay for itself in time saved. For cutting in, the best brush has a long handle and the bristles are cut at an angle instead of straight across.

If you are painting a house and the homeowner does not specify the degree of gloss for the paint, it is usually best to use satin gloss or semigloss paint. These paints are usually more durable than the high-gloss paint or the flat paint.

When you buy paint or caulk, ignore the big number on the container, which is supposedly the number of years the product will last. Some manufacturers are in a contest with each other to see who can claim the biggest number. Just buy the "top of the line" product of a reputable manufacturer.

If you have two or more cans of the same kind of paint from the same manufacturer, you can usually mix them to get intermediate colors. You cannot tell what the resultant color will be until the mixed paint is dry. Put a spot of the mixed paint on a piece of paper and use a hair dryer to dry it, which will take a minute or less.

When you have many cans of paint, you want to be able to stand back 6 or 8 feet from the shelves where your paint is stored and quickly spot the cans you are looking for. I put a 2-inch by 4-inch white self-stick label on each can (Fig. 29-1). Be careful not to cover any important information. Then I mark the label: BLACK EXT GLOSS OIL, or perhaps YELLOW INT FLAT. Most of my paint is latex. If it is oil based, I add OIL. In addition, when I first open a new can of paint, I dip a fingertip into the paint that sticks to the lid, and I make a 3-inch diameter spot on the front of the can and another on the lid. Then, whether the cans are on a shelf, or on the floor, I can instantly see what is in each can. Typical labels are shown below.

BLACK	YELLOW
EXT	INT
GLOSS	FLAT
OIL	

Some materials, such as latex-based paint and latex caulk must be stored where they will not be subject to freezing. Read the labels on any can of coating, adhesive, etc. If it doesn't say "Protect from Freezing," don't worry about it. If the label says "alkyd" (a type of oil) or "flammable," or "freeze thaw stable," the product will not be harmed by cold.

PUTTY

There are four kinds of putty that you will have use for.

Epoxy Putty   Epoxy putty is excellent for attaching two parts when they do not fit very well. Unlike other glues, it will stay put until it hardens. It is sometimes used to seal leaks in plumbing systems.

Glazing Compound   This is sometimes called *metal-sash putty*. It can be used when installing window glass in either wooden-frame or metal-frame windows. It may take many weeks to harden.

Plumber's Putty   This is a nonhardening putty that is used when installing faucets and drains.

Glazier's Putty   This has been used for centuries when putting glass in wooden windows. It hardens in a few days. It is also good for filling small holes prior to painting.

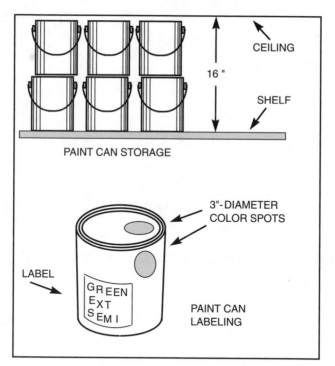

FIGURE 29-1 Paint can labeling and storage.

GLUES

Construction Adhesive	138	Epoxy Putty	139
Contact-Bond Cement	138	Goop	139
Crazy Glue, Superglue	138	Hot-Melt Glue Gun	139
Epoxy (5-Minute Clear Epoxy)	139	Yellow Carpenter's Glue	140
Epoxy Paste	139		

There are many varieties of glue, some general purpose and some special purpose, and new ones seem to come to market every year. When I see a new kind of glue, I usually buy a small amount and experiment with it to see if it is in some way better than what I have been using. The glues that I have found most useful are listed in alphabetical order.

CONSTRUCTION ADHESIVE

Construction adhesive, such as "Liquid Nails," is inexpensive. It comes in cartridges that are used with a caulk gun. It is waterproof and easy to use and is good for big jobs such as wood construction, paneling, plywood, and drywall. I also use it when constructing my corrugated-cardboard storage boxes. Try not to get it on your skin, it is hard to remove.

CONTACT-BOND CEMENT

Contact-bond cement is a very strong rubber cement. It is used for gluing laminates, veneer, cardboard, etc. You can also put this cement on the threads of a screw or bolt to stop it from loosening, but you will still be able to remove the screw when necessary.

CRAZY GLUE, SUPERGLUE

These glues are used for very small jobs where the mating parts fit perfectly. They set in seconds. They have a shorter shelf life than most glues; they sometimes become unusable in a year. I keep them in the refrigerator where the shelf life is longer. Try not to get these glues on your skin; they can glue your fingers together.

EPOXY (5-MINUTE CLEAR EPOXY)

This glue is a thick liquid, clear or colored, that hardens in 5 minutes. It is good for small jobs where the parts to be glued fit closely to each other. It hardens so fast that you can simply hold irregularly shaped parts together until the glue sets. One such use is to repair broken ceramic objects. If you buy nonclear epoxy, try to get the kind that is white rather than gray. There are also epoxies that take several hours to harden, which gives you more time to work.

EPOXY PASTE

Epoxy paste is similar to the clear epoxy, but it contains a filler and it forms a thick paste that doesn't run as much while it hardens. It is good for larger jobs and for glue jobs where the mating parts do not fit closely.

EPOXY PUTTY

Epoxy putty is even thicker than the paste. It will fill large gaps in poorly-fitting joints. It can be molded into various shapes and is quite strong after hardening. Epoxy putty is sometimes used to seal leaks in plumbing systems.

GOOP

Goop™ is a general-purpose glue that needs no mixing. It is good for small jobs. I carry a tube of Goop in my car. It is not as strong as epoxy, but is easy to use.

HOT-MELT GLUE GUN (Fig. 30-1)

The glue gun is a useful and inexpensive tool. You put a "stick" of glue in it, the gun melts the glue and you squirt the molten glue wherever it is needed. The glue hardens as it cools, usually in just a matter of seconds. Glue guns come in various wattages; I like the higher-wattage guns (160 watts). The glue sticks come in various lengths, I suggest the longer sticks of glue because you won't have to stop in the middle of a job to insert another stick of glue.

The glue sticks also come with various melting points. I like the glue sticks with the higher melting points. I once built a robot for a friend. It was made of old vacuum cleaner parts. I glued it together with hot-melt glue that had a low melting point. The friend put the robot on a windowsill in the sun and, in the summer, the glue softened and the robot collapsed.

If you have a hammer or other tool with a loose handle, it can usually be fixed quickly and easily with a glue gun. The major limitation of the glue gun is that you can only use it for small jobs because the glue cools and hardens so fast. Some people use carpenter's glue to glue large pieces of wood but they "tack" the pieces together with hot-melt glue in a few spots. The hot-melt glue holds the pieces together while the carpenter's glue sets up. Hot-melt glue is not as strong as epoxy, but it is very convenient and easy to use.

You will get stronger joints with hot-melt glue if you keep the glue gun in each spot for several seconds so that the glue has time to bond with the surfaces before it hardens.

YELLOW CARPENTER'S GLUE

This is an easy-to-use glue for general-purpose wood gluing. It needs several hours or overnight to harden. It is not as waterproof as epoxy.

Some of these glues come in a plastic bottle with a cap that turns. You turn the cap one way, then squeeze the bottle to dispense the glue. Then you turn the cap the other way and it closes the bottle and a tiny tip extends through the cap to keep the opening clear. My experience is that these dispensers soon become clogged with hardened glue and are unusable. I prefer the bottle that has a tapered round or triangular cap. You remove the cap, squeeze out the glue, and replace the cap.

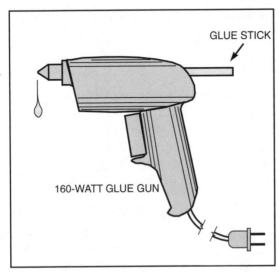

FIGURE 30-1 Glue gun.

LUBRICANTS

CRC or WD40 (in a Spray Can)	141	Plumber's Heat-Proof Grease or	
Light Household Oil	141	Silicone Grease	142
Paraffin Wax	141	Silicone Lubricant (in a Spray Can)	142

A lubricant is the opposite of a glue; it makes things slide on each other without sticking. The lubricants that I have found most useful and wouldn't want to be without are listed.

CRC OR WD40 (IN A SPRAY CAN)

These are good penetrating lubricants. They help to loosen rusty nuts or bolts and are claimed to retard rusting. Be careful about using them indoors because they have a strong, persistent, unpleasant odor.

LIGHT HOUSEHOLD OIL

This oil comes in a small flat can with a spout and a screw-on cap or other closure device. Make sure the container can be closed tightly or it will leak if it is not in an upright position. You can use this oil to lubricate motors, hinges, and almost anything that has moving parts.

PARAFFIN WAX

This wax is used for rubbing on the sides of window frames and adjoining parts to make sticky windows and screens slide smoothly up and down. You can buy paraffin wax or use a candle. If you don't have wax for this purpose, you can use a cake of soap, although it's not as good. Sometimes wax is rubbed on the threads of a wood screw to make the screw go into the wood more easily. I usually keep a candle in my toolbox. If I forget to remove the candle from the toolbox in summer, when the temperature in the car reaches 130 degrees or more, the candle often melts and makes a mess.

PLUMBER'S HEAT-PROOF GREASE OR SILICONE GREASE

This grease comes in a small can. It is useful for lubricating valve stems of faucets and other plumbing purposes. It is also good for gate hinges and other outside uses because it is heatproof and waterproof. Silicone grease is used for the same purposes.

SILICONE LUBRICANT (IN A SPRAY CAN)

Silicone spray is good for many purposes including many places on cars. You can use it on the rubber gaskets around the car door to make the door easier to open. You can spray it into door and window locks to make them work smoothly. Silicone spray is also good for lubricating moving parts in computer printers, etc. Unlike almost all other lubricants, silicone does not damage rubber parts. However, you should be careful to keep it off rubber drive members such as belts and drive wheels, because it may cause them to slip.

A nonfunctioning electric switch or lamp socket can sometimes be resurrected by spraying silicone into it. (Be sure the device is not plugged in.) Be careful to not let the spray get in your eyes; it can be very painful.

TAPES

Black Plastic Tape	143	Packaging Tape	144
Duct Tape	143	Two-Faced Foam Tape	144
Fiberglass Tape	143	Making Tape Easier to Use	144
Masking Tape	143		

There are dozens of kinds of tapes for almost all imaginable purposes. The ones I would always want to have on hand are listed alphabetically.

BLACK PLASTIC TAPE (³/₄-INCH-WIDE)

This tape, sometimes called electrical tape, is used for electrical work. It also comes in other widths and colors. It is waterproof and can be used indoors or outdoors.

DUCT TAPE

Duct tape is usually gray or aluminum in color and 2 inches wide. This tape, originally intended to seal joints in air ducts, has many other uses. Some people think that all you need to repair ANYTHING is lots of duct tape. Most duct tapes do not hold up well when used outdoors. If you must use duct tape outdoors, buy the special variety that is intended for exterior use.

FIBERGLASS TAPE

Open-weave, self-sticking fiberglass tape is used when doing drywall work. It is very strong and you will find other uses for it as well.

MASKING TAPE (1-INCH-WIDE)

Masking tape is used when painting, and for many other purposes. Don't leave a roll of masking tape where it is exposed to sunlight, the adhesive will harden and the tape will become useless.

PACKAGING TAPE

This tape is similar to scotch tape. It is about 2 inches wide. It is especially useful when preparing packages for mailing. The clear tape is better than the light tan variety because you can put it directly over the address label without concealing it. The tan variety is good for covering up unwanted printing when you are reusing a box.

TWO-FACED FOAM TAPE

Two-faced foam tape is good for attaching objects to walls, glass surfaces, and ceramic tile surfaces. Buy the good-quality tape intended for automotive use so that you can also use it for reattaching automobile trim. Be careful about using this tape on plastic or painted surfaces because it may be difficult to remove without leaving permanent marks.

MAKING TAPE EASIER TO USE

After you have removed as much tape as you need from the roll you are using, it is a good idea to turn under the end of the remaining tape, or to push the end of the tape off the side of the roll. If you don't do this, the next time you use that roll of tape you will waste time trying to find where the end is and then trying to get a fingernail under the end to get the tape started again.

WOOD

Buying Wood   145   Pressure-Treated Wood   146
Boards   145   Studs   146
Plywood   145

BUYING WOOD

You should be aware that lumber sizes are described in bizarre and inconsistent ways. For example, a 1 × 8 × 8-foot board is not 1 inch thick, it is approximately $3/4$ inch thick. It is not 8 inches wide, it is approximately $7^1/2$ inches wide. However, it is exactly 8 feet long. Similarly a 2 × 4 × 8-foot stud is approximately $1^1/2$ inches thick, $3^1/2$ inches wide, but exactly 8 feet long. When you buy plywood, however, you get what you pay for. A 4-foot by 8-foot sheet of $3/4$-inch plywood is indeed exactly 4 feet by 8 feet and is just a tiny bit less than $3/4$ inch thick.

When you buy boards or studs, you should look them over closely before buying. Sight along them and don't buy them if they are not straight or if they have large knots at places which would weaken them.

BOARDS

If you have a few boards at home, you will find many uses for them and it will save you many trips to the lumber yard. I suggest that you buy a few white pine boards 1 × 8s × 8 feet. You can cut them shorter or slice them narrower as needed.

PLYWOOD

There are many varieties of plywood and similar products, such as flakeboard, oriented-strand board (OSB), etc., and new products are constantly appearing. Some have special smooth surfaces that are ideal for painting signs. Some have waterproof glue, which makes them good for outdoor use. When you have a particular job to do, you should carefully consider the pros and cons before you decide which of these products to use.

Because there are so many varieties, and because these sheets of plywood take up a lot of room, I would not buy any plywood until it is needed.

You will gradually accumulate pieces of plywood, hardboard (Masonite), pegboard, paneling, etc. These sheets of material should be stored leaning against a wall and as nearly vertical as possible. If they are leaning against the wall from a foot away, they will often take a permanent bend and become useless for many jobs. The smaller pieces should be stored in front so you don't have to look behind anything to see what you have.

PRESSURE-TREATED WOOD

Pressure-treated wood is wood, usually yellow pine, that has been impregnated with chemicals to prevent rot and termite attack. Because pressure-treated wood is so frequently used, I like to have a few pieces at home to save unnecessary trips to the lumberyard. I like to have a few 2 × 4s by 8 feet, a few 4 × 4s by 8 feet, and a few 1 × 6s by 6 feet. These boards can be stored outdoors because weather won't hurt them. The 1 × 6 boards will tend to warp if they are not lying on a flat surface or if they are exposed to sunlight. You can lay the 4 × 4s on the ground, put the 1 × 6s on them, then lay the 2 × 4s on top. When you buy pressure-treated wood, try to get the newer kind that contains no arsenic.

When you put a screw through a piece of pressure-treated wood and into something else, a fence post for example, it is a good idea to drill a clearance hole for the screw in the pressure-treated wood. Otherwise, the wood will tend to split, often several weeks later, especially if the screw is only a few inches from the end of the board.

If you want to paint pressure-treated wood, the best procedure is to first let it weather for a few months. Then, when there has been no rain for a few days, and the wood is perfectly dry, paint it. If you must paint damp wood, use latex paint.

STUDS

Studs are the vertical members that are inside most walls. They are usually made of fir or spruce wood. I like to have on hand a few 2 × 4s × 8 feet and perhaps a few 2 × 3s × 8 feet. In some newer houses, the studs are 2 × 6s; this allows use of thicker insulation. Still other new houses use steel studs. Because steel studs are becoming more popular, it is worthwhile to call your local home center to see if they are planning a demonstration of these studs.

OTHER USEFUL MATERIALS

Cement Mix, Mortar Mix, Concrete Patch	147	Sandpaper	149
Drywall	148	Sash Chain	149
Duct Seal	148	Sheet Metal	149
Fiberglass Fabric	148	Spackle, Patching Plaster	149
Metal Strapping	148	Vinyl Siding	150
		Wire: Steel and Aluminum	150

Here is an alphabetical list of other useful materials.

CEMENT MIX, MORTAR MIX, CONCRETE PATCH

These compounds are used for repairs to interior or exterior masonry surfaces. If you want the patch to match the color of the surface being repaired, you can add a small amount of latex paint (usually black or brown) to the mix. But you won't know the true color of the patch until you mix a small amount and let it harden and dry. You will never get a perfect match, but you can come close.

I have had good results using these mixes to fill large holes in rotted sills and other exterior wood members. Scrape out the soft rotted wood, pack the cavity tightly with the mix, keep it damp for 24 hours, and then keep the area painted to prevent further rot. If you cover the patched area with fiberglass cloth, that is even better.

If these compounds are kept in a plastic bucket with a tightly fitting lid, they will keep for years. If the mix came in a paper sack instead of such a bucket, wrap the bag in several layers of plastic trash bags, close tightly, keep it off damp floors, and it will also last for years. When you use these mixes after long storage, see if they have lumps. If they have soft lumps that crumble at a touch, the mix is OK. But, if you find hard lumps that do not crumble very easily between the fingers, the mix should be discarded. If it is used, it will lack strength and hardness. I suggest that you have some cement mix on hand and buy the other compounds when they are needed.

If you are using patching cement, you will get better adhesion if you first wire-brush the surface even if it appears perfectly clean. Brush vigorously in two perpendicular directions. The best procedure is to wire-brush and then spray with water or bonding agent until the surface will absorb no more but there is no liquid on the surface, trowel on a small amount of the cement using a lot of pressure, and then apply the rest of the cement and trowel to the desired shape.

DRYWALL

Drywall is a sheet of plaster with paper on both faces. It comes in several thicknesses, but the $1/2$-inch thickness is by far the most widely used. It is good to have a piece of it on hand for small repairs. Store it in a vertical position.

DUCT SEAL

Duct seal is a thick, pliable, nonhardening substance similar to modeling clay. It is used to seal joints in air ducts and to seal holes in siding where pipes or wires go through an outside wall. It is also good for holding a screw on the end of a screwdriver. Buy some, you will need it sooner or later, and it keeps forever.

FIBERGLASS FABRIC

Flat-weave fiberglass fabrics of various widths are useful when painting surfaces that have holes or cracks. This material looks like fiberglass screening, but it is very thin and flat, and, with two coats of paint on it, it is virtually invisible. The fabric bridges the holes and gaps so there is no need to fill them before painting. The fabric is held in place by the paint, or you can use caulk to hold the fabric in place before painting. You can buy this fabric in paint stores, and wider widths of it, often colored black, can be found in roofing supply stores.

METAL STRAPPING

You can buy metal strapping in rolls of various widths and thicknesses. *Stainless steel* strapping about $3/4$ inch wide is useful for repairing outdoor furniture and big wooden flower tubs. It is also used to attach TV antennas to chimneys. *Galvanized steel* strapping about an inch wide with holes every inch is useful for fence repair and for supporting pipes and tubing along a basement ceiling.

SANDPAPER

There was a time when all sandpaper was more or less the same. It was made with flint, which resembles ordinary sand, and glued with water-soluble glue to a sheet of heavy paper. Now there are dozens of kinds of sandpaper. I like the aluminum oxide and silicon carbide papers best, although they are the most expensive, because they last longest before they get worn and dull and you have to throw them away and start using another piece. Open-coat sandpaper is best when sanding soft wood or painted surfaces because it has less tendency to clog up.

In addition to the 40-grit, 80-grit, and 160-grit sandpaper suggested to have in your car, you might want some 400-grit waterproof sandpaper for sanding surfaces, such as a car body or a refrigerator, to prepare for painting. If you do this job, keep the work wet with a hose or a sponge to wash away the paint dust as it is created. If your hardware store doesn't have this fine-grit sandpaper, you can buy it at auto supply stores.

SASH CHAIN

If you work in an old house with sash cords and sash weights for the windows, you may be asked to replace the cord with chain. Sash chain is also used for some bathroom skylight windows.

SHEET METAL

I suggest buying a roll of aluminum flashing that is 12 inches wide. Get the kind that is painted white on one side and dark brown on the other side. You will find many uses for it. I carry mine in my car. I find that pieces of sheet aluminum of various thicknesses are also very useful. Get the soft grade that is easy to cut and bend. If I come across a piece of galvanized sheet steel, I buy it and eventually find uses for it.

SPACKLE, PATCHING PLASTER

These compounds are used to fill holes and cracks in interior surfaces preparatory to painting. They come in many varieties. Some harden in minutes, some in hours, some are ready to use, others are powders that must be mixed with water. You should have at least one kind on hand. Store the powder variety in a closed container in a dry environment and it will keep for years. You should also have some exterior spackle, the kind that is waterproof after it hardens.

If you add latex paint to the patching plaster powder instead of water, you will have spackling compound of any desired color.

VINYL SIDING

You may pass a house where vinyl siding has been installed. You may see a lot of smaller pieces in the trash or the Dumpster. Take some of these pieces. They are very useful for small repairs. The siding with a wide flat area is better for your purposes than the kind with a midrib. Vinyl siding can be cut with tin snips and bent into almost any shape, almost as though it was sheet metal. I often attach house numbers to a piece of white or ivory vinyl siding and then attach it to a house or mailbox.

WIRE: STEEL AND ALUMINUM

I find it useful to have on hand several sizes of galvanized steel wire and aluminum wire, both solid and stranded. Wire is useful for making hooks for special purposes, repairing fences, staking recently planted trees, and supporting TV antennas.

LADDERS

Useful Ladder Sizes	151	Mitts and Stabilizers	152
Fear of Ladders	151	Using Two Ladders	153
Ladder Safety	152		

USEFUL LADDER SIZES

I have found the following sizes of ladders to be sufficient for doing most jobs.

Stepladders   Stepladders should be 2 feet high, 4 feet high, and 6 feet high or 3 feet high, 5 feet high, and 7 feet high.

Extension Ladders   You will need one ladder that extends to 10 or 12 feet and another ladder that extends to 16 or 20 feet.

When you buy extension ladders, try to get ladders that have a flat area on top of each rung rather than perfectly round rungs; they are much easier on the feet.

There are some fancy combination ladders that can be configured in many ways. They are good, but expensive. If you have shiny new ladders and have to store them outdoors, you may want to paint them some dark, dull, ugly color so no one will be tempted to steal them. Fiberglass ladders are heavier and more expensive than aluminum ladders but they are safer if you are going to be working near power lines because they don't conduct electricity. All of my ladders are aluminum.

FEAR OF LADDERS

There are some people who, upon first finding themselves 5 or 6 feet above the ground on a ladder, experience the kind of terror and panic in the pit of their stomachs that would be more appropriate had they suddenly found themselves dangling from a hang glider over the Grand Canyon in a thunderstorm. How do I know that there are such people? Because I am one of them. The good news is that you *can* get over this fear. At least this is what worked for me.

I leaned my 20-foot extension ladder against my house wall. Then I went up four rungs, which is 4 feet. Because the ladder was springy and swaying a bit in the breeze, I could not muster the courage to go any higher. So I just stood there for 10 or 15 minutes until my subconscious finally realized that, no, this was not going to be a near-death experience. The next day I went one rung higher and even rocked back and forth a bit. It took about 3 weeks to get accustomed to working calmly when my feet were 15 feet above the ground. You can do it too.

What if you absolutely, positively, *will not* go up a ladder? Don't despair, there is a lot of work that does not require a ladder. But you will be missing out on many good jobs, so try to become ladder compatible. I have often been hired to do work that the homeowner could have done himself, except that he had ladder phobia.

If you have a long extension ladder, you can mark the center of it with a band of paint. That is where you can pick up the ladder to carry it without one end being heavier than the other and falling into the ground.

LADDER SAFETY

Please see Chap. 46, Work Safely.

MITTS AND STABILIZERS (Fig. 35-1)

It's a good idea to buy ladder mitts for your ladder. These rubber mitts prevent the ladder from scratching the walls that you lean it against. You can improvise ladder mitts by taking two strips of carpeting and wrapping them around the ends of the ladder and tying them on. There are also ladder stabilizers. The stabilizer attaches to the top of the ladder. It is like a wide bar with two curved feet that lean against the wall. This not only makes the ladder more stable, it allows you to put the ladder in front of a window but not leaning against the window.

USING TWO LADDERS

Most stepladders have a shelf that flips out and can be used to hold a can of paint. However, I find it better to have the paint on a second step ladder which is standing alongside the one I am using. That way, I don't have to be as careful how I move, lest I spill the paint. This is especially helpful when you are working with a full can of paint.

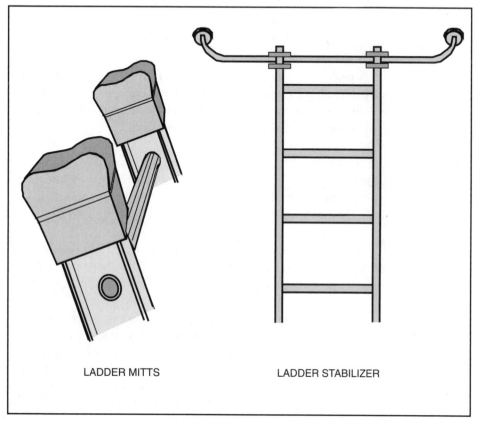

LADDER MITTS   LADDER STABILIZER

FIGURE 35-1 Ladder mitts, ladder stabilizer.

WORKBENCH WITH VISE

You should build or buy a sturdy workbench, the heavier and sturdier the better. As an example, if the top of your bench is made of 2 × 8s or 2 × 10s and the legs are made of 4 × 4s braced diagonally with 2 × 4s, that is the kind of heavy construction that is desirable.

The bench need not be huge, although, if you have plenty of room, I would suggest having a big bench with lots of drawers. A bench 3 feet wide and 8 feet long is ideal. You could add a backstop board, a few inches high, along the back, to stop things from falling off behind the bench.

If your bench is not very heavy and extremely rigid, you should find a way to anchor it firmly to the floor or the wall. Paint the top of your workbench with gloss paint to seal it against dirt, oil drips, etc. Light gray is a good color.

On your bench, you should have a big, heavy, swivel vise. (See Fig. 37-1.) The vise should be bolted down on a corner of the workbench. If you are right-handed, the right-hand corner of the bench is probably best. I like a vise that opens at least 4 inches, with jaws that are at least 4 inches wide. Why the emphasis on a heavy bench and a heavy vise? There will be times when you will want to put a piece of metal in the vise and shape it by pounding it with a heavy hammer or putting a length of pipe on the piece and bending it to shape. The vise is also often used as an anvil; you put a piece of metal on the back end of the vise and hammer it into the desired shape.

The vise should open, close, and swivel smoothly and easily. Don't buy a cheap vise. Spend whatever it takes to get a good one; it will last a lifetime.

OTHER USEFUL EQUIPMENT

Car-Related Items	155	Pipe Clamps	157
5-Gallon Buckets	155	Portable Folding Worktable	157
Halogen Work Light	156	Rope (Big)	157
Hand Truck	156	Sawhorses	158
Outdoor Table	157	Vise	158

In addition to the tools and materials already suggested to have at home, the following equipment items are recommended. If you acquire them over time, as opportunity and finances permit, you will find many uses for them.

CAR-RELATED ITEMS

For work on cars you should have:

12-Volt Tester   This small inexpensive device is like a pen with a small light, a metal tip, and a wire with a clip on the end. You attach the clip to any metal part of the car or engine and then touch the metal tip to wherever you are testing for voltage. If the voltage is there, the light goes on.

Battery Charger   An inexpensive 12-volt charger, capable of recharging a battery overnight is sufficient for most needs.

Jumper Cables   Don't buy the cheapest jumper cables. Pay a little more and get good ones.

5-GALLON BUCKETS

You are probably familiar with the white 5-gallon buckets from drywall compound and many other products. These buckets are very useful and it's a good idea to have several of them. Drywallers will often have empty ones that they don't want. You can often find these buckets in Dumpsters at construction sites. Here are some typical uses for these buckets.

- I often go to someone's home to do several jobs. There may be an electrical job, a plumbing job, and a small paint job. Before I leave the house, I take three buckets and put all the tools and materials for each job in its own bucket. This saves time at the work site.
- These buckets are useful when cleaning paint brushes. You can put some water or solvent in the bottom and work the brush back and forth very vigorously without splashing paint on yourself or the surroundings.
- Buckets are useful for mixing up small quantities of patching plaster or cement.
- The buckets are useful when doing gardening work. You can carry water or dirt in them when transplanting, or you can put weeds in them to take to the compost pile or trash can.
- You can use a bucket to throw trash into as you work. Be sure the outside and bottom of the bucket are clean before you bring it into someone's home.
- You can sit on a bucket when you are painting or working near floor level. You can turn one of these buckets upside down and set a can of paint on it. This will save having to bend down as far as you would if the can was on the floor.

If you stack these buckets to save space, be careful not to push them tightly together; you will have great difficulty getting them apart again.

HALOGEN WORK LIGHT

If you are doing extensive work such as painting in a large dark room or hallway, your drop light will not provide sufficient light. You should have a 300- watt or a 500-watt halogen work light. They are not expensive, and they provide lots of light, but be sure to read the instructions carefully before you set one up for use.

HAND TRUCK (Fig. 37-1)

An old hand truck will work just as well as a new one. Look for a sturdy hand truck with large wheels. The bigger the wheels are, the easier it will be to truck objects across soft or soggy ground and the easier it will be to move heavy objects up or down stairs. If you are moving something big and heavy, such as a washing machine or a refrigerator, you should use a few ropes to tie the load tightly to the hand truck.

OUTDOOR TABLE

If you have room for it, get a wooden picnic table for your backyard, the kind that is made of redwood boards. If you are assembling or painting something large, this is an ideal place to do it, especially if your indoor workbench is cluttered with tools and other objects, as most workbenches are. This is also a good place to work on mowers or other gasoline-powered devices. That way, you won't smell up the house with gasoline fumes or risk an explosion.

PIPE CLAMPS (Fig. 37-1)

Pipe clamps are clamps that you attach to a length of iron pipe to make a long clamp. I like to have two pipe clamps, each one on a 4-foot length of pipe. These are useful when you are working with a wooden door that is coming apart at the joints. You reglue the joints, then you use the pipe clamps to pull the door back together until the glue sets. You may also use pipe clamps when building or repairing furniture.

PORTABLE FOLDING WORKTABLE

A portable folding worktable is a combination sawhorse, vise, and portable workbench. One such table is called Workmate™. It is not essential to have one, but it can be helpful if you do a lot of carpentry. If you buy one, get a good sturdy one; some of the cheap ones have flimsy plastic parts that can break or fall off.

ROPE (BIG)

Try to get a big long rope, preferably one that is $3/4$-inch nylon and about 100 feet long. If you can get a few big pulleys that can handle this rope, that is even better. You will use this rope when you do tree work, for example, to make sure the tree falls where you want it to. You may use it to pull down a branch that has fallen from a high part of the tree and is now lodged somewhere in the tree. You may use it to pull objects up to a roof or to lower objects down from a roof. It is also useful, along with the pulleys, when you want to use your car or truck to pull a bush out of the ground.

SAWHORSES

You should have a set of folding sawhorses, preferably ones that open and close quickly and easily.

VISE

See Fig. 37-1.

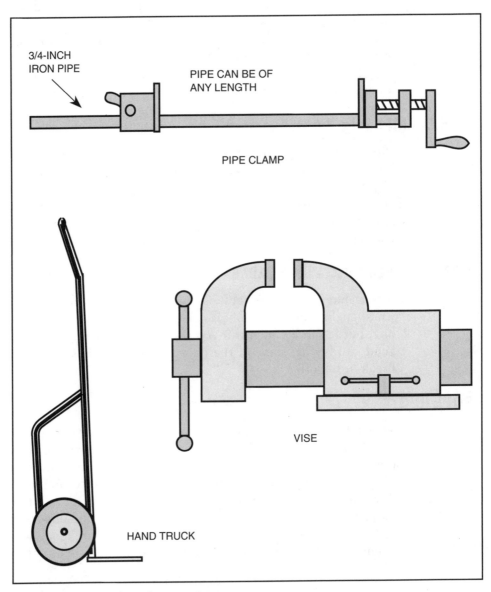

FIGURE 37-1 Hand truck, pipe clamp, vise.

BOXES

| Plastic Compartment Boxes | 160 |
| Corrugated-Cardboard Boxes | 160 |

Unlike the person who is only concerned with various projects around the house, you must have all your tools, hardware, and materials ready to go. Furthermore, you should be able to find what you need quickly. It will take a lot of thought and a lot of time to get your items organized and labeled so that you can just grab what you will need, put it in your car, and be on your way. But this is time well spent, so, no matter how long it takes, do it right.

One of the most capable handymen I ever met was a fellow named Mac. Mac was a retired shipbuilder and he once said to me, "Give me a set of blueprints and I can build an entire ship single-handed." I believed him. I never saw Mac have to stop to figure out what to do next on any job. But Mac did not have his materials well organized. One day he and his helper spent half an hour going through a big pile of items looking for a particular plumbing fitting that he was sure he had. Eventually they gave up, and Mac had to send the helper out to buy another one. The moral of the story is: If you have something and can't find it, you are worse off than if you didn't have it at all, because you will waste a lot of time looking for it.

This chapter, and the next two, are about how to organize and store your possessions so that you can find the items you need without wasting a lot of time looking for them.

You will gradually accumulate hundreds of hardware items. This is desirable because it will save you innumerable trips to the store. You should almost never find yourself making a special trip to a store to buy something that is small, inexpensive, and frequently used. The first time you buy a switch or an outlet, for example, buy a few extras. However, the problem will soon arise: how and where to store all these items. The answer: Keep the items in sturdy, clearly labeled plastic boxes with compartments, or, for larger items, modified cardboard boxes, and store the boxes on shelves.

PLASTIC COMPARTMENT BOXES

These boxes come in many sizes from 3 inches by 6 inches by $3/4$ inch deep (or smaller) up to 8 inches by 12 inches by 2 inches deep (or larger). They have a hinged lid that snaps shut. The boxes that snap shut in two places are better than the ones that have only one snap. Some of these boxes have no compartments, some have as many as 16 compartments. The size of box you choose, and the number of compartments, will depend on what you intend to store in that box. It is well to have one or two unused compartments to allow for future need.

I keep my compartment boxes on a shelf with one end facing out and the hinged side of the lid on the right. This is the most convenient way if you are right-handed. Because they are usually small and light, they can be stacked several deep. I put a stick-on label on the end of each box to indicate the contents. Put the label on the same end of each box so that if you are looking at the label, the hinges of the box are on the right.

CORRUGATED-CARDBOARD BOXES

For the items you wish to store that are too big for plastic compartment boxes, you will have to use cardboard boxes. When you first start out, you can probably get some empty shoe boxes at the local shoe store to hold items such as pipe fittings, electrical outlets, etc. But shoe boxes are flimsy and are just temporary until you can get or make something better. You can also use cigar boxes, but if you take them with you to a job, you should put a rubber band around each box so it won't spill its contents if your car hits a bump. If you have an old inner tube, you can cut rubber bands from it that are perfect for keeping cigar boxes closed.

What you want are boxes that are very sturdy, easy to open and close, and shallow. Why shallow? Because what you *don't* want is to have to empty out your box of parts at the work site, root around in the pile to see if you can find what you need, and then have to scoop up all the pieces and dump them back into the box. You should be able to just open the box and see all the contents with little or no poking around. The boxes should be sturdy enough so that you can stack them three or four deep without the bottom box collapsing from the weight.

A step up from shoe boxes are the boxes that automobile brake shoes come in. You can probably find a place that services brakes and get lots of these boxes. These boxes are shallow and very sturdy, but you may have to cut down the flaps somewhat to make the box easy to open and close. You may also have to run a band of strong tape around the box near the top to stop the box from opening out flat. If you look around and ask around in your vicinity, you may find other sources of suitable small boxes.

Still another possibility are the plastic kitchenware containers such as those from Rubbermaid and Tupperware. Be sure the lids stay firmly on but are easy to remove when necessary.

When I began accumulating items, I was fortunate because I was given empty boxes from IBM punch cards. These boxes are approximately 8 inches wide, 16 inches long, and 3 inches deep. I have about 200 of them, clearly labeled and sitting on shelves where I can find what I need very quickly. For larger items, I also have many boxes that are approximately 12 inches wide, 18 inches long, and 7 inches deep.

Medium-sized boxes are available at the liquor store. For larger boxes, I go to the local supermarket and get corrugated-cardboard boxes. Boxes whose bottoms are long and narrow are preferable to boxes whose bottoms are nearly square because you can put more of them in the same shelf space and let the front ends of the boxes extend over the front of the shelf. Look for sturdy boxes. The boxes from tomatoes and bananas are often very sturdy. If the bottom is not strong and solid, cut a piece of cardboard from another box, sized to fit the bottom of the box you are working on, and lay it in, or glue it in if the existing bottom is not strong and tight. If you are doing a lot of gluing like this, the best way is to get a tube of Liquid Nails or other construction adhesive and use it in a caulking gun.

Because most cardboard boxes will be too tall for your needs, you now have to cut them down to the desired height. See Fig. 38-1. Suppose the box you are working on is 18 inches high and you want the finished box to be just 6 inches high. Measure up 6 inches from the bottom of the box and make marks at all four corners. A felt-tip pen is fine for this. Using a straight edge, draw lines connecting these corner marks. Now add to the original 6 inches the desired width of the flaps that you will interweave to close the box. If the bottom of the box is 10 inches wide, you will add 5 inches for the width of the flaps. Draw a second line around the box 5 inches above the first line. In other words, the second line is 11 inches above the box bottom. Now take a sharp utility knife and cut the box off at the 11-inch height.

Now take a quarter or half dollar and, pressing firmly, run the corner of the coin along the lines where you will fold down the flaps. The idea is to make a crease along the fold lines. Now make two cuts at each corner, from the top of the carton to the fold lines. These cuts should be about $1/4$ inch apart and they, in effect, remove the corners of the box. Remove the thin strip of cardboard that is left. This will make closing the box easier. Now fold the flaps *outward* first, then inward. That's it. You now have a strong shallow box. It will stay shut if you interleave the flaps as you close them. Reinforce the bottom if necessary. After a bit of practice, you will be able to do this entire procedure in a matter of minutes.

Even better than boxes that close by interleaving the flaps as described above are boxes with a removable top. Such boxes are easier to stack and they can slide past each other even when they are stacked several boxes deep. If you can find sturdy boxes with removable tops, use them, otherwise, use boxes with flaps. Some of the boxes from computer paper are suitably sturdy and can be cut down to make them shallower.

Some moving and storage companies sell sturdy corrugated-cardboard boxes with removable tops. Try to buy the kind that has single-thickness sides, because this kind of box can be cut down in height without weakening the box.

If the widths of most of your boxes are the same, your shelf space will be utilized the most efficiently. If the lengths of your boxes vary, some of the boxes will just stick out farther in front of the shelf. The depths of your boxes may vary, depending on whether you made the box to hold large or small items.

In many cases, you will have several different items in the same box, so you will need some way to keep those items separate. Get some quart cartons and some half-gallon cartons from milk or orange juice and cut them down to the height of your box plus extra for fold-down flaps. Fit these inside your box and put your small parts in them. Print the contents of each small box on one of the flaps. Baby food jars are also very convenient for separating different small parts. Paint the lids of the jars white, and print the contents of each jar on the lid.

For very small items, you can use the plastic containers from 35-millimeter film. Camera stores often have lots of these. Try to get the ones with gray lids; you can write directly on them with a permanent-ink felt-tip pen. If you have containers with black lids, stick a round self-stick label on the lid and write on the label.

There is one more step. In addition to having your items in sturdy boxes that you can take with you to the job, the boxes must be marked so that you can quickly select the ones you need.

I paint one end of the boxes with semigloss latex paint. I use yellow for electrical parts, light green for plumbing parts, pink for objects related to computers or electronics, half yellow and half pink for telephone parts, and white for everything else. I have four wide-mouth jars, about pint size, one for each color of paint. I smear a thin film of grease on the threads of the jar and the lid so that the paint will not harden on the threads and make the lid hard to remove. After the boxes are color coded this way, and the paint is thoroughly dry, take a Magic Marker or a felt-tip pen, preferably with permanent ink, and print in large black capital letters what the box contains (IRON PIPE FITTINGS, POWER STRIPS, etc.). The idea is that you want to be able to stand back 8 or 10 feet from several shelves full of these boxes and immediately find the ones you need. If you have to change the labeling, the ink is removable with alcohol, or you can just paint over it and start again.

You can, of course, use a paper label instead of painting the end of a box, but my experience is that the labels tend to fall off after a few years. If you use self-sticking labels, brush a coating of rubber cement onto the cardboard box and let it dry before sticking on the label. That will keep the label on much longer. If you use the kind of gummed label that you moisten before attaching, don't use the rubber cement.

There are a few mathematical symbols that are useful when you are labeling your boxes. One is > which means greater than. So you might have a box labeled: NAILS > 2″. This box contains nails that are longer than two inches. Of course, this box will not contain a jumble of nails of all lengths. It will have a small box of nails that are $2^{1}/_{4}$ inches long, a box of $2^{1}/_{2}$-inch nails, etc. If the V is pointing to the left, it means less than. For example WOOD SCREWS < 1″ means wood screws that are less than 1 inch long. These symbols are often combined with the equal sign, thus ≥ means greater than or equal to. For example: $^{1}/_{4}$″ bolts ≥ 3. This box contains $^{1}/_{4}$-inch-diameter bolts that are 3 inches long or longer.

As you acquire more items, some of the items in one box will have to be transferred to a larger box or subdivided into two boxes. When I first started out, I had only a few boxes. One was marked "PLUMBING PARTS." As I acquired more plumbing parts, I used two boxes, one for copper tubing fittings and one for iron pipe fittings. Then I further subdivided the copper tubing fittings into two boxes, one for $^{1}/_{2}$-inch fittings and one for fittings for tubing greater than $^{1}/_{2}$ inch in diameter.

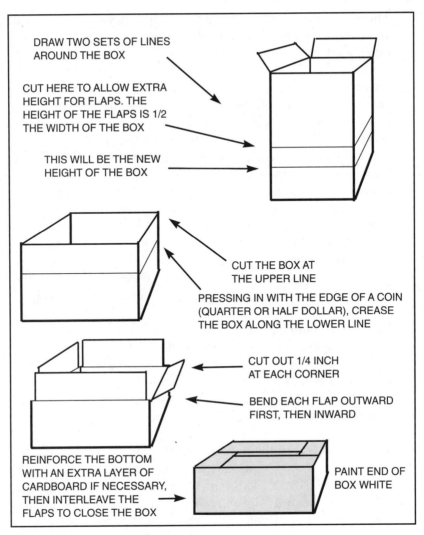

DRAW TWO SETS OF LINES AROUND THE BOX

CUT HERE TO ALLOW EXTRA HEIGHT FOR FLAPS. THE HEIGHT OF THE FLAPS IS 1/2 THE WIDTH OF THE BOX

THIS WILL BE THE NEW HEIGHT OF THE BOX

CUT THE BOX AT THE UPPER LINE

PRESSING IN WITH THE EDGE OF A COIN (QUARTER OR HALF DOLLAR), CREASE THE BOX ALONG THE LOWER LINE

CUT OUT 1/4 INCH AT EACH CORNER

BEND EACH FLAP OUTWARD FIRST, THEN INWARD

REINFORCE THE BOTTOM WITH AN EXTRA LAYER OF CARDBOARD IF NECESSARY, THEN INTERLEAVE THE FLAPS TO CLOSE THE BOX

PAINT END OF BOX WHITE

FIGURE 38-1 Cutting a box to size.

SHELVES, HOOKS, RACKS, BUCKETS

Shelves	165	Racks	167
Hooks	167	Buckets	168

SHELVES

As you accumulate many boxes of items, you must have shelves upon which to keep them. You can't just have piles of boxes sitting on the floor. So now the problem becomes, where to build those shelves. And keep in mind that there is an iron law of nature: "Your possessions will multiply to fill or exceed all available shelf space."

Wherever you have a place where you can build some shelves, do so. Ideally, you will have a big basement with an outside door. Or, you may have a big garage, or you may have or could build a shed on your property. Another possibility: You may know someone with an unused garage who will let you keep your possessions there in return for taking care of their repair needs. If none of these are available, look around your house. Maybe you have an unused room. You might get some ideas from a book on making storage spaces.

I like the shelving systems that consist of standards that attach to the wall at each stud (Figs. 39-1 and 39-2). These standards look like U-shaped channels and they have rectangular slots spaced 1 inch apart center to center. These standards come in several lengths. You then insert brackets into the slots and the brackets support the shelves. The brackets come in lengths from 6 inches to 14 inches or more to match the width of the shelves. The nice thing about this system is that you can easily move the brackets up or down to change the spacing of the shelves. Try to buy the standards and brackets that are made of steel; the heavier, the better. Those made of aluminum tend to be flimsy and weak.

You can also buy steel industrial-type shelving systems, the kind that consists of four vertical corner angles with holes every inch and individual shelves, 1 foot by 4 feet, that bolt to the angles to form a top, a bottom, and as many shelves as you wish in between. These systems are very strong. You can fasten them against a wall or, if you fasten them to the ceiling or have two of them back to back, they can stand in the middle of a room. You can often find these shelving systems for sale, used but usable, at industrial supply or store supply places or at going-out-of-business sales.

Still another method of erecting shelving is to use L-shaped shelf-support brackets. These are screwed to the wall, into the studs, 16 inches apart, and the shelves then rest on the brackets. This is the least expensive way to put up shelves. The only disadvantage of this method is that it is not as easy to change the spacing between the shelves as with other methods.

The most underutilized space in most houses is the wall space just below the ceiling. I have shelves around the walls of my kitchen that are 16 inches (41 centimeters) below the ceiling, just low enough so that I can stack two gallon-size cans of paint, one on top of the other, on them. (See Fig. 29-1.) I have approximately 50 gallons of latex paint stored up there—interior paint, exterior paint, semigloss, satin gloss, flat, and in many colors. It may not look nice and it is not guaranteed to win the approval of your significant other, but if you have nowhere else to store paint, these shelves will do the job. When you build such shelves, keep in mind that paint is much heavier than an equal volume of water, so make those shelves strong. Depending on your height, you may want to have a small stepladder or a sturdy wooden box nearby to stand on when using the shelves.

Sometimes there is a considerable amount of space under a flight of stairs. This can also be a good place to build some shelves.

I like shelves that are 12 inches deep. I can put boxes that are up to 18 inches long on these shelves with the extra length extending out from the shelf. The shelves should be sturdy and supported every 16 inches if you are attaching them to a wall that has studs at that spacing. Try to use real wood or plywood (³/4-inch or thicker) for the shelves. Particleboard is not as strong as wood or plywood and it tends to sag over time. But it is inexpensive and you can use it if it is supported every 16 inches along its length and at both ends (Figs. 39-1 and 39-2).

I like the bottom shelf to be 16 or 17 inches above the floor. That is high enough to accommodate two 1-gallon cans or one 5-gallon bucket sitting on the floor underneath it. If the floor is sometimes damp, as in some basements and garages, and if some of the 5-gallon buckets are metal, put something impermeable to moisture (plywood, vinyl flooring, tar paper, etc.) under the buckets to keep them off the floor. Otherwise, the bottoms of the buckets, if the buckets are metal, may rust out. The other shelves should be spaced so that you can put your storage boxes on them two deep, or three deep for very shallow boxes. If you have several sets of shelves for your items, keep the items you use most often near the door. That way, you won't have to carry them as far.

I keep the boxes I use most at waist or chest height. I keep heavy boxes that I rarely use on the floor or the lower shelves, and light boxes that I rarely use on the top shelves. Try to keep all of your electrical-work boxes near each other, your plumbing-related boxes together, etc.

Typically, when I am preparing to go to a job, I will take several of the compartment boxes and either a few of the larger boxes or a few items from some of the larger boxes.

If one of my storage boxes is empty, I turn it upside down on the shelf. The reason is that if I am looking for something and I see that box upside down, I know that I am all out of whatever it had contained. If I no longer want to use a box for whatever it is labeled, I turn the labeled end of the box to the wall. I have a separate section of shelf for these boxes that are ready to be reassigned.

HOOKS

You will find many uses for big hooks on the wall to hold coils of wire, rope, etc. You can buy hooks or make them from shelf-support brackets (the ones that resemble a large letter L, mounted upside down on the wall. Bend the end up at 45 degrees so objects don't slide off. See Fig. 39-3.

RACKS

You should have some racks, preferably on the basement ceiling, where you can store long lengths (up to 8 feet, if possible) of wood, pipe, tubing, etc. If you have the kind of basement ceiling that has exposed joists, you can put strips of wood across the bottoms of the joists and store a lot of boards, pipes, etc., between the joists.

When you are starting out, all this work with boxes, shelves, hooks, and racks will take a lot of planning, a lot of time, and a lot of work. Do it carefully, and it will pay for itself a hundred times over.

BUCKETS

You can use 5-gallon plastic buckets to store lengths of wood, pipe, angle iron, metal or plastic tubing, metal rod, etc. I have several such buckets holding useful items. The items should be long enough to extend beyond the top of the bucket, but not so long as to cause the bucket to tip over. You can see at a glance what is in each bucket and select what you need.

You can use some $^1/_4$-inch-thick hardboard or plywood to make two vertical dividers for a bucket. See Fig. 39-4. The dividers fit into the bucket at right angles to each other and divide the bucket into four sections. One of the dividers is slit from the top down to the middle and the other is slit from the bottom up to the middle. The dividers interlock. You can now keep four different categories of items in one bucket. For example, steel rods and tubes in one section, steel bars and angles in one section, aluminum shapes in one section, and copper and brass items in the fourth section. Even if you keep the same items in all four sections, it is still desirable to have the dividers because they keep the items more nearly vertical, thus saving floor space.

You can also buy divider systems that are designed to fit into these buckets so the buckets can hold small items.

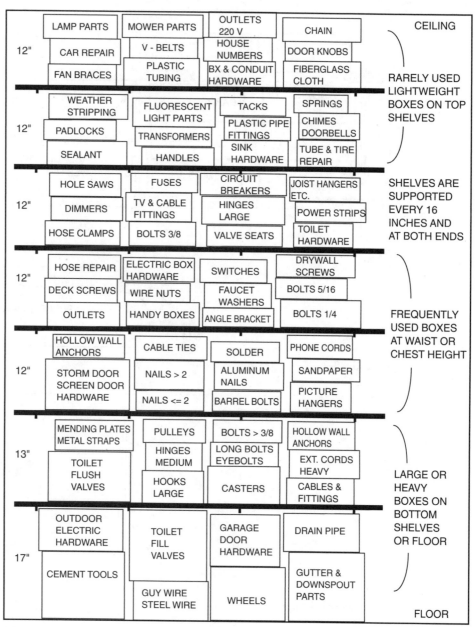

FIGURE 39-1 Boxes on shelves.

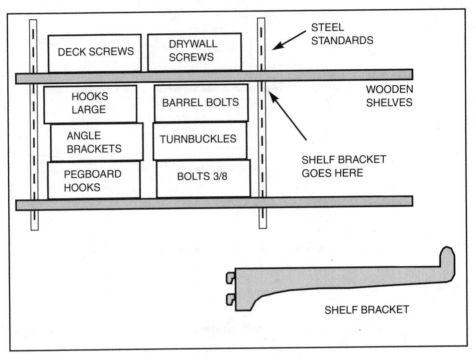

FIGURE 39-2 Boxes on shelves, close-up view.

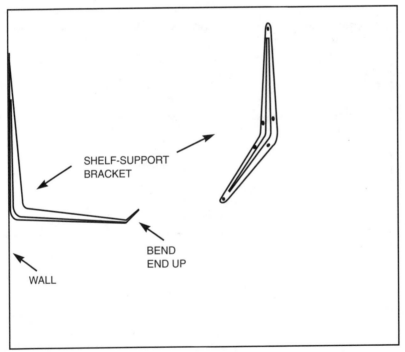

FIGURE 39-3 Shelf-support bracket used as a large hook.

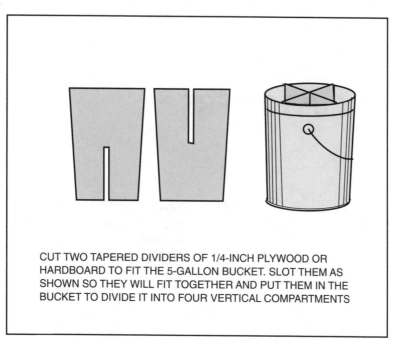

CUT TWO TAPERED DIVIDERS OF 1/4-INCH PLYWOOD OR
HARDBOARD TO FIT THE 5-GALLON BUCKET. SLOT THEM AS
SHOWN SO THEY WILL FIT TOGETHER AND PUT THEM IN THE
BUCKET TO DIVIDE IT INTO FOUR VERTICAL COMPARTMENTS

FIGURE 39-4   Bucket dividers

FINDING CUSTOMERS

Business Cards	172	Newspaper Advertising	175
Distributing Your Cards	173	Phone Answering Machine	175
Be Friendly	174	Realtors	175
Car Sign	175	Storekeepers	176
Lawn Sign	175	T-Shirts	176
Make an Offer	175		

BUSINESS CARDS (Fig. 40-1)

When you are ready to start seeking customers, the first thing to do is to get 100 or more business cards printed up. There are mail-order companies that will do this for a reasonable price, or you could try your local copy shop.

If you have access to a computer, you can design and print your own business cards. You can create and print a whole page of cards and then cut them to size. Most paper used with computer printers is of a thickness called "20 pound." Such paper is too thin to be cut into business cards although you can use rubber cement to attach a card to a heavier backing. You can buy heavier paper that is usable with most printers. I use 35-pound paper (sometimes labeled 35/70). It is a bit on the thin side for a business card, but it is good enough and I don't have to be bothered with adding a backing.

Still another method is to print up a page of business cards on 20-pound paper and, using a copier that can print on heavier stock, such as manila file folder, make copies of the sheet of cards and then cut them apart. The final size should be standard business card size, 2 inches × 3$\frac{1}{2}$ inches.

Your cards should be printed in black ink on white or pastel paper. Keep it simple, pretty pictures do not help. Don't use fancy fonts that are hard to read. All you need is your name, address, phone number, and a description of your work. See Fig. 40-1.

Use all capital letters. Make sure the printing, especially the phone number, is large and easy to read. Many of your customers will be older people whose eyesight may be weak. If you have an e-mail address, include it on your business card.

In a pinch, until you can get professional-looking business cards printed up, you can stick some of your return address labels on 2-inch $\times$ 3^1/$_2$-inch cards, add the word HANDYMAN and your phone number, and hand those out.

When you buy supplies at a store, you can present one of your cards. Some paint stores and other suppliers may give you a discount when they see that you are a professional.

Keep four or five of these cards in your wallet at all times and keep a stack of them, at least 25, in your car at all times. Don't miss any opportunity to give one of your cards to a prospective customer. Keep in mind that you want to find customers who live nearby, preferably within 10 or 15 minutes driving time.

DISTRIBUTING YOUR CARDS

Bulletin Boards   Put a card on supermarket bulletin boards, church bulletin boards, and the bulletin boards in hardware stores, home centers, etc. If there is room on the bulletin board, you can put up larger advertisements with tear-off tabs with your phone number. Check from time to time to see that your card is still there and not covered up.

Friends, Relatives, Neighbors   Give cards to friends, relatives, and neighbors. Ask them to pass the cards on to anyone who needs work done.

New Housing Developments   If new houses or apartments are being built in your vicinity, go there when people are just starting to move in. Hand out your cards and put one under each door. This is fertile ground for new customers because the people have left their old handyman behind when they moved and there is always something to be done in a new place.

People at Home Centers   If you go to a home center and see someone who looks like he might need your services, perhaps a customer who looks baffled and confused, walk up to him, smile, and say, "Hi, my name is John. May I give you one of my handyman cards?" Hand him the card as you speak.

You can have flyers printed up that describe the services you offer and put them under windshield wipers of cars in the parking lot.

On one occasion, I helped a gentleman carry his purchases to his car. I gave him one of my cards. He called me the next day and gave me several months of work fixing up a huge old house that he and his wife were selling. And after they moved, they gave me more work in their new house. All for the price of a card and a few minutes of my time.

People at Yard Sales   If you go to a yard sale, give one of your cards to the person holding the sale, and one to any likely looking prospects who come to the sale. At one yard sale, being held by a local dentist, I chatted with him and his wife, then gave them one of my cards. The dentist had me do several weeks of work on his house and then sent me to his sister-in-law who gave me several more weeks of work. If you go to a community yard sale held by people in an apartment complex, that is an excellent opportunity to hand out your cards.

People You Work For   If you work for someone, leave a few of your cards with him and ask him to give one to any neighbor who might need to have work done.

BE FRIENDLY

Learn to be outgoing and friendly. On one occasion, I was doing a paint job, when a little old lady, probably about 80 years old, came walking by. I caught her eye, gave her a big smile, and said "Good morning." She was absolutely surprised and pleased. She was obviously accustomed to being ignored and here someone had taken the trouble to greet her. On her way back, she stopped and watched me for a while. I was wondering why she was so interested in what I was doing.

"Are you a painter?"

"I'm a handyman, but I do a lot of painting." I gave her one of my cards.

"My house needs painting, would you like to do it?"

"Yes ma'am."

CAR SIGN

You can put a sign on your car that says "HANDYMAN JOHN," and your phone number. If you do this, your car must be neat and clean and the sign must be very professional looking.

LAWN SIGN

With the permission of the homeowner, you can put a sign on her lawn while you are working there. Get the kind of sign that is held in the ground with two thin wires You can push them in and pull them out in seconds, without any tools, and they leave no visible holes.

MAKE AN OFFER

You can also get work by seeing something that needs fixing or painting and asking the owner if he would like you to do it. I got my first sign-painting job by telling a shop owner that his sign needed repainting. He asked me what I would charge to paint it, I gave him a price, and he said, "Do it."

On another occasion, I was asked to fix a window for a homeowner. I noticed that, although the home had a large two-car garage, there was no room for either of the cars because there was a mountain of bicycles, skis, golf equipment, and folding chairs on the garage floor. I asked if he would like me to put up some shelves, hooks, and racks to get all that equipment off the floor. He told me to go ahead and later told me how delighted the family was to be able to use their garage again.

NEWSPAPER ADVERTISING

You can advertise in your local newspapers if the rates are reasonable. Some papers run specials from time to time with very low rates.

PHONE ANSWERING MACHINE

You must have a phone answering machine in good working order. Check it for messages twice a day or oftener. Before leaving a job, call your answering machine; there may be a message there that you should respond to before going home.

REALTORS

Realtors often have need of a handyman to do fixing or painting in a house they are going to sell. Visit your local realtors, get on good friendly terms with them, and leave a few cards with them. They can be extremely helpful.

STOREKEEPERS

Storekeepers also need things fixed. Give a card to the owner of any store you go to. Don't overlook the owner and workers in your local restaurant. I was once in a camera shop. The owner was trying to fix a small lamp. I showed him how to do it. He then gave me a lot of work in his shop and in his home. Then his daughter called me and I did a lot of work for her.

If you are bidding on a job for a store which sells things you use, such as a food store, you can offer to do the work for a certain dollar value of merchandise (sometimes called a "store credit"). This gives you an advantage over other bidders because the actual cost to the store owner is much less.

T-SHIRTS

You can wear T-shirts with HANDYMAN JOHN and your phone number. If you are doing an outside job, people who pass by will sometimes ask you to do work for them.

```
┌─────────────────────────────────────────┐
│           HANDYMAN DAVE                  │
│                                          │
│    REPAIRS OF ALL KINDS & PAINTING       │
│                                          │
│  FREE ESTIMATES    SMALL JOBS WELCOME    │
│                                          │
│    987 EASY ST.    JOYVILLE, PA 99999    │
│                                          │
│           (123) 456–7899                 │
└─────────────────────────────────────────┘
```

FIGURE 40-1 Business card.

KEEPING YOUR CUSTOMERS HAPPY

Be Reliable	177	Don't Break Anything	180
Be Considerate	177	Latest Gadgets	181
Be a Friend	178	Recommendations	181
Be Polite	178	The Written Estimate	181
Customers Can Help You	178	When to Decline a Job	182
Customers Vary	179	When You Don't Know How to Fix It	183
Difficult Customers	179		

BE RELIABLE

In my years as a handyman, I have heard many complaints about other handymen. And it is almost always the same complaint. "He isn't reliable. He said he would be here Tuesday and I stayed home all day and he never showed. He didn't even call." Or, "He said this job would be done by Wednesday, and it's now Friday and the job still isn't done."

So I urge you, be reliable. If you tell the customer that you will be there on Monday between 9 A.M. and 10 A.M., *be there*. If something unexpected prevents you from being on time, call as soon as you are aware that you can't make it. "I'm sorry, I had car trouble, or an emergency call," or whatever the problem is. Remember that nowadays, most homeowners are busy; even if they don't have a regular job, they usually have errands to run every day.

Don't overpromise. If you don't know when you can do a job, tell the person you will call them as soon as you know when you can do it.

BE CONSIDERATE

Try to adapt your schedule for the convenience of the homeowner. I like to start early each day, especially in summer. But one of my customers doesn't get up until 11:30 or 12:00. So, when I work for her, I find other things to do in the morning.

If you must have a radio or boom box to accompany you while you work, make sure it is not so loud that it annoys the customer.

Don't smoke in someone's house. It can leave a bad smell which lasts for hours.

If you leave ladders or other large objects at the job site until you finish up, be sure they will not be in the homeowner's way.

You will know that you have satisfied customers when they call you again and ask for additional work.

BE A FRIEND

Remember that you are selling a service. In addition to doing good work at a reasonable price, you want the homeowners to like you. Smile when you greet them; it doesn't cost anything. Take a few minutes to ask how they are, "How are the kids? How was your vacation?"

BE POLITE

Learn to say yes sir, yes ma'am, please, and thank you.

CUSTOMERS CAN HELP YOU

Another reason to be on good friendly terms with your customers is that they may be helpful to you in various ways. Some of my customers have offered me furniture, books, sports equipment, computers, etc., that they no longer needed. My office desk at home is made from a huge solid-mahogany front door that was given to me by one of my customers. In many cases, even though I didn't need the items that customers offered me, I did know someone who was happy to get them. So this is another service you can provide for your customers; enable them to swap things with each other.

When I get to know my customers, I ask them what kind of work they do, or did before they retired. On one occasion, I needed several vinyl outdoor signs made up. One of my customers had recently retired from that business and he got me the signs at cost. Another of my customers helped me start learning about computers.

CUSTOMERS VARY

The incomes and personalities of your customers will vary widely. You should learn to adapt yourself to whatever their needs and desires are.

If a person of limited means lives in a house where the paint is peeling, you might just paint and caulk where absolutely essential to prevent deterioration of the woodwork or penetration of water and damage to the interior. This could save the customer a lot of money. Other customers will want all areas painted, even if most of the areas don't need it, just to make everything look as nice and new and shiny as possible.

Similarly, one customer might want a fence which is falling down fixed at minimum expense. I might just drive a few steel fence posts into the ground and lash them to the falling fence to keep it up for a few more years. Another customer might want the entire fence replaced.

I was hanging pictures for a woman who had moved to a new house. She had me hold up each picture while she stood across the room saying, "Up a little, down a little, left a little." It took more than 2 hours to put up 10 pictures. I didn't mind, except that my arms were getting tired, because I was being paid by the hour. A month later I was ready to hang pictures for another woman who had moved. I asked her where she wanted them and she told me to hang them wherever I thought they looked right. When I finished, she glanced into the room and said, "That's fine."

Another time I was asked to replace a white telephone jack with a beige one. The jack was near the floor and behind a chair, so no one would ever see it. I politely suggested that it was a waste of money, but the homeowner wanted it done, so I did it.

DIFFICULT CUSTOMERS

On extremely rare occasions, you may find yourself dealing with a difficult customer. In 20 years of doing handyman work, I remember only a few such experiences.

In one case, I was asked to paint a basement laundry room that also contained the furnace, hot-water heater, and other appliances. I gave the woman a price, based on my guess that I could do the job in 2 days, and she told me to go ahead. When I finished and asked her to look it over, she actually lay down on the floor and looked up behind some equipment and told me I had to paint there also. I told her that those places were very hard to get to and no one could ever see them. She told me that she could see those places and I had to paint them.

It took me an extra day to clean and paint those inaccessible areas. Whenever she asked me to do work again, I gave her a high price and, in most cases, she found someone else to do the job. That was fine with me; let someone else have that aggravation.

Another time, I worked for a woman who was sure I was going to over-charge her for everything she wanted done. She had probably had bad experiences with other tradesmen. She made the job so unpleasant that I never worked for her again. But these were only two bad experiences in 20 years. Most of your customers will be extremely nice people. Many will become permanent friends.

DON'T BREAK ANYTHING

This may seem obvious and not even worthy of mention, but it is something to keep in mind at all times. It is easy to become so engrossed in what you are doing that you become oblivious to your surroundings and one careless move could cause the early demise of some prized possession. Some homes have expensive, delicate, fragile furniture, lamps, antiques, and doodads of all kinds. I once saw a young man, on his first day on the job, break an expensive antique plate, the homeowner's pride and joy, and irreplaceable. The homeowner was in tears and, of course, he never worked there again.

I know a professional cleaning woman. She comes to people's homes and offices with a small crew of helpers and they clean everything like a whirl-wind. But if there are "breakables," she won't let her people get near them. She insists that the homeowner move them to a safe place.

I can think of only two occasions on which I broke something. One time I pulled on a garden hose and it knocked over a flower pot and broke it. Another time, I cut a large branch off a tree. It fell and bounced in a way I had not expected and it broke a lawn ornament when it fell.

On another occasion, I was working with a long thin strip of wooden molding. The back end of it knocked over a tall thin table with several fragile doo-dads on it. Fortunately, the thick carpeting prevented anything from breaking, but it taught me a lesson; remove all breakables from the room in which you are working.

You must be scrupulously honest. If you break something, tell the homeowner immediately. "I'm sorry, I broke your 'whatever,' I'll pay for it or replace it." If you find yourself breaking things frequently, you are either trying to do too much in too little time, or you are in the wrong line of work.

LATEST GADGETS

You can be very helpful to your customers if you keep abreast of new gadgets that simplify jobs around the house. As an example, one of my customers wanted to be able to hear his doorbell even if he was in his basement office, or on the second or third floor of his big old house. I was about to start doing this the hard way by using a bigger bell transformer and additional ringers, and running wires through walls and floors. Just then, a catalog arrived in my mail with the perfect solution to this problem. It consists of a small sending unit that you attach on or near the front door and several inexpensive remote units that you plug in wherever you want to hear the bell. It worked perfectly and the customer was very happy.

Of course, I made less money with this new gadget, but you should always think in terms of what is best for the customer. It will always pay in the long run. The moral of the story: Try to keep informed about new devices which may relate to the work you do.

RECOMMENDATIONS

On occasion, a homeowner may ask you to recommend a roofer, or a plumber, or some other tradesman. You must be very careful. If you recommend someone, and the customer is not pleased with his work, the customer will blame you. I usually suggest that the homeowner ask around in the neighborhood for someone who has had good experience with a tradesman. Sometimes, if I know someone whom I consider very reliable, I give the homeowner his name, but I always add, "You should get one or two other bids and go with the person you feel best about."

THE WRITTEN ESTIMATE

When you are asked to bid on a job, you give the customer a written price. It is usually referred to as an estimate, but it is actually the final price unless the customer asks for changes or additional work. The estimate should be printed clearly in ink on your letterhead. Be sure to include the date, the name, address, and phone number of the customer, and a detailed description of everything you will do. Keep a carbon copy for yourself.

A typical estimate, written on your letterhead, might look like Fig. 41-1.

One of my first jobs was to repair a wooden fence. I told the owner that I would replace the missing pieces and paint the new pieces, but I did not write it down. More than a month later, he asked me to do the job. He was expecting me to paint the whole fence, which led to an argument. It was my fault for not giving him a detailed written description of the work to be done. Fortunately, he liked my work, and subsequently he gave me more jobs.

Here is another example: A neighbor wanted her attic insulated to R30. She got three estimates. One man told her he would do it for $375. He borrowed an old envelope from her and scribbled that figure in pencil on the back of the envelope. The second man gave her a price of $395. He printed this neatly in ink on one of his letterheads, including details of exactly what he would do. The third man gave her a price of $925. She wisely rejected the high bid of $925. That guy had larceny in his heart and very likely would not have done the work properly. Then she went with the $395 bid because the man made a good impression with his neat and workmanlike behavior.

WHEN TO DECLINE A JOB

There are times when you should decline a job that is offered to you. As they say in Vegas, "You have to know when to hold and when to fold." Here are a few examples where I felt compelled to fold:

- I was asked to cut a big branch off a huge tree. I like tree work but, after looking this over, I realized it was a job for a tree man who had the necessary experience and heavy equipment. So I reluctantly declined.
- I was asked to paint a big old house. The entire exterior was wood, the windows, the siding, the doors, etc. This would have taken several weeks and would have paid very well. But, when I examined the house carefully, I saw that it had gone unpainted for too long. Much of the wood, especially the window sills and frames, was spongy and rotted. I know from experience that such wood will not hold paint. I explained to the homeowner that I could paint the house and it would look fine at first. But, within a year or less, the new paint would be peeling and the rot would continue. There was nothing I could suggest other than to get a siding man to cover everything with vinyl or aluminum. It would cost a lot more than painting, but it would be permanent.
- A homeowner for whom I had done many jobs asked me to fix his old furnace which wasn't working properly. When I removed the front

panel, I saw a rat nest of wires, some of them dangling loose, some taped together with masking tape. Obviously, an amateur had been messing in there. The thermostat was a very old model, of a type I hadn't seen before. It also had extra unidentified wires hanging loose. Despite his urgings, I told him I would not touch that mess. I had no confidence that I could fix it and I might leave him without any heat at all.

- Always put the customer's best interest first. I was asked to fix a toaster oven. I saw that it needed a new heating element. I also saw that other parts of the oven were so rusted and corroded from years of use that something else might go at any time. I explained to the homeowner that I could fix it, but, for a few dollars more, she could buy a new one and be much better off. She took my advice. So I lost a job, but gained a loyal customer.

- On another occasion, a woman for whom I had done a lot of work asked me to coat her blacktop driveway. I told her I could and I gave her a price. But I also told her that, because it was a big driveway, she might get a better price from a professional company with a tank truck and a power sprayer because they could do it in a fraction of the time it would take me. She did get a better price from them but, of course, she was grateful, and she gave me many other jobs.

WHEN YOU DON'T KNOW HOW TO FIX IT

There is no disgrace in not knowing how to fix something. Even the most experienced handyman cannot possibly know everything. No homeowner will think less of you if you confess to ignorance of some subject. If I am asked to fix something that I am unfamiliar with, I usually do one of four things, depending on how I size up the situation.

- I say, "I'm not familiar with that, but I'll take a look at it and if I can't fix it, I won't charge you for the time I spend looking at it."

- I say, "I'm not familiar with that, but let me talk to my man at the plumbing supply place and then I'll let you know if it is something I can do."

- If the item is small, I may say, "I'll take it home and look at it when I have time. If I can't fix it, I won't charge you anything for looking."

- If it is not a very expensive item, and it appears that it would take me a lot of time to figure out what is wrong and even more time to fix it (if possible), then I say, "I'm afraid I can't be of much help to you with that, you are probably better off buying a new one."

HANDYMAN DAVE

REPAIRS OF ALL KINDS & PAINTING

FREE ESTIMATES   SMALL JOBS WELCOME

987 EASY ST.   JOYVILLE, PA 99999

(123) 456–7899

XXXXXXX@aol.com

10/2/05

Work for Jane Doe

777 Maple Ave.

(123) 456-7788

Install railing on basement stairway and	
paint to match existing woodwork	$ 60
Clean gutters	$ 30
Install 3 new screens on upstairs windows	$ 120
TOTAL	$ 210

FIGURE 41-1 Typical estimate.

HOW MUCH TO CHARGE

Fixed Price	185	Minimum Charge	187
Time and Material	186	Poor or Affluent?	187

There are two main ways to charge for a job. One is to charge a fixed price for the job, the other is called "time and material." In most cases, especially when just starting out on your career, or whenever you work for a new customer, you should give a fixed price. When people get to know and trust you, you can charge time and material.

FIXED PRICE

You look at a job and try to guess how long it will take. At first, you will probably be way off but, in time, you will eventually get fairly good at estimating how long a job will take. Then you multiply the number of hours it will take by your desired hourly rate. Then you add on the cost of materials, and that is the price you give the homeowner. This method has the advantage for the homeowner that she knows how much the job will cost before she decides whether she wants you to do it. It is also the only way she can compare your bid with others that she may get. Also, if a problem arises which causes the job to take longer than expected, it is your problem, not hers. Many handymen use the fixed-price method exclusively.

The advantage for you when the price is fixed is that, if the job takes less time than you expected, you make more per hour than you had anticipated. Another advantage is that you need not keep track of the hours you work, and if you stop for a while to talk to someone, it doesn't matter. The disadvantage for you is that, if you underestimate the time required, you could end up working for far less than you expected. As an example, a customer once asked how much I would charge to remove three bushes from her front lawn. I figured I could just put a chain around each bush, attach the chain to my car bumper, and yank those bushes right out of the ground. I gave her a price and she told me to go ahead. But it turned out that those bushes had very long, strong, deep roots and I had to do a lot of digging and chopping to get them out. I ended up making less than half my expected hourly rate. But that's the way you learn.

TIME AND MATERIAL

You keep an accurate record of the hours worked and charge your hourly rate plus the cost of materials. The advantage to the homeowner is that he often gets a lower price because you don't have to add a percentage onto the estimate (some tradesmen use the figure 15 percent) for the unexpected problems that may or may not arise. The advantage for you is that you don't have to attempt to guess how long a particular job will take (often very difficult). And you also don't need an accurate estimate of the cost of material.

What should your hourly rate be? Ask around. People who work in lumberyards have a good idea of what carpenters charge. People who work at home centers or hardware stores can be helpful. Ask tradesmen whom you meet. Look at classified ads and see what hourly wages are being offered. Once you have a good idea of your possible competitor's hourly rate, you can charge the same or a little less. If you think a competitor could do the job in less time than you (and this is a near certainty when you are first starting out), you can lower your bid accordingly.

When I first started, I worked on the assumption that it would take me twice as long to do most jobs as it would take a professional who had done that job, or a similar one, a hundred times. Sometimes, when I was very anxious to get a particular job, usually because I knew it would be a valuable learning experience, I would give a very low price to make sure I got the job. As I acquired skill, and more power tools, I gradually raised my rates.

How can you know how long a job will take? This is always a guess. I found that, in the beginning, I always underestimated the time required. Here is a suggestion. Sit down, get in a totally relaxed mood, close your eyes, and imagine yourself doing the job. Try to estimate the time required for every single step, however small. Write down these numbers and add them up. For example: Spread out drop cloths. Set up ladder. Scrape where required. Sandpaper where required. Wipe off dust. Apply spackle wherever needed. Caulk all cracks. Apply paint. Remove ladder. Clean up. Clean brushes and rollers. Put everything back in car. If you do your estimates this way, you are more likely to come close to guessing the actual time that the job will take. After a while, you will be able to look at a job and make a reasonably good guess as to how long it will take.

When I started out as a handyman, I would occasionally realize, after I finished a job, that there was a better way to do it that would have taken less time. In those cases, I would charge for how long it should have taken, rather than for how long it did take. The goal is to have your customers always know that they will get the lowest price from you.

MINIMUM CHARGE

Suppose you are called out to do a job and, when you arrive, you find that it takes only a few minutes to solve the problem. Maybe something wasn't plugged in properly, a valve somewhere wasn't turned on, or a circuit breaker needed resetting. How do you charge for this? Many handymen have a minimum charge, perhaps an hour of their time. I see this as entirely reasonable, and if you have plenty of work and plenty of customers, there is no reason not to do it. I don't charge anything for such calls. You may lose a little money doing this, but you can be sure that the person will be grateful and probably give you work in the future.

POOR OR AFFLUENT?

If you are working in an affluent neighborhood, your hourly charge can be somewhat higher than in a poor neighborhood. The important thing to most wealthy people is that you be absolutely reliable and that your work is flawless and exactly as they request.

BEFORE YOU GO TO THE JOB

Driving Instructions	188	Questions to Ask	189
Job List	188	What to Take	190

Depending on where you are going, what you are going to do when you get there, and whether you have been there before, these are some of the subjects to be discussed and questions you may want to ask on the phone before you drive to someone's house.

DRIVING INSTRUCTIONS

You should have good maps of all the areas in which you may work. Study the map before you call the homeowner. Make a pencil sketch of the route that looks best to you. Then, when you call the homeowner, ask if that is the best way to get there. There may be a better route, or one-way streets, detours, construction, or other problems that you should know about. Your sketch should include two streets before every turn and two streets after each street where you should have turned. That way, you are less likely to miss a turn because of a missing or twisted sign. Your sketch should also include the homeowner's phone number. If you are delayed for any reason, you can call and explain.

JOB LIST

Go over the list of jobs they want done. Sometimes people plan to ask you to do additional jobs after you arrive. You should know about these additional jobs before you leave home. That way you can bring the necessary tools and materials. Many people don't understand that you can't possibly bring everything for every possible job.

QUESTIONS TO ASK

Here is a list of questions that you might wish to ask before going to someone's home.

Anybody Home?   Will the homeowner be at home all day, at home part of the time, or at work all day? If they will be home all day, fine. That is usually best. If they will be home part of the time, when do they expect to be at home? Try to get any questions asked and decisions made when they are there. If they will be at work all day, get their phone number at work so you can reach them if questions arise. Will they leave the back door unlocked or leave a key somewhere?

Burglar Alarm   If there is a burglar alarm, is it completely deactivated so that you will not set it off accidentally and have to convince the police that you are not a burglar? (I have done this.)

Electricity   Is there outside electricity? Is it turned on inside? If there is no outside electricity, is there a porch light where you can remove the bulb and insert your screw-in outlet? Will they be sure to leave the porch light turned on?

Key   If the work you are to do is all outside work, you might want to ask about having a key or leaving a door unlocked so you can use the bathroom if necessary.

Ladders   If ladders will be needed, does the homeowner have the necessary ones? That can save you the time and trouble of lugging your ladders out and back.

Meters   Where is the gas meter, the water meter, and the electric circuit breaker panel or fuse box?

Parking   Where can you park? Can you park in their driveway? Would they prefer you to park on the street?

Pets   Are there any pets? Is the dog friendly? Do you have to be careful not to leave any doors open so that the pets will not escape?

Stores   Where is the nearest lumberyard, paint store, hardware store, plumbing supply, etc.? What hours are they open? Are they open on Sunday?

Telephone What should you do if the phone rings? If you have no instructions, don't answer. But they may want you to answer in case they have to reach you from work. Or, you may have to get a call from someone. If the phone rings, answer as follows: "Smith residence, Mrs. Smith is not here, this is John the handyman, can I take a message?" If the owner is home and you have to make a call, don't just pick up the phone and start dialing. Ask first, "May I use your phone?"

Trash Cans Are there large trash cans somewhere that you can use?

Trash Day When is trash day? What time do the trash men usually come? Some of your work may create a lot of trash; for example, bundles of branches. You want to get that stuff to the curb when it will not have to sit there for days waiting to be picked up. In some cases, when there is no good way to handle the trash at the work site, I take it home with me and dispose of it on my trash day.

Water Is there an outside hose spigot? Is the water turned on inside?

WHAT TO TAKE

Another thing you should do before you go to a job is to look around at all your tools and materials. If you think there is even a remote possibility that you might need a particular tool or material, take it with you. Far better to have it and not need it than to need it and not have it.

An example would be if you are asked to hang a cabinet on a wall. The homeowner may not know what kind of wall it is. So take whatever tools and hardware you will need to do the job whether the wall is thin wooden paneling, plaster and lath, drywall with wooden studs, drywall with metal studs, or masonry (stone, cinder block, concrete).

When a homeowner asks me to come out and estimate a job and it is a small job (only a few hours), I usually take whatever I think will be needed to do the job. I give her an estimate and tell her that I could do the job then and there or she could let me know at some future time if she wants me to do it. In most cases, she tells me to go ahead and do it. This saves me the time required to load up again and drive out there again, so I might make the estimate a bit on the low side.

BEFORE YOU LEAVE THE JOB

The Approval Tour   191
Other Things You Should Do   192

THE APPROVAL TOUR

If the homeowner is at home, you should insist that she walk around with you and check out everything you have done. There are several reasons for this. One is that you won't get a call a month later, "You know that thing you said you fixed, well, I just went to use it and it doesn't work." This does happen, usually because something unrelated to your work goes wrong.

As an example, I once installed a new electric outlet on the second floor of an old building. I should have insisted that the owner check it out, but I didn't. A few weeks later, he called to complain that the outlet did not work. It turned out that someone on the third floor, which was on the same circuit, had plugged in a defective iron and blown the fuse. The owner was skeptical that I had done the job right the first time. Had I insisted that he see for himself that the outlet worked before I left, this problem would not have occurred.

Another reason is that, although you were sure you did exactly what the homeowner wanted, you might have misunderstood. Some people are not very good at communicating their thoughts. Remember, the customer is always right. Just say, "I'm sorry, I misunderstood what you wanted, and I'll fix it right now." Sometimes you did exactly as you were asked, but when the homeowner sees it, she has second thoughts. For example, she might say, "You know, now that I look at it, I think I would like to have that top shelf a few inches lower."

Still another reason is that you may have installed something whose operation may appear simple and self-evident to you, but the homeowner may require some instruction.

If something that you installed for the homeowner came with an instruction book, warranty, or other paperwork, give this paperwork to the homeowner and urge her to send in the warranty and keep the instruction book in a safe place where she can find it if needed.

OTHER THINGS YOU SHOULD DO

Clean Up   Don't leave any mess (sawdust, shavings, scraps of wood or sheet metal) anywhere; always clean up after yourself.

Electricity, Gas, and Water   If you had the gas turned off to do your work, make sure to relight any gas appliances that have pilot lights. If you had the electricity turned off, reset the electric clocks and VCRs, or at least tell the homeowner that they need resetting. If you had the water turned off, you may want to run some water from a few faucets. If air got into the pipes during your work, these faucets may spit and sputter and the homeowner may think something is wrong.

Leave Old Parts   If you installed new parts, show the customer the old parts before you, or they, throw them away. That way, they can see what you did.

Look Around   Walk around the house and grounds to wherever you had been working to make sure you did not leave any tools or other items behind.

Paint   If you painted any doors or windows, make sure they open and close properly and were not glued shut by the paint. If you painted something and it is not thoroughly dry, put up a WET PAINT sign. Tell the homeowner how long to wait before touching or using the item.

Recheck   Recheck everything that you fixed to make sure it is working perfectly.

Bill   Take one of your letterheads from your car. A letterhead is a sheet of paper with the same information at the top as is on your business card. At the top of the sheet, print the date and the name, address, and phone number of the homeowner. Print, legibly and neatly, a list of everything you did and your charges. Do this on a clipboard with a carbon copy for yourself. Give this bill to the homeowner. If she pays you, mark PAID at the bottom and sign it or initial it. Clip the carbon copy to that customer's page in your three-ring book. If I am doing a big job, I sometimes ask to be paid at the end of each week.

Call Home   Another thing you might want to do before you leave a job is to call your answering machine to see if there are any messages. Perhaps you will want to look at a job or buy something on your way home.

WORK EFFICIENTLY

Time Is Money	194	Wall Calendar	195
The "Buy" List	194	Scheduling Your Workday	196
The "Hours" File	194	Pocket Paper	198
Maps	195	Checks	198
Phone Books	195		

TIME IS MONEY

Your most valuable commodity is your time. If you plan carefully, you can get much more done each day, which means you can earn more each day. When you first start out, you should not be concerned with speed. You should concentrate on giving the customer the best possible job at a reasonable price. After you acquire some expertise, you can start thinking about saving time. Here are some methods I have evolved to save time.

THE "BUY" LIST

I have a clipboard at home on which I list items to buy. I list items I need now and items I am running low on and will need soon. Then, when I must go to the store, I buy whatever I am in immediate need of and the items I will soon need. This saves unnecessary trips to the store. For example, I notice that I am running low on 1-inch drywall screws. I write that on my list. When I shop, I buy a box of these screws and I have them on hand when I need them.

THE "HOURS" FILE

This is a stack of 3×5 cards in a card file box or even just held together with a rubber band. On these cards I print the name of all the stores where I buy supplies, their phone number, and the hours when they are open. I may also include the names of the people I deal with at those places. I also make cards with the same information for the bank, post office, and library. Some places open at 7 A.M., some at 8 or 9 or 10. Some places have different summer and winter hours. The cards are arranged alphabetically. This information helps me schedule my day's activities.

MAPS

I like to have a map (or maps) of the areas in which I work tacked up on a wall. It should be a map that shows all the streets. Realtors often have good street maps of the area. Sometimes there are good maps near the front of yellow-page phone books. If there has been a lot of home building and road building in your area, try to use maps no more than a few years old. I have a magnifying glass hanging near the map to use in seeing the fine details. Then, if I have to go somewhere I have not been before, I can make a sketch of the best route and I take the sketch with me. I keep several map pins with this map so I can insert them in the map and visualize my daily journey.

It is also a good idea to stick map pins in the map at the locations of all the hardware stores, home centers, lumberyards, etc., in your area. Study the yellow pages to find where they are. When you have time, visit each of them and get an idea of what you can expect to find at each place. That knowledge will save you a lot of time.

PHONE BOOKS

You should have up-to-date phone books of the areas where you live, where you work or may work, and where you may be buying supplies.

I like to have all my phone books stacked in one place on a shelf near the phone. I put my phone books on the shelf with the spine of the book to the left and the bottom edges facing out. I mark the necessary information about each book on these bottom edges. This is helpful because the spines of most phone books are so cluttered with advertising that it is not easy to tell what area the book is for. I use a black marking pen and make large capital letters (see Fig. 45-1). YEL means yellow pages, WHT means white pages. This enables me to instantly select the phone book I want.

WALL CALENDAR

A useful tool for planning your work is a wall calendar that shows several months at a time. When I found that I could not buy a calendar exactly like the one I wanted, I designed my own. Here is how I make my wall calendar.

I buy a roll of white wrapping paper that is 28 inches wide. I cut a piece 48 inches long and tape it to an interior door with a few pieces of masking tape. Then I draw horizontal lines an inch apart and vertical lines 4 inches apart. I use a T square resting against the side of the door to draw the horizontal lines and a straightedge to draw the vertical lines. This divides the paper into 1-inch by 4-inch rectangles, one for each day. Each week occupies a space 1 inch high and the full width of the paper. Then I darken the lines that divide the months and label each month in the top center rectangle of that month. There are 14 possible layouts for the months, so be sure you are using the right one for that particular year. The yellow pages of the phone book often have a chart showing the calendar layout for each year.

Next, I pencil in the day of the month for each day. I make these numbers large and dark so I can read them easily while seated at my desk and talking on the phone. Then I pencil in all the holidays, birthdays, car inspection dates, bills due, taxes due, dates when various people will be on vacation, daylight saving time, etc. (see Fig. 45-2). I fasten the calendar to a door or a wall near my desk.

Now, when someone calls and asks for work to be done, I can glance at my calendar and see when I can schedule it. As soon as I agree to do a job on a certain day, I mark it on my calendar. The first thing I do upon arising each morning is to look at my calendar and see what I have to do that day. Then I cross off the preceding day. When there are only a few months remaining on my calendar, I move the existing section of calendar up and add another section below it.

SCHEDULING YOUR WORKDAY

Suppose you arrive at the customer's house at 9 A.M. and there are several jobs you plan to do that day. There are many things you should take into consideration when deciding the order in which to do them.

- If one of the jobs you will do is urgently needed by the homeowner, for example, hot-water heater not working, do that first.
- Some jobs will require that the homeowner be there to make certain decisions. Schedule these jobs for when the person will be at home. If he has to leave for work soon after you arrive, get the decisions made before he leaves.
- There may be inside work and outside work to be done. If rain is forecast for the afternoon, get the outside work done in the morning.
- In wintertime, when the days are short, do the outside work while there still is daylight.
- If the trash man comes at noon, get any trash you may create to the curb before noon.

- If there is work to be done in the attic, which may become fiery hot in the afternoon, do that work before the sun starts beating down on the roof.

- If you are doing a patching job or a painting job, which may require two applications, do the first application immediately upon arriving so that you can do the second application before you leave. This could prevent having to come back a second day.

- Exterior paints requires a minimum temperature to work best (usually 55 degrees). In cool weather, you can do the exterior painting in the early afternoon when it is warm outdoors. If you are painting the whole house in cool weather, you can start on the east side where you will be in the morning sun and then work around the house, staying in the sun as much as possible.

  If you must paint when the temperature is below 55, some paint stores sell paint which is specially formulated to work at temperatures as low as 35 degrees. If you use paint at a temperature below the recommended minimum, the paint job will look fine at first, but it may crack and peel in a year or less.

- In hot weather, you can start on the south side, before the sun gets too hot, then the west side, the north side, and finally the east side, thus staying in the shade.

- If you are painting, try to first paint the areas where someone might brush against the wet paint, so that those areas will be dry before anyone comes by.

- Will the homeowner start preparing dinner at 4 o'clock? Get any work you are doing in the kitchen done before that time. Will kids be coming home from school at 3 P.M.? Get the work in the kids' rooms done before 3 o'clock.

- Is there a job that may require you to go to the hardware store to buy something? Do that job early enough so that the store isn't closed when you learn what you need and go to buy it.

- Are other workers coming to work in the same room as you? Schedule that work before they arrive or after they leave.

- Still another consideration, in some areas, is the rush hour madness. You may want to start an hour earlier or leave an hour later than you otherwise would have, to avoid this stress-inducing ordeal.

- When you are first starting out, you may be somewhat nervous when you arrive at a new customer's home. In my case, I would do a very easy job first, then I would be in a more relaxed and confident mood to do the rest of the work.

POCKET PAPER

When working at someone's home, I carry a sheet of paper folded up and kept in a shirt pocket. I bring this pocket paper with me when I leave my house. At the top of this sheet, I write the date and the name and phone number of the customer and, if necessary, a sketch of how to get there. On this paper, I have also written a list of jobs I intend to do that day and everything I will need to do those jobs. As I load these items into the car, I circle them on the paper to be sure I don't forget anything. The paper may also contain a list of items to buy before going to the work site. In the same pocket, I carry a mechanical pencil that has a pocket clip. The pencil will stop the paper from falling out if I am bending over. The pencil should have soft, dark lead (grade B or 2B).

As I work, I make frequent notes on this pocket paper. I may be painting something and the homeowner may say, "Can you take a look at the kitchen window? It's hard to open." I write "fix kitchen window" on the pocket paper so I don't forget to do it when I finish painting. If I do fix the window, I encircle it on the paper to indicate that I did it. Don't cross it out, you want a legible record of what you did. If I find that, for some reason, I can't fix the window, I encircle that note with a dotted line to indicate I tried to fix something but couldn't. Then I explain to the homeowner what the problem is. Some other typical notes that I may write on the pocket paper during the course of a day may be:

- Start 9 A.M., $1/2$ hour for lunch, finish 4 P.M.
- Sharpen $1/4$-inch drill bit.
- Buy 80-grit sandpaper.
- Measure doorway for folding door.
- Get paint chart, get homeowner to select the color.
- Take chair home to fix.
- Bring chain saw.
- Go to bank, deposit check, get $100.

When I get home, I clip the pocket paper for that day onto the customer's page in my three-ring book (see Chap. 52, Record Keeping and Finances). I keep these papers until I make up my bill and get paid. Then I keep them a full year, just in case there are any questions.

CHECKS

Most people will pay by check. Deposit these checks immediately. Some people are careless about their checking accounts and if you wait several days to deposit the check, there may not be sufficient funds in the account, not out of any intent of the customer to cheat you, but because they wrote other checks subsequently assuming that you had already deposited yours.

Carry some deposit slips and ATM (automatic teller machine) envelopes in your car and stop at the bank on the way home. Keep a ballpoint pen in your car. The pens that write blue are better than the ones that write black; the black pens often won't work in cold weather.

I know a man who sells and installs carpeting. He has an account at every large and midsized bank in Philadelphia. When he gets a check, he drives to that particular bank immediately and deposits it. That way, if the check was good when it was written, the money goes into his account the next day. You need not go to such lengths, but do deposit your checks as soon as possible.

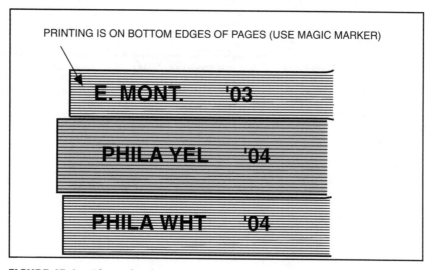

FIGURE 45-1   Phone books.

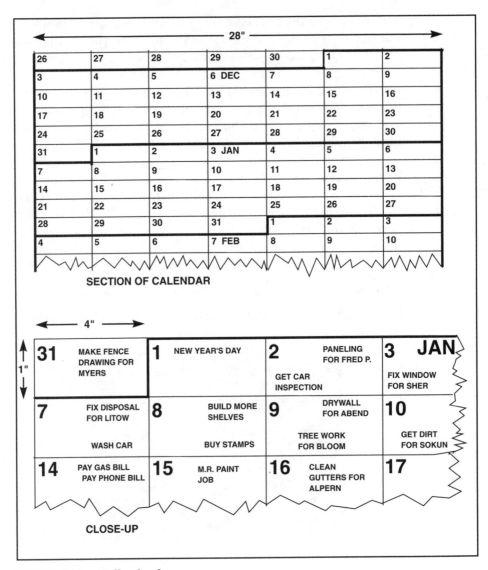

SECTION OF CALENDAR

CLOSE-UP

FIGURE 45-2 Wall calendar.

WORK SAFELY

Avoiding Accidents   **201**
First Aid   **202**
Ladder Safety   **203**

AVOIDING ACCIDENTS

Most accidents occur toward the end of the day when you are tired or when you are in a hurry. So be especially careful at those times.

Children   Don't let little kids stand nearby if you are using power tools or an axe or a sledgehammer or if you are doing something that might harm them if they do something unexpected.

Electricity   Turn off the electricity before you do electrical repairs. If there is someone else in the house, put a "DO NOT TURN ON" sign on the breaker that you turned off.

Falling Trees   Learn how to make a tree fall where you want it to, or don't cut it down.

Flammable Liquids   Don't use flammable liquids indoors. Don't store flammable liquids (alcohol, paint thinner, gasoline, turpentine) inside your house. You can buy small plastic sheds to store such materials away from the house.

Gas Appliances   Always read the safety instructions that come with any appliance. Turn off the gas before you disconnect a gas appliance such as a stove. If there is a shutoff valve for the stove, use that. If not, turn the gas off at the meter. But remember to relight any pilot lights that may go out.

Heavy Objects   Learn how to lift heavy objects without damaging your back. Don't try to lift objects beyond your ability.

Loose Handles   Don't use hammers or axes that have loose handles.

Nasty Insects   If you see bees or wasps entering a hole in the house near where you are working, be very cautious. They will usually not bother you if you are at least 10 feet away. You can sometimes seal up such holes with caulking early on a cool morning before the insects warm up. Be cautious about turning over flat rocks; there are some wasp colonies that live in the ground.

Nasty Plants   Learn to recognize poison ivy, stinging nettle, and any other nasty plants that may be growing in your area.

Power Tools   Never be in a hurry when using power tools, especially chain saws. Wear safety goggles when required.

Roof Work   If you must work on a sloping roof, use a safety harness unless the slope is very shallow.

Sunscreen   Use sunscreen if you are fair-skinned and will be working in the sun.

FIRST AID

Take a first aid course. Carry a first aid kit in your car. If I get a bite, or a sting, or brush against poison ivy, here is what works for me: I moisten the area with a little water, then I rub a cake of soap on the skin until there is a thick soapy paste on and around the affected area. I let it dry and the itch or sting from the nettle or insect bites soon goes away and I do not develop ivy poison. When I shower and the soap washes off, the itch resumes until I repeat the soap application. Some people like to put mud on a bee sting. Others use meat tenderizer.

Cuts   I get occasional nicks and cuts while on the job. The important thing about such minor wounds is to keep them clean. If I don't have a Band Aid with me, I take a piece of paper towel or toilet paper, put it against the wound, and tape it on with masking tape, or whatever kind of tape is handy. This tape should be replaced with a "real" Band Aid or medical adhesive tape as soon as you get home. Any tape other than the special tape made for medical use is very irritating to the skin. I find that small superficial cuts heal faster if I just keep them clean and don't use iodine, peroxide, alcohol, etc.

Splinters Getting occasional splinters is inevitable. If you have a magnifying glass and a pair of sharp tweezers, you or a friend can usually extract them. You might have to cut the skin a little to get at the splinter. I use a sharp-pointed X-acto knife for this purpose. Splinters from pressure-treated wood do not turn black and are harder to see.

LADDER SAFETY

A fall from a ladder can ruin your whole day. Be sure the mechanisms that lock the upper section in place are working properly. Sometimes a few drops of oil are required to make them function smoothly. Inspect the rope that raises the ladder and the pulley that the rope runs through. Oil the pulley. If the rope is worn, replace it. If the ladder is not on level ground, put something secure under one leg (a flat rock, a brick, a 2 × 4, a wooden wedge).

If there is any possibility that the ladder may slip, I run ropes from the bottom of the ladder to a bush, or tree trunk, or fence post, and other ropes from the middle or top of the ladder to whatever is available. Sometimes I run a rope from the ladder through a window and tie it to a radiator or the leg of a heavy piece of furniture. Be cautious about working on ladders in windy weather or at the end of the day, especially if you are tired.

Be very cautious about standing on rickety old ladders. Don't lean the top rung of a ladder against a tree trunk. That ladder will feel very stable when you are near the bottom but, when you get near the top, it will tend to twist and turn and throw you off. Lean the side rails of the ladder against a strong branch instead.

Don't carry heavy objects up a ladder. Attach a rope to the object, go up the ladder, then pull the object up.

IMPROVISING

45-Degree Cut	204		Missing Shingle	207
Attach a Screw	205		O Ring That Leaks	207
Bamboo Water Pipe	205		Oil	207
Cannibalization	205		Paintbrush	207
Caulk Backing	205		Phillips Screwdriver	208
Clamping Device	206		Pilot Light	208
Drainpipe	206		Sawhorses	208
Electric Wire	206		Small Hole	208
Hammer Handle	206		Tub Drain Leak	208
Hinge Pin	206		Washers	209
House Numbers	206		Water Valve	209
Madison Bars	207			

When you are fixing something at home, you will have all your resources, tools, and materials available to you. But when you are at a job site, there will be times when you *wish* you had something, but you *don't* have it. In some cases, you will have to go home and get it, or buy one locally, or postpone that particular work until your next visit to that house. If none of these options are convenient, you can often use your imagination, "think outside the box," as the current popular phrase goes, and find a nonstandard way to get the job done. In other words, improvise. The variety of time- and laborsaving improvisations is literally endless. Here, alphabetically, are just a few examples:

45-DEGREE CUT

Suppose you have to cut some wood strips at a 45-degree angle and you don't have your miter box or a 45-degree triangle. Take a sheet of paper and make a fold starting at one corner. Make the fold so that the sides of the paper adjacent to that corner lie one on top of the other. You now have a 45-degree angle. Use the angle to draw a pencil line for the 45-degree cut.

ATTACH A SCREW

You may want to attach a screw to the end of your screwdriver in order to start the screw in some hard-to-reach place. If you don't have the special screwdrivers that are magnetic or have other provisions to hold the screw, you can often use a bit of duct seal or caulking or putty or chewing gum or any thick sticky substance to hold the screw on the screwdriver until you get it started.

BAMBOO WATER PIPE

The check valve on a customer's washing machine split open one Sunday, spilling all the water in the machine onto the laundry room floor. The check valve is really only needed when the machine is installed in a basement that has no drain and the machine must pump the wastewater up to a drain in the floor above. In this case, the check valve wasn't needed and could have been replaced by a piece of 1-inch-diameter copper tubing about 6 inches long. But there was no way to get such a piece of tubing on this Sunday. As I wandered around the customer's premises looking for a substitute, I saw a length of bamboo that had come with a rug rolled on it. I had heard that bamboo is used in the orient for piping liquids. If it works in Mongolia, maybe it would work in Pennsylvania.

I selected a section of the bamboo that was the proper diameter and cut out a piece 6 inches long. I put it into the machine in place of the check valve and it worked perfectly for several years.

CANNIBALIZATION

I was fixing a second-floor toilet one night and I needed a new brass rod that connects the float to the fill valve. There was no easy way to get one, but I recalled seeing an unused toilet in the basement. With the homeowner's permission, I took the float rod from the basement and used it upstairs. This process of using parts from one device to fix another similar device is called cannibalization.

CAULK BACKING

A twisted plastic bag can be used for caulk backing. You press the bag part way into a deep crack to limit the amount of caulk required.

CLAMPING DEVICE

A customer needed a small clamping device that was missing from the luggage carrier of her foreign car. The dealer said he could get one in a week, but she needed it that day. Looking at the remaining clamp on the other side of the rack, I noticed that it resembled some devices I had at home that were intended to hold kitchen cabinets together. With a minor modification, one of these devices did the job. She is still using it.

DRAINPIPE

There was a leak in the drainpipe under a sink. I didn't have the right replacement parts. I taped the "wound" with several wraps of black vinyl electrician's tape. Because there is very little water pressure in the drain line, this held until I came back a few days later with the proper replacement parts.

ELECTRIC WIRE

You may be running an electric wire or a phone wire through walls, floors, or ceilings. The usual procedure is to drill a hole at each end, then put a fish wire through, attach your electric wire or phone wire to the fish wire and pull it back through the holes. A fish wire is a long flat wire that comes on a reel. But what if you don't have a fish wire with you. If the distance inside the walls and floors is not too great, you can take a wire coat hanger (the thinnest wire is best), straighten it out, and use it as a fish wire.

HAMMER HANDLE

Drywall screws can be used to tighten a loose hammer handle. Drive two of them into the head end of the handle.

HINGE PIN

A bolt, lag screw, or large nail can be used as a hinge pin.

HOUSE NUMBERS

I had to attach some self-stick numbers to a mail box. The mail box was covered with black gritty dirt, which would have prevented the numbers from sticking, and I hadn't thought to bring a rag or a brush to wipe it clean. I was about to sacrifice my undershirt to this task when I saw a bush with large soft leaves. I pulled off several of the leaves and used a bunch of them to wipe off the dirt. It worked perfectly.

MADISON BARS

I needed two Madison bars to install an electric box in a wall. A Madison bar is a flat piece of thin sheet steel in the shape of the letter F and about 5 inches high. I didn't have any Madison bars but I found a tomato can in the trash and cut two Madison bars out of it with tin snips. Ugly? Yes. But they don't show and they did the job.

MISSING SHINGLE

I had to replace a missing shingle (often called a "slate") on a slate roof. I was trying to keep the cost of the job to the homeowner as low as possible. I cut a piece of sheet aluminum to the size of the missing shingle and painted it dark gray. I then slid the aluminum shingle into place and pulled it out again. It brought a lot of dirt out with it. I kept doing this until it came out clean. Then I used silicone caulk to coat the parts of the shingle that would not show and slid it back into place. This makes an inexpensive and long-lasting repair.

O RING THAT LEAKS

You are repairing a plumbing device that is leaking because of a worn O ring. Since O rings come in so many sizes, you may not have a correct new one readily available. So remove the existing O ring from its groove. Cut or tear a strip of Teflon tape the width of the groove and wind a few turns of it around the bottom of the groove. Replace the O ring. This will often stop the leak for weeks or even months, but it should be regarded as a stopgap measure and the proper new O ring should be installed when possible.

OIL

I needed a few drops of oil to lubricate the hinges on a squeaky door. I didn't have any oil with me, so I pulled the dipstick out of my car engine and the few drops of oil that came with it were sufficient to silence the squeaks. If you need some grease and don't have any, many homes have a jar of petroleum jelly in the medicine cabinet that you can use.

PAINTBRUSH

You need to clean a paintbrush that has been used with latex paint, but you don't have a bucket. You can rinse out the brush in a toilet and flush down the paint before it stains the porcelain.

PHILLIPS SCREWDRIVER

I needed a Phillips screwdriver but I had only a slot-type screwdriver. I went outside and used the concrete sidewalk as a grindstone. I scraped the screwdriver back and forth until I had ground it into a V shape which fitted the Phillips-head screws. It didn't take very long. Very crude, admittedly, but desperate situations call for desperate measures.

PILOT LIGHT

You may have to relight the pilot light on a hot-water heater. First you have to get your head down to floor level. Then you have to remove one or two small sheet metal doors. Then you have to hold down a button and light the pilot light, which can be as much as 12 inches inside the guts of the water heater. You probably do not have a match 12 inches long (although they do exist). When I had this problem, I would usually look under a nearby tree or bush, hoping to find a dead dry twig 15 inches long. I would light the end of the twig and poke it in to reach the pilot light. This worked, but one day I saw a better way. A man from the gas company attached a paper match to the end of his steel tape measure. He lit that match with a second match. Then he extended the tape 15 inches and relit the pilot. He did the whole procedure in a matter of seconds. Watch and learn!

SAWHORSES

You may be doing some carpentry and you need a pair of sawhorses to support a board that you must cut. If the homeowner has two trash cans of the same height, they will often serve as saw horses.

SMALL HOLE

You need to drill a small hole in wood and you don't have the right size drill bit to put in your electric drill. Using cutting pliers, cut the head off a nail. Use the cut end as a drill bit. Use a light pressure and a slow speed and this drill bit will usually do its job.

TUB DRAIN LEAK

After several decades of service, it is not unusual for leaks to develop in the drain line from a bathtub. These leaks are usually, but not always, where two fittings join. The problem is that the leaky joint is often highly inaccessible. Sometimes you can barely get a few fingers of one hand to the leaky spot. To do the job "by the book," which means disassembling the system and replacing the corroded fitting, you might have to saw some floorboards and cut and then replace some water supply lines. The job could take many hours.

I get the leaky spot dry, then I take a strip of thin strong cloth about $1^1/2$ inches wide and 8 or 10 inches long. A strip longer than this will be unwieldy. I coat the cloth lightly on both sides with silicone caulk and wrap it tightly around the leaky spot. I then wrap it again with another such strip of cloth. I have found that this makes an effective and permanent repair.

WASHERS

I needed some metal washers about the size of a penny. I didn't have any, but I did have a few pennies. I drilled the proper-size holes in them and the problem was solved. How do you drill a hole in a penny? Either grip it very firmly with pliers and hold it against a board, or put the penny on a board and tighten two or three screws down against the edge of the coin before drilling. If you have a heavy-duty punch, you can just punch the hole in the penny.

WATER VALVE

I had to fix a water valve that was leaking around the stem. Usually, this can be fixed by tightening the packing nut, this compresses the packing and stops the leaking. But sometimes the packing is so worn that this does not work. The right way to fix this is to replace the packing. I didn't have any packing material (usually a mixture of graphite and asbestos fiber) but I did have a roll of Teflon joint tape. I twisted the Teflon tape into a string and wrapped the string around the valve stem to add to the existing packing. This works and lasts a long time. Some people recommend taking a piece of cotton string, coating it with Vaseline or grease and wrapping that around the stem to act as packing.

The moral of the story is: When you need something, and you don't have it with you, look around and let your imagination work to find a way to get the job done.

BIG PAINT JOBS

Timesaving Ideas   210
Paint Left-Handed   211
Selecting the Brush or Roller   212
What Color?   212
Stubborn Paint Can Lids   212

Closing the Can   213
Cleaning Brushes   213
Cleaning Roller Covers   214
Cleaning Your Skin   215

TIMESAVING IDEAS

Here are some timesaving ideas that can cut several hours from the time required for a big paint job. By big, I mean a job that takes several days.

Some paint jobs are best done with an oil-based paint; for example, for priming metal which could rust, or priming exterior bare wood. But most jobs can be done with latex (water-based) paint. Use latex paint whenever possible because it is easier to use, easier to clean the brushes, dries faster, and smells less.

If I use a roller with oil-based paint, I throw away the roller cover because it takes a lot of time to clean and the solvent (paint thinner) to clean it costs as much as a new roller cover.

If I am doing one room, I use a brush to get the areas that the roller cannot reach, then I use a roller. If I am painting two or more rooms the same color, it pays to use a paint stick. A paint stick is a special roller attached to a hollow handle. The handle can hold about a quart of paint. This enables you to put the paint on about four times as fast as with an ordinary roller. The downside is that it takes time to clean the paint stick.

If the paint job is to take several days, I take a 5-gallon bucket and line the bottom with several layers of newspaper. I put a few stones around the edges to keep the paper in place. I fill the bucket with water to within a few inches of the top. Then, after each day's work, I suspend the brushes and rollers in the water.

Paint brushes always come with a hole near the end of the handle. This hole is very convenient to hang the brush on a pegboard hook. But to suspend the brush in water, it helps to drill another hole in the handle. This second hole should be about $3/16$ inch in diameter and located about $1/2$ inch above the metal ferrule that holds the bristles. Put one end of a short piece of wire through this hole and bend the other end of the wire over the rim of the bucket. This hole will also be useful for attaching a brush to a brush extender.

If I am going to use the same color paint the next day, I wrap the brushes and the rollers tightly with plastic bags before suspending them in the water. This keeps the paint in so you don't have to work the water out of the brush the next day. Wrapped and suspended like this, brushes and rollers will stay ready to use for a week or more. If I am going to use a different color the next day, I don't wrap them in plastic. Overnight, most of the paint will fall out and settle to the bottom on the newspapers.

After the job is done, I carefully pour off the water, leaving the newspapers with the paint on them on the bottom. After the remaining water evaporates, I can remove the papers with the dried paint on them and put them in the trash.

If I am using oil-based paint and have to use the same brush or roller cover the next day, I pour some paint thinner onto the brush or roller cover and wrap it tightly in plastic bags. I leave it outdoors, because of the smell, but not where the sun can reach it, until the next day.

In some cases, such as when painting masonry basement walls, the fastest way to do the job is to pour a gallon or two of the paint into a 5-gallon bucket and dip the roller directly into the paint. You can buy a grid, designed to fit into these buckets, to roll the excess paint off the roller.

PAINT LEFT-HANDED

Can you paint with your left hand? If not, it is a skill worth acquiring, and with some practice you can learn to do it. There are three situations where left-handed painting is helpful. One is when you are working high on a ladder. Being able to paint with your left hand as well as your right will allow you to paint a wider area before you have to come down and move the ladder. The second situation is when you are painting a large area with a brush. Your right hand, wrist, and arm may tire, especially if you are using oil-based paint which exerts more drag on the brush. You can paint for a while with your left hand and allow your right hand to rest. Finally, when you are painting a door or window that has a lot of small panes of glass, you will find that, with some of the surfaces, it is easier to see what you are doing if the brush is in your left hand.

SELECTING THE BRUSH OR ROLLER

When you are estimating how long it will take to do a paint job, you should take into consideration the time required to clean the brushes and roller covers. If the paint job is big, the time required to clean these tools is insignificant, so you should choose whichever brushes and rollers will do the job in the least amount of time.

However, if you are painting a small area, the time required to clean the brush or roller cover could be greater than the actual painting time. That is not efficient. As an example, suppose you have to paint a flat surface which is just 2 feet by 2 feet. You could paint that surface in seconds with a roller, but you might then spend 10 minutes cleaning the roller cover.

You could do the job in 1 or 2 minutes with a 4-inch-wide brush, but you might spend 5 to 10 minutes cleaning the brush. Probably the best compromise would be to use a thin brush that is 2 or 3 inches wide. Thin brushes hold less paint that thick ones, but they can be cleaned much more quickly. In this case, the painting would take about 2 or 3 minutes and the cleaning another 2 or 3 minutes.

You could also use a disposable brush made of plastic foam. In this case, you don't spend any time cleaning the brush.

WHAT COLOR?

If a customer asks my opinion regarding what color to paint something, I am reluctant to make a suggestion because they are the ones who have to live with it. I bring them a paint chart and let them make the decision. Exception: I often suggest that the insides of closets be painted white, preferably semigloss, because that makes it easier to see what is in there.

STUBBORN PAINT CAN LIDS

Ordinarily, all it takes to remove a paint can lid is a bit of prying with a screwdriver. But, on occasion, you may experience great difficulty in removing a lid. This is because paint, in addition to being a good protective coating, is also a good glue. If a lot of paint accumulated in the rim of the can, and the can has not been opened for a long time, the lid may simply refuse to open. The only result, when you pry at the lid with a screwdriver, is that the lid bends upward at the point at which you are prying. This only seems to happen with gallon cans. For some reason, the quart cans are easier to open.

Try using two screwdrivers, about an inch apart. If that does not work, go get your paint can opener if you have one. (See Fig. 14-2.) It is better at removing lids than is a screwdriver. Still no success? I find that if I place two paint can openers about an inch apart and pry simultaneously, and move them around the lid, prying a little at a time, the stubborn lid usually comes off.

When you encounter one of these difficult lids, before you remove it mark an arrow on the lid and another on the side of the can and line up these arrows when you replace the lid. When you first open a can of paint, if you wipe a thin film of grease around the groove in the rim of the can, and around the rim of the lid, this problem can be avoided.

CLOSING THE CAN

Before I open a used can of paint, I make a mark at the top of the can and a mark next to it on the lid. Then, when I replace the lid, I line up those two marks. That makes it easier to replace the lid and have it fit tightly. If the can is nearly empty when I close it up, I make a horizontal pencil line on the front of the can to indicate how much paint is left. Then, the next time I need that kind of paint, I can judge whether there is enough left in that can to do the job.

When you replace a lid on a can of paint, it is a good idea to first lay a rag or a few sheets of newspaper on the lid. Then tap around the lid with a hammer to replace the lid tightly. The rag or paper prevents paint that has gotten into the rim of the can from splattering on you and whatever is nearby. Turn the can upside down for a moment before you put it away, this seals any tiny openings that might let air in.

CLEANING BRUSHES

Cleaning a paintbrush is a task you will have to do many times, so it pays to find ways to minimize the time required. If time permits, hang the brush in water overnight. The water should cover the bristles but no further. Most of the paint will fall out. Then proceed as follows. Shake out the brush, then put some water in a bucket, work the brush back and forth vigorously, pour out the water, shake out the brush, and repeat until the water is almost perfectly clear. Sometimes I work the bristles between my fingers to help get the paint out. The final rinse should contain a little soap or dishwasher fluid.

Then I wrap the brush in a piece of paper, leaving the end open. The purpose of the paper is to keep all the bristles straight as they dry and not have any of them sticking out at an angle. I put a rubber band around the ferrule, not around the bristles, to hold the paper in place, and then I hang up the brush to dry.

In a few cases, you will find that there is a sticky residue on the bristles even after thorough washing in soapy water. In those cases, a quick rinse in a very small amount of paint thinner will remove the residue.

If the brush was used for oil-based paint, use paint thinner instead of water, and do the job outdoors. I often leave the brush outside a few days until the odor is gone.

CLEANING ROLLER COVERS (Fig. 48-1)

If you have to clean roller covers very frequently, here is a timesaving method, for latex paint only. First you must make a special tool. Remove a roller from the handle it came with. You then have a wire frame with two plastic ends. Put a $1/4$-inch-diameter wood or metal rod about 18 inches long into this roller and use epoxy glue, or whatever method is convenient, to fasten it in.

When you are ready to clean a roller cover, put this modified roller into your electric drill. Now you need two 5-gallon buckets, one empty, the other filled with water to about 3 inches from the top. Put the roller cover to be cleaned onto the roller. Put the roller into the empty bucket and spin it. Centrifugal force will cause much of the paint to fly off.

Now dip the roller into the water for a few seconds and spin it again in the empty bucket. Repeat this procedure a few times. Most of the paint has now been removed. Now spin the roller in the water for 10 or 15 seconds. Use a variable-speed drill and spin it slowly at first, then faster, but not fast enough to splash water all around. Spin again in the empty bucket, and repeat a few times. The roller cover is now clean. Remove it from the roller and stand it on end until it is dry.

CLEANING YOUR SKIN

Whenever I paint, I always have a rag in one back pocket. I use it to wipe off any paint that gets on me or anywhere else it does not belong.

Paint that dries on your skin can be removed by brisk rubbing with a hot soapy washcloth. For some reason, oil-based paints seem easier to remove the following day. The most difficult substances to get off your skin are roofing cement and construction adhesive (such as Liquid Nails). These compounds are removable with paint thinner.

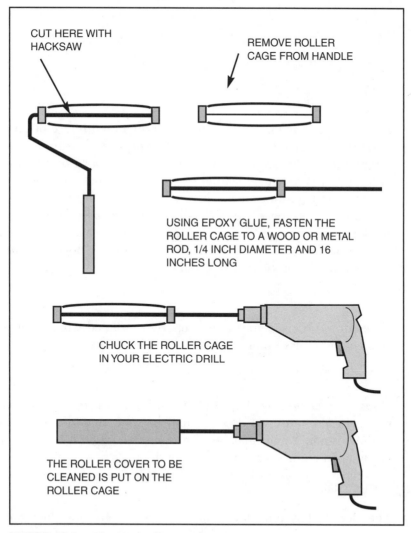

FIGURE 48-1   Cleaning roller covers.

OLD HOUSE VERSUS NEW HOUSE

Attics	216	Paint	217
Doors	216	Plumbing System	217
Electrical System	216	Walls	218

If I was given the choice of doing work on an old house or doing work on a new house, I would choose the new house every time. There are many things you could, or will, run into in an old house that will make the job more difficult. The usual situation in an old house (pre-1940) is that nothing is plumb (plumb means perfectly vertical), nothing is level (perfectly horizontal), nothing is flush (flush means that adjacent surfaces meet correctly), and nothing is square (square means that adjoining members meet at right angles. So you often have to ask a higher price for the work. Some of the potential problems are listed below.

ATTICS

Attics in old houses are rarely properly ventilated which makes working in them on a hot day an ordeal.

DOORS

Doors may be odd-sized in old houses. Standard storm or screen doors may not fit in old houses. A doorway may be $^1/4$ inch wider at the top than it is at the bottom. A door may be so warped that when it is closed at the top, it is still open an inch or more at the bottom.

ELECTRICAL SYSTEM

The electrical system in an old house is ancient and does not conform to the new code. Here are some of the problems you may find.

- Some old houses still have knob-and-tube wiring (a very ancient method). You cannot connect new wiring to such circuits and meet the electrical code requirements. Sometimes the electrical supply to the house is insufficient to allow you to add circuits for new appliances.

- The electrical boxes in the walls are often very small and packed solidly with old wires. The insulation on these wires may have deteriorated to the point where it is more like dried mud than the rubber and cotton it once was. When you pull these wires out of the box to connect them to a new switch or outlet, the insulation breaks off in big pieces. After you connect a new switch or outlet, it may be very difficult to get it back into the box so you can replace the cover.

- You cannot tell which of the wires was once white (the neutral wire) and which was black. The white wire has turned black with age and they are both black now. The copper wires themselves may have turned black with surface corrosion so you have to scrape them until you see shiny copper before you connect them to anything.

- There is often no ground wire, so you cannot install a grounded outlet without running a ground wire to a suitable ground.

- There may be a fuse box instead of a circuit breaker panel. If a circuit breaker has tripped, you can see that immediately. If a fuse has blown, you may or may not be able to tell by looking.

PAINT

Paint in old houses often contains lead. So, if you are sanding a surface to prepare it for painting, you should wear a dust mask and use a vacuum cleaner or a damp cloth to clean up any paint dust that you create.

PLUMBING SYSTEM

Here are some of the problems you may run into when working on plumbing in an old house.

- The plumbing fixtures are ancient; it may be impossible to buy replacement parts. The plumbing may be the original galvanized iron pipe instead of copper tubing. This will greatly increase the time it takes to do anything. The drainpipes are often cast iron which is much harder to work with than the copper or plastic drainpipes in new houses. There may be no clean-out plugs in the drainpipes.

- There may be no shutoff valves for the individual plumbing fixtures. You may have to make several trips to the basement to turn water on and off as you do plumbing repairs. Sometimes the shutoff valve for the whole house is corroded and can't be turned. You may have to turn off the water at the curb; this requires a special long-handled wrench, sometimes called a "curb key."

WALLS

The walls in old houses may present the following problems:

- You cannot be sure of what is inside the walls. The studs may be located 16 inches on centers, but often they are not. It is harder to locate the studs because of the lath and plaster which cover them. Some studs may be missing.
- It can be much harder to run new wires through old walls. There are often hidden obstructions such as pieces of wood or brick or stone, lumps of plaster or cement, etc. Sometimes the space between the inner wall and the outer wall is less than 1 inch.
- Some old houses have mud pack foundation walls. These walls are made of stones with something resembling dried mud between them and a layer of cement on top of the mud. It is very difficult to put shelves or paneling onto these walls in the basement and, on the outside of the house, pieces of the cement are always breaking off.

THOUGHTS AND SUGGESTIONS

Aluminum-Base Bulbs	219	Flashlights	227
Asbestos Anxiety	220	Guarantees	227
Big Wash Jobs	220	House Numbers	227
Bundling Branches	220	Measuring for Ceiling Installations	228
Buying New Products	221	More Than One Way to Do a Job	228
Buying Replacement Parts	221	Murphy's Law Jobs	228
Computer: Do You Need One?	222	New Installations	229
Customer May Give Inaccurate Information	222	Pocketknife	230
Cutting Plastic	223	Pro Bono	230
Doors That Stick	223	Screws, Not Nails or Glue	230
Finding Hardware and Materials	224	Setting Fence Posts without Digging	231
Fixing Things Even If You Don't Know How They Work	225	Taking Things Apart	231
		When Business Is Slow	232

Here are several unrelated thoughts and suggestions that may some day be helpful to you.

ALUMINUM-BASE BULBS

There was a time when the bases on light bulbs, and the sockets that they screwed into, were made of brass. Now, however, to save a fraction of a cent on each bulb and each socket, they are often made of aluminum. Ordinarily, this is not a problem. However, when the light fixture is outdoors or in a damp location, there is a tendency for these two aluminum surfaces in contact with each other to corrode and stick tightly together, especially if the light is off for long periods of time. Then, when you try to remove the bulb, either the bulb breaks, or the socket breaks, or the socket turns until the wires break.

To prevent this, when I put an aluminum-base bulb into an outdoor fixture, I sometimes wipe a thin film of grease or petroleum jelly onto the bulb base before screwing the bulb in. Then, when the bulb needs replacing, it unscrews easily.

ASBESTOS ANXIETY

There has been a lot of frightening talk about asbestos. It is really only hazardous if there is asbestos dust in the air that you breathe. Asbestos in vinyl-asbestos flooring or in asbestos-cement siding is no threat. If you are in an old house and there is asbestos insulation on or near the furnace and it is crumbling and getting into the air, that is cause for concern. You can wrap such asbestos securely with fiberglass cloth and the house will be safe for the current inhabitants. This may not meet the code requirements if the house is to be sold.

BIG WASH JOBS

On occasion, you may have to wash the outside of a building or perhaps walls and ceilings inside a building in preparation for painting. If the surfaces are very dirty and the only water you have has to be carried from some distance, you have a problem. The water you are using gets dirty quickly and you have to go get more. Here is a method that minimizes the time you spend bringing more clean water to the job.

Get a 5-gallon bucket of water and a big rectangular sponge or a sponge mop and start washing the walls. When the sponge gets dirty, instead of rinsing it in the water, wring it out onto the ground or into an empty bucket. Put one side of the sponge against the surface of the water for just a second, then turn the sponge over and put the other side against the water, again for just a second. The sponge will now have absorbed some water, but very little of the dirt in the sponge will get into the water in the bucket. Wring out the sponge and repeat the procedure a few times until the sponge is nearly clean. Then proceed with your washing. When you use this method, the bucket of water will last much longer before it eventually gets too dirty to use.

BUNDLING BRANCHES (Fig. 50-1)

I often have to tie branches into bundles. To facilitate this, I carry in my car a piece of $^1/_4$-inch-diameter rope about 12 feet long, with a pulley on one end. When I have to tie branches from a tree into bundles, I lay this rope out straight on the ground. Then, as I cut branches from the tree or pick up fallen branches, I cut them to length, if necessary, and lay them across the middle of the rope. The length to which I cut them depends on what the local ordinance requires for them to be picked up by the trash men, usually 4 feet maximum. I lay some of the branches with the leafy end on one side of the rope and some the other way.

When the pile of branches is as big as I want it, I put the end of the rope through the pulley and start pulling to tighten up the bundle of branches. I keep pushing the bundle away from me with one foot while pulling on the rope. When the bundle is as tight as I can get it, I tie the rope temporarily to one of the branches. Then I tie the bundle with strong twine. If the branches are long, I tie the bundle in two places. Now I untie my pulley rope and the bundle of branches is ready for disposal.

BUYING NEW PRODUCTS

By new, I mean new to you, something you are not yet familiar with. When I buy a product that I have not used before, I always read the instructions before leaving the store. Sometimes the instructions require some additional material or items; for example, a special solvent might be required. That way, I don't have to go back to the store again to buy the solvent.

On one occasion, I bought a plumbing device. I sat in my car for 20 minutes trying to understand the poorly written installation instructions. Then I went back into the store to ask for help. That was better than to take that device to the job site before finding out that I didn't know how to install it.

BUYING REPLACEMENT PARTS

When you buy a replacement part, for example, a plumbing part or an appliance part, whenever possible take with you the old part and also, if possible, the parts that the new part must fit into. Take the whole appliance if it is not too big. That will prevent the disappointment of getting back to the job with the new part and finding that it does not fit. If you cannot bring the old part and the parts it fits into, make a careful, detailed, pencil sketch of the situation, including all relevant measurements. If the old part has a number or any other identifying marks on it, write them down and take them along. If the device for which you are buying a new part has a name, a model number, or a serial number, take those with you. These numbers are often on a small metal tag somewhere on the back, bottom, or inside of the appliance.

COMPUTER: DO YOU NEED ONE?

You don't really need a computer to be a successful handyman. However, if you like computers, you will find occasions where they can save time. Here are a few examples.

- I once worked for a businesswoman who had several projects going at once. She asked me to keep track of how much time I spent on work related to each project. She also wanted separate numbers for time and materials. A spreadsheet on my computer proved to be ideal for this task.

- I was asked to build an extensive fence around a customer's property. I made a drawing on my computer of what I thought they wanted. When I showed them the drawing, I learned that they wanted something quite different. I changed the drawing and got their approval before I bought any materials. The great advantage of the computer in such cases is that it is so easy to make changes.

- If you have Internet access, you can visit the many sites that tell how to build and fix things.

- And, of course, a computer is helpful when you calculate your yearly earnings and if you do your own taxes.

CUSTOMER MAY GIVE INACCURATE INFORMATION

A customer called and asked me to replace the switch at the top of her cellar stairs. I took an assortment of switches, but when I arrived, I found that the switch was fine, and the problem was a defective fluorescent tube in the basement lighting fixture. I had to go out to buy a new fluorescent tube whereas I could have brought one with me. This was poor planning on my part. I should have asked what kind of fixture the switch controlled and, in addition to the switches, brought an assortment of tubes and repair parts for such fixtures.

Similarly, if a customer calls and asks you to replace a defective bulb or fluorescent tube, it might be wise to take with you, in addition to bulbs and tubes, a few switches, in case that turns out to be where the problem lies.

A customer told me that water came in through one of her windows whenever it rained. It turned out that the window was fine; the water was coming in through a roof leak and running down inside the wall and then dripping out at the top of the window.

Another customer asked me to fix her leaky garden hose. I found that there was nothing wrong with the hose, but the spigot (sometimes called a "hose bib") needed repair.

The moral of the story is: When a customer has a problem and tells you what is wrong, you should be aware that the customer's diagnosis may be incorrect. You should try to think of *everything* that could possibly be causing the problem and be prepared to deal with whatever the actual cause of the problem turns out to be.

Another example, quite common: I am asked to come over and do a small paint job. The homeowner tells me that she has the necessary paint. When I arrive, she can't find the paint, or there is not enough left in the can, or the lid was not on tightly and the paint has dried out and hardened. As a result, whenever I am asked to do a small paint job, I bring every can of paint I have that might be the proper color and if the customer's paint can't be used, mine often can.

CUTTING PLASTIC

If you are cutting thin ($1/8$ inch or less) plastic sheet, you can use a specially shaped drawknife to score the plastic deeply, then snap if off. (See Fig. 8-1.) You can buy these drawknife blades to go into an ordinary utility knife. You can cut thicker plastic, such as Plexiglas or Corian, with a jigsaw or saber saw but you must be careful not to generate any heat or the material will melt. Use a new blade with sharp coarse teeth, use a low speed, use a light pressure, and keep the cut cool with water from a sponge or spray bottle.

DOORS THAT STICK

You may have to fix a door that sticks, making it hard to close and even harder to open. It may be difficult to determine the exact spot(s) where it is sticking. Take a crisp dollar bill, insert it at the edge of the door so it is halfway inside and halfway outside. Close the door until it just touches the jamb and slide the dollar bill up and down and across the top until you find where it cannot pass. That is the spot that needs attention.

You can also use the dollar bill on a closed refrigerator door between the door gasket and the refrigerator. In this case, the bill should stick at every point around the periphery of the door. If there is a place where the bill slides easily, cold air will leak out there and waste energy. The gasket needs fixing or replacing.

FINDING HARDWARE AND MATERIALS

If you look around on trash day, you will often find boards, plywood, pipes, and an endless variety of items that may come in handy some day. Don't take big items unless you are sure you have plenty of space to store them until they are needed. Some of the objects that I may take, when I see them in the trash and they are in good condition, are:

- Angle iron
- Handles
- Hardware of all sorts
- Knobs
- Latches
- Long electrical cords
- Small appliances
- Steel pipe and tubing
- V belts
- Wheels
- Wire nuts

Before you start taking objects from the trash, find out what the local ordinances are regarding "scavenging." In most cases, the authorities don't care as long as you don't make a mess. But, in some places, they are very strict and you might have to pay a fine.

In many cases, the problem with the discarded item is minor and easily fixed. Then you have something you can use, or give to a friend, or sell. If you can't fix it easily, or don't want to fix it, you may wish to keep a few parts and toss the rest. I have a box of wheels from mowers and I have often found what I needed to fix a mower or a wagon or an exercise device in that box. V belts are also worth saving. If they are in good condition, they can serve temporarily until a new belt can be procured. I am convinced that at least 50 percent of the objects that Americans throw away could be rejuvenated or could have been saved from an early death by a few drops of oil in the right places.

Be a Dumpster diver. When building or renovation is going on, you can often find lots of useful items in the Dumpster. Pieces of wood, plywood, paneling, siding, electrical cable, angle iron, pipe, etc., that are too small for the contractor to keep, may be perfect for a job you will do.

FIXING THINGS EVEN IF YOU DON'T KNOW HOW THEY WORK

There are many cases in which something is not working properly and you can fix it even though you don't have a full understanding of how it works. Here are a few examples.

You may be asked to fix an electrical appliance, for example an iron, a vacuum cleaner, a washing machine, an overhead garage door. First make sure that the outlet where the appliance is plugged in is working properly. There may be a blown fuse or circuit breaker, or the outlet itself may be defective. Then examine the plug, the cord, and the on–off switch. In many cases, you will already have found the problem. If the device has a belt, see if it is working properly, not broken or loose and slipping. Unplug the device and see if you can turn by hand whatever is supposed to turn.

Next, look at any moving parts and see if anything is obviously broken. Lubricate any places where the original lubricant may be gummy or dried out. I have fixed some very complicated slide changers, three-speed record players, and floppy disk drives by watching them as they failed to do what they were supposed to do and lubricating the moving parts. If the device has a motor, sniff at it. If it has a strong burned smell, chances are the motor is defective. This usually takes care of many cases, but leaves some where more knowledge is needed and you will have to decide whether you want to tackle the job.

I have fixed nonfunctioning computer printers and other computer components by first turning off the power and unplugging the equipment from the electric outlet or power strip. Then I find the cord that connects the printer to the computer. I pull the connector off the printer and push it back on several times, then I leave it on. I do the same at the other end of the cable where it connects to the computer. This often solves the problem. The reason that these connectors often fail to connect is that some of the voltages used in computer systems are very low, 3 volts or less (as compared to 115 volts for most house wiring). These low voltages cannot "punch through" the thin films of oxidation or corrosion that sometimes form on connector pins. By pushing the connectors on and off, you scrape away the oxidation or corrosion. The same procedure, applied to phone lines, may solve the problem of a nonfunctioning phone, modem, or fax machine.

Sometimes a simple visual inspection will reveal what is wrong. On one occasion, a woman called me on a Saturday morning. She was in a state of near panic. Her refrigerator had stopped working and she couldn't get the repairman until Monday. Meanwhile, the hot weather would cause all her food to spoil. I told her that I didn't know much about refrigerators and I doubted I could help, but I would come over and take a look. When I arrived and moved the refrigerator away from the wall, I saw a heavy solid copper wire, with orange insulation, dangling from the control mechanism at the back of the refrigerator near the top. After poking around a bit, I saw where that wire had been connected to the motor at the bottom of the refrigerator. Obviously this was the problem, or at least part of the problem. I resoldered the wire and the refrigerator worked perfectly.

But, if you are a good handyman, not only do you fix devices, you try to determine why the device stopped working and see if you can prevent it from happening again. I asked her if she had been poking behind the refrigerator with a broom or mop. She hadn't. So why had that heavy wire broken? After some thought, I realized that it was just simple vibration. When the motor ran, that wire vibrated, and eventually, after 4 years of vibration, it broke. This is called metal fatigue. I added a small clamp to hold the wire tightly and prevent vibration so the problem would not recur.

There is another lesson here. This was a design flaw in the appliance. Whoever designed that refrigerator did not consider what would happen to that unsupported wire after several years of vibration. Engineers who design things are not omnipotent, they do make mistakes, as witness the frequent expensive automobile recalls to correct design flaws.

Here is another example of fixing something without knowing much about it, a case in which luck played a major part. I was asked to look at a copier which had stopped working. The machine no longer pulled in the blank paper onto which the copy would be printed. I told the customer that I would look at it but I doubted I could do anything about it.

When I opened the top of the machine, I saw a small spring, no bigger than half a match stick, lying loose. Obviously this was at least part of the problem. It was lucky that that spring had not fallen down into the guts of the machine where I would never have seen it. But where had that little guy come from? Now I got even luckier. There was an identical spring at the other end of the intake roller so I could figure out where the loose spring belonged. I replaced the spring. But what would stop it from popping off again? On close inspection, I saw that the tiny plastic hook that held one end of the spring was cracked and bent out of shape, a manufacturing defect. I made a replacement hook from a paper clip and the copier has been behaving itself ever since.

FLASHLIGHTS

You should always have a properly working flashlight in your car. You may have a good-quality, relatively new, flashlight. You put new batteries in it just recently. Yet, the flashlight acts erratically. Sometimes it comes on brightly, sometimes you have to shake it just to get it to light dimly. Often, the problem is with the bulb. Unscrew the front of the flashlight. Look at the bottom tip of the bulb. There is usually a little blob of solder there. This solder tends to oxidize and stop conducting electricity. If the solder is dark gray, sand it lightly with fine sandpaper or scrape it lightly with a sharp knife. Also look at whatever metal part in the flashlight makes contact with the bottom of the bulb. If that part is not clean and shiny, scrape or sand it until it is. This often solves the problem, at least for a time.

Another problem with flashlights that are kept in a car is that, in very hot weather, the batteries can go bad in a few months even if you do not use the flashlight. So check your flashlight regularly to make sure it is OK.

When you buy batteries for your flashlight, it is a good idea to take a permanent-ink, felt-tip pen and mark the date of purchase on the batteries. When the batteries are a year old, replace them, even if they have rarely been used. That way, your flashlight is less likely to suddenly die while you are using it.

If you frequently find yourself working in dark basements or attics where there is no easy way to plug in your drop light, buy a 6-volt lantern. It will last longer than a regular flashlight and give much more light.

GUARANTEES

On rare occasions, a homeowner will ask if I give a guarantee for the things I build or fix. If they ask, I usually guarantee the jobs for 90 days. If I built some simple sturdy wooden structure, such as a bookcase or a flight of stairs, I give a 5-year guarantee. There are exceptions. If I manage to get an old appliance working again, but I have no confidence in how long it will work, I explain the situation to the homeowner and I write on the bill "NO ASSURANCE OF HOW LONG THIS WILL CONTINUE TO WORK."

HOUSE NUMBERS

Many houses have hard-to-read house numbers or none at all. I always suggest that a legible house number be installed. The mail carrier knows where you are, but UPS, FedEx, and emergency vehicles (police, fire, ambulance) may not. I like to have on hand 5-inch-high black plastic numbers from zero to nine. The 1, 2, and 3 are needed oftener than the higher numbers, so I would buy at least five of those and at least three of the others.

These numbers can be attached directly to the house, but if they are attached to wood, it will be difficult to paint around them, so I often attach the numbers to a piece of vinyl siding or painted aluminum and then screw that to the house. It can be removed when painting and then replaced.

MEASURING FOR CEILING INSTALLATIONS

Suppose you want to install something, perhaps a fan or a light fixture, at a location on the ceiling that is, for example, 6 feet from one wall of the room and 8 feet from another wall. When you get up on your stepladder and attempt to measure these distances, you may find that your steel measuring tape cannot be extended that far without losing its rigidity and flopping down. Or, if you turn the tape over so that the graduations face the ceiling, the tape may remain rigid, but you can't see the markings.

The solution is to mark the 6-foot point and the 8-foot point on the back of the tape before you go up the ladder.

MORE THAN ONE WAY TO DO A JOB

Some jobs can be done in more than one way. Some plumbing jobs can be done with copper tubing or plastic tubing. Some construction can be done with wood or metal. I suggest that you do these jobs one way the first time and another way the next time you have a similar job. You can then decide which way is best for a particular job.

MURPHY'S LAW JOBS

Murphy's law (attributed to an army captain named Murphy) states that if something can go wrong, it will go wrong. From time to time, you may do a job in which it seems that Captain Murphy himself is perched on your shoulder, waving his evil magic wand, and making everything go wrong.

- Something that should come apart easily, does not, or worse, some vital part, weakened by years (or decades) of hidden corrosion, breaks as you try to remove it.
- Something that should go back together easily, does not. Something that should fit perfectly, does not.
- The local hardware store is all out of something that they should have and you must have.

- The toilet that you went to fix is different from any you have ever seen and parts for it may not be available anywhere.

- Partitions have been built up close to a toilet or other appliance that you must fix and you must force yourself into an awkward, uncomfortable, even painful position, to do the work.

- A suspended ceiling has been installed in a basement and you must remove a lot of the panels to find the electrical or plumbing lines that you need. It may be a struggle to get all those panels back in place because of various obstructions.

- An unexpected obstruction inside a wall may prevent you from running an electrical line where you intended.

- A valve intended to turn off the water for the entire house may be stuck in the open position and impossible to turn. If it does finally turn, it leaks, and you have to fix that also.

- Decorative interior window shutters may have been installed which prevent you from installing or removing storm window screen or glass inserts.

- Wiring in an attic may have been covered up with loose fiberglass insulation and you cannot see where the electrical lines run.

- A window through which you had intended to crawl to get to the porch roof may not open.

The list of things that can go wrong is endless. You can only grin and bear it and realize that occasionally a job will take two, three, or even four times as long as you expected.

NEW INSTALLATIONS

If you are replacing existing electrical or plumbing parts, you are usually on pretty safe ground. However, this is not always true. The applicable building code may have changed since the original installation, and your work should conform to the new code. One example is that GFCI (Ground Fault Circuit Interrupt) outlets may be required where they previously were not required. Another example is if a gas hot-water heater is being installed in an earthquake-prone area, the code now may require a flexible gas supply line and one or more metal straps to fasten the heater to a wall.

Similarly, if you are installing new electrical lines or plumbing fixtures in new locations, it is not enough that your installation works properly, it must also conform to the electrical code or the plumbing code. These codes exist to assure safety and you should know the code before you install something. There are books that describe these codes and it is a good idea to have such books. But, usually, if you tell the clerk at the supply store what you intend to do, he can tell you how to be sure it conforms to code. The codes vary from place to place.

Your local government usually has a building inspector who can tell you what you need to know. Some libraries have copies of the codes. Many areas have electrical and plumbing inspectors and require that new installations be approved by these inspectors.

POCKETKNIFE

In addition to all the tools in my toolbox, I always carry a pocketknife in my pants pocket. I like the kind that has one large blade for cutting, a screwdriver blade, and a tapered gouge-like blade, sometimes called an awl, which is used to make small holes in wood to start screws. The awl blade can also make holes in leather belts. Keep the knife sharp and keep it oiled so it is easy to open. Don't carry this knife on your person or in your carry-on luggage if you are going to fly somewhere. Even better, leave it at home.

PRO BONO

Pro bono is a Latin term whose approximate meaning is, "for the good of the public." It is a term that lawyers use when they do work without charging for it. You may encounter a person who needs some work done but can't afford to pay for it, perhaps an old person, a woman with children and little or no income, or a person who can't work because of health problems. In such cases, I either do the job without charge or charge just for the materials. I may have a used but usable plumbing fixture or electrical appliance that I donate to this person. Or, I may build them some shelves with used lumber that I have on hand.

If you can spare the time, I suggest you do this once in a while. It will give you a good feeling, and remember, "Man does not live by bread alone."

SCREWS, NOT NAILS OR GLUE

From time to time you will be asked to build something, usually of wood. It might be shelving or a rack designed for a special space or a special need. I always use screws to construct these projects, rarely nails, and never glue. The reason is that, if I make a mistake, or the customer wants some changes, it is much easier to take the object apart and reassemble it.

If you are asked to build a low plant stand or bench to hold flower pots, keep in mind that, sooner or later, someone is going to use it as a footstool and stand on it. So make it strong enough to hold a person.

SETTING FENCE POSTS WITHOUT DIGGING

Steel pipes, usually $1^3/8$ inches in diameter or 2 inches in diameter, are often set into the ground to serve as fence posts. If the post does not have to support a gate, it is often not necessary to dig a hole for the post and pour in concrete. There is an easier way to set the pipe in the ground.

Take a piece of pipe, check with a level to be sure you are holding it vertically, and drive it into the ground 2 or 3 inches. Use the heaviest sledgehammer you can handle.

Now pull the pipe out of the ground. It will have a short plug of dirt in the end. Drive this plug out with a long wood or metal rod or a thinner pipe.

Repeat the first two steps, being careful not to go down more than 2 or 3 inches each time. If you do more than this short distance, it may be hard to drive the dirt plug out of the pipe.

As the hole gets deeper, it may become difficult to pull the pipe up and out to remove the dirt plug. Put a large pipe wrench on the pipe and turn the pipe slowly as you pull up on the wrench handle.

When I set posts like this, I like them to go at least 2 feet into the ground, and even deeper if the dirt is soft or sandy. Make a mark on the pipe at the desired depth and when the mark reaches the ground, you are done.

TAKING THINGS APART

If you are taking something apart to fix it, an appliance for example, and you are not familiar with it, you should proceed carefully. You want to be sure you can get it back together correctly. Make pencil sketches of what fits where. Make marks on adjacent parts and line up those marks when reassembling. Keep all the fasteners, and other parts that you remove, in a container that contains nothing else. Be especially careful if there are two sets of bolts or machine screws, identical in all respects, except that those in one set are slightly longer than those in the other.

When reassembling, if, for example, there is a part that is held on with four fasteners, put all four in place and hand-tighten before you use a tool for final tightening.

WHEN BUSINESS IS SLOW

There will be times when you haven't much work to do. You may have no requests for jobs, or you may have outside work to do and you must wait a few days until it stops raining. Make good use of this "free" time.

Are all your tools in perfect condition? Does anything need repair or lubricating or sharpening? Is everything put away where it belongs and can be found immediately when needed? Are you running low on some hardware items or some material? Add those items to your buy list. If the buy list is long enough, it may be time to do some shopping.

Is it time to build more shelves to accommodate your growing inventory? Is there something you can do to your vehicle to make it more useful or to prepare it to pass inspection?

If you have steady customers, you can call and ask if they need any work done. They may have something that they had been planning to ask you to do.

You can hand out more of your business cards. You can go to the home center and familiarize yourself with some of the thousands of items in stock. You are sure to come across some things that are new and interesting. Pay special attention to items that are stocked in large quantity because they are the items you are most likely to have use for some day.

You can refamiliarize yourself with your how-to books. You can go to the book store or library and look for books or magazine articles that are relevant to your work. If it is close enough to tax time so that you have some or all of the information you need to do your taxes, do as much of the paperwork as you can now. The earlier you do this job, the better, because, at tax time you may have lots of work, or your accountant may be too busy to see you.

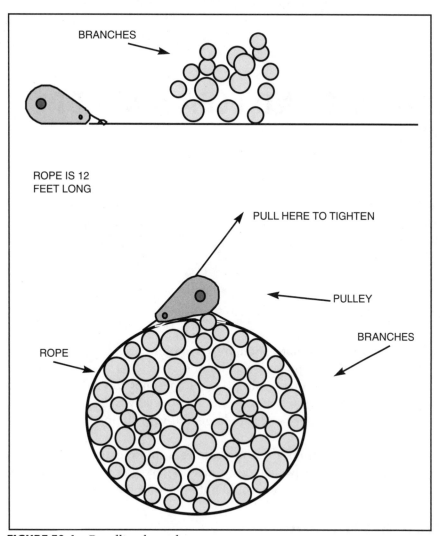

FIGURE 50-1 Bundling branches.

YARD SALE AND FLEA MARKET TACTICS

Items to Take with You   234   Buying Work Clothing   239
Bargaining   236   Flea Market Suggestions   239
Buying Paint   236   People You Meet   239
Buying Used Tools   237   Antiques and Collectibles   240

If you are fortunate enough to live in an area that has lots of yard sales and flea markets, you can get many of the tools and hardware items that you will need, and at bargain prices, sometimes for as little as one-tenth of what you would pay in a store. This is especially helpful when you are just starting out and your needs are large and your finances small.

I sometimes think of a yard sale as a minivacation. You go places you would not otherwise have gone, you meet people you would not otherwise have met, and you buy items you would not otherwise have bought.

ITEMS TO TAKE WITH YOU

Here are some suggestions for items to take with you when you go to yard sales or flea markets:

Backpack   Take a backpack or shoulder bag so that you can put purchases in it as you buy them and still keep both hands free to examine other items.

Business Cards   Have several of your business cards in case you meet someone who might use your services.

"Buy" List   Take a list of items you would like to buy. Be sure to include the dimensions of what you need.

Cap or Visor   Wear a cap or visor to keep the sun out of your eyes in case the sun is just rising behind the tables that are displaying the items for sale.

Catalogs   Take tool and hardware catalogs so you can compare the asking prices with what the items cost new. After a while, you will have such a good feel for what things should be worth that you won't need these catalogs.

Dollars and Quarters   Take lots of dollars and quarters in case the seller does not have the right change for a large bill.

Drill Gauge   A drill gauge is a flat piece of steel, or plastic, with holes for each size drill bit. You will need this because, when you buy a used drill bit, the size marking on the shank of the bit is often obliterated.

Flashlight   Have a flashlight with you, or in your car, because some people have items for sale in a dimly lit garage or basement.

Magnet   Take a small magnet so you can tell what is steel and what is stainless steel, aluminum, or brass. Iron and steel are magnetic. Most, but not all, stainless steel is not magnetic. Stainless steel kitchen knives usually are magnetic. Bronze, copper, brass, zinc die castings, and aluminum are not magnetic.

Magnifying Glass   You may need this to read the fine markings on drill bits to see the size and the type of steel (high-speed steel or carbon steel).

Measuring Tape   You will use this to measure hardware items and clothing items to see if they are the size you need.

Overlay Map   I live in a suburb of Philadelphia where there may be 15 or more yard sales on a Saturday morning. I find an overlay map to be very helpful in planning my morning's activities. Here is how to make one.

Get a good street map of your area. Realtors often have these. Mount the map on a stiff backing, thick cardboard, or $1/8$-inch-thick hardboard. Don't make it larger than about 15 inches square or it will be difficult to handle in your car.

Make a large red mark at the location of your home. Then cover the map with clear plastic film or thin Plexiglas.

Yard sales start at various times, some as early as 7 A.M. and some as late as 10 A.M. I use felt-tip pens to locate the sales on my map, a different color for each opening time. I then plan the most efficient route. As I visit each sale, I circle that location, so I know I have been there. Next week, I wipe the plastic clean with alcohol and start again.

Pencil and Paper Take pencil and paper in case you need to write down someone's phone number.

BARGAINING

Try to arrive at the first yard sale at least $1/2$ hour before the advertised opening time. Look for tools before you look at anything else; there will be other buyers for tools and the bargains will go fast. If you don't see any tools, ask the seller if he has any tools or hardware for sale. Sometimes he will take you to the basement and show you some. If you buy several tools at once, you will often get a better price than if you buy them one at a time. If you see a tool you want but think the price is too high, just offer less, but do it in a polite way. No one is offended by such offers and the worst that can happen is that the seller will say no. Sellers are more likely to make price concessions toward the end of the day.

BUYING PAINT

You can get a lot of good bargains when you buy paint at flea markets or yard sales. But you should be aware of certain things.

First of all, try to buy the "top of the line" of whatever manufacturer made the paint. If the can says "OUR BEST," or "OUR FINEST," that is the top of the line. If the can lists the ingredients and gives the percentage of each, that is a good sign. If you are buying latex paint, the 100 percent acrylic paint is better than the acrylic-vinyl mixture. If the percentage of "vehicle," which in latex paints is water, is 50 percent, that is good paint, if it is 70 percent, that is cheap paint. If the pigment in white paint is at least 30 percent titanium dioxide, that is good paint. If the pigment is mostly silicates (clay) and carbonates (chalk), that is cheap paint. It is not usually practical to open the can to inspect the contents but you can judge how much paint is left in the can by the weight. Look at the lid. Was it replaced tightly when the paint was last used? If the lid was not put on tightly and there are gaps where air might get in, the paint is probably no good.

If you are buying an oil-based paint (look for the word alkyd, or flammable), shake the can. If you can hear and feel the liquid sloshing around, that paint is probably OK. If you can't hear it sloshing around, don't buy it. Be aware that oil-based paints can settle out hard and require a lot of stirring, preferably with an electric drill and a special stirring tool, before they are usable.

If you are buying a latex (water-based) paint, you have to be concerned as to whether that paint was subjected to freezing. Freezing will ruin a latex paint, the solids will settle out and cannot be remixed with the liquid. Shake the can. If you can hear and feel the paint sloshing around but the liquid sounds thin and watery, that paint may have been ruined by freezing. Shake the can vigorously, if the sound changes from thin and watery to thick and creamy (like a milk shake) the paint is probably OK. Ask the seller if the paint was stored in a place where it might have frozen. Most people at yard sales will tell the truth about what they are selling.

I buy any can of high-quality paint I come across if it is white, which is by far the most widely used color. I also buy any can of paint if it is a color I do not have.

Another way to get good paint at low cost is to look for "returns" whenever you are in a store that sells paint. Some people will buy several cans of paint of a specially mixed color and, if they have unused cans left over, the store will sometimes buy those cans back and offer them for sale at low prices. If I come across such a can of paint and it is white or a very light color, almost white, I buy that paint and I always find a use for it.

BUYING USED TOOLS

Here are some suggestions for buying used tools.

Drill Bits   If you want to buy drill bits, take a magnifying glass and a drill gauge with you. Look at the shank of drill bits to see if you see HS. This means high-speed steel. Don't buy a drill bit unless it is high speed. The cheaper carbon steel drill bits are only good for wood, plastic, aluminum, and other relatively soft materials. They get dull very quickly if they are used for drilling in steel. High-speed bits rarely show any rust; if the bit is rusty, it is more likely carbon steel. One way to tell whether a drill bit you own is carbon steel or high-speed steel is to hold the bit lightly against a spinning grinding wheel. A carbon steel bit will throw off a thick shower of bright white sparks, a high-speed steel bit will throw a thin stream of yellowish or orange sparks.

Electric Drills   If you see an electric drill for sale at a good price, here are a few considerations. If the drill looks worn, battered, and scratched from years of hard use, don't buy it. Plug the drill in. Does it run smoothly and reasonably quietly? If the gears make a lot of noise, don't buy it. Is there only a small amount of sparking at the brushes? If there is a lot of sparking and a smell of ozone, don't buy it. Does the chuck key fit the chuck properly? Look at the gear teeth on the chuck and the chuck key. If they show a lot of wear, don't buy the drill. If the teeth do not show much wear, but the key is hard to turn, the chuck probably just needs a few drops of oil to open and close easily. Similar considerations apply to circular saws and other portable power tools.

Files   If you are buying a file, run your finger, against the grain, over the teeth at the very ends of the file where it has not had much wear. Now run your finger over the middle of the file. You should feel the same "bite" as you did at the ends. If not, that file will not work very well if at all.

Handsaws   If you are buying a handsaw, feel the teeth at the end of the blade nearest the handle. These teeth are usually as sharp as when the saw was new. Then feel the teeth near the middle of the blade. Do they feel nearly as sharp? If so, that saw will work well. If not, don't buy it.

Another thing to look at when buying a used handsaw is the "set." This means that every other tooth of the saw should be bent outward to one side and the "in-between" teeth should be bent outward to the other side. If the saw does not have enough set, it will bind and stick and will not cut properly. To see the set, sight along the line of the teeth.

If the saw is sharp and has good set, but is a little rusty, you can remove the rust with fine sandpaper and then wax the blade with automobile wax. The wax prevents further rust and also reduces friction and makes the saw easier to use. It is a good thing to do even with nonrusty saw blades.

Phillips Screwdrivers   These screwdrivers are very difficult to regrind. I would not buy a Phillips driver if the point shows damage.

Pipe Wrench   If you are buying a pipe wrench, feel the teeth. If the teeth are sharp, even if the spaces between the teeth are filled with grime, the wrench will work like new once the grime is removed.

Pliers   If you are buying cutting pliers, close the pliers and hold them up to the light. The jaws should meet along their length and not let any light through between them.

Scissors If you are buying scissors, test them on a thin sheet of paper to make sure they cut cleanly and easily all the way to the tip. Scissors can be sharpened easily unless they have been ground improperly, in which case they are ruined forever.

BUYING WORK CLOTHING

You will need a lot of work clothing, and yard sales are a good place to buy them at low cost. Here are some timesaving suggestions. Take a pair of work pants that are a perfect fit for you and lay them out flat. Measure the inseam (from the crotch to the bottom of the leg). Measure the waist. Measure from the crotch to the waist. Make a drawing of a pair of pants laid out flat, and put these dimensions on the drawing. Take the drawing with you or remember the dimensions. When you see a pair of pants at a yard sale, measure the pants to see if they are what you need. If the legs are too long, that is easy to remedy. If the other dimensions are not right, don't buy the pants.

Similarly, with shirts and sweaters you can measure the shoulder width and the length of the sleeve to decide whether it is worth trying the item on to see how well it fits.

When I see a belt for sale, I hold the belt buckle about 3 inches above my navel. If the belt then reaches to the ground, I know it is the right length for me. If a belt is too long, it is, of course, easy to cut it shorter and punch a few extra holes in it if necessary.

FLEA MARKET SUGGESTIONS

At a flea market, in addition to the items mentioned here for yard sales, you might take a folding shopping cart to carry your purchases, especially if the parking area is far from the market area.

Be cautious of the dealer with sets of shiny new tools at very low prices. These tools are usually, though not always, inferior. Look for used tools that no longer look pretty. The uglier the better, because the uglier the tool, the lower the price. A hammer with a dirty handle and some rust on the head will do the job as well as a shiny new hammer but it will sell for much less. A screwdriver or chisel or drill bit with a worn tip can be restored to perfect working order in a few minutes on a grinding wheel.

PEOPLE YOU MEET

If you see the same people again and again at yard sales, take the time to become acquainted with them. They may be of help to you. One such fellow gave me much good advice about fixing electronic devices and another was very helpful with auto repair suggestions. A third fellow told me how to fix a mower that I was having trouble with. There may also be times when you can swap tools or materials with these people. You can ask them what items they are looking for and tell them your needs. Then each of you can buy items for the other.

ANTIQUES AND COLLECTIBLES

We have all heard stories of people who bought something at a yard sale which then turned out to be very valuable. This happens much less frequently than in the past because more and more people are becoming aware of what is valuable. But it still happens occasionally. I knew a woman who bought a string of real pearls for 10 cents and an antique dealer who bought a rug for $30 and sold it the next day for $150. I have a friend who is very knowledgeable about military items. He makes money on things he buys at yard sales. If you go to a lot of yard sales, you might want to look at collectibles in addition to useful items for your work. If you make the acquaintance of a dealer at a yard sale, and if he or she is willing to tell you what to look for, you might get lucky too. If you are really interested in collectibles, there are, of course, books on the subject.

RECORD KEEPING AND FINANCES

Checking Account	241	Receipts	242
Three-Ring Notebook	241	Taxes	242

CHECKING ACCOUNT

If you open a separate checking account for your handyman business, it will simplify your record keeping, but it is, of course, an additional expense. So, when you are first starting out, you could use your existing checking account. But be sure to label all your deposits and expenditures so that you can easily extract the information you need for tax purposes and for payments and expenses calculations.

THREE-RING NOTEBOOK

I keep most of my records in a three-ring notebook. I use lined three-ring paper. One page is for each customer, in alphabetical order by last name. I put reinforcements on the top and bottom holes of each page. At the top right of each page, I print the customer's last name, first name, telephone number, address, etc. I also print the names of the spouse, kids, and (sometimes) the pets.

Smith, Fred
(111) 222 3333
123 Pine Road
E-mail address (if any)
Sarah (wife)
Joan (daughter)

When a customer calls to request work, I write down, on his page, the jobs he has requested. I also print his last name on the first page of my three-ring book which is labeled "WORK TO DO." On the first page of my book, I have a list of customers who want work done but, to determine the jobs needed, I turn to their particular page. When I finish up somewhere, I cross that name off the first page.

When necessary, I put a large-sized paper clip on a customer's page. This clip is used to hold small papers relating to that customer (pocket paper, receipts). I never take the three-ring book with me. I keep it at home; the information in it is too vital to risk losing. At the back of the three-ring book I keep several blank pages with reinforcements already attached. Thus I am ready to start a new page whenever I get a new customer.

If you prefer to keep your records for your customers in hanging file folders, or in your computer, there is no reason not to do it that way. If you use a computer, you must make backups.

RECEIPTS

Whenever you buy something, you will, of course, be given a receipt. In some cases the receipt is printed clearly in dark ink and it shows what you bought, when you bought it, and where you bought it. But sometimes the receipt is just a narrow strip of paper, printed in very faint purple ink, and with nothing on it but numbers for the price, the tax, the amount you gave, and the change you were given. In this case, turn the receipt over and, on the back, write the name of the store, the item you purchased, and the date. Why? In case whatever you bought is defective, you must have the right receipt to return it. It does not happen often, but it can happen. Keep all your receipts; a cigar box will serve nicely. You will need them for tax purposes and for calculating your earnings.

TAXES

The tax codes are so complex that, in many cases, it is better to find an accountant, someone whose charges are reasonable, to do your taxes, rather than try to figure them out yourself. The accountant can probably save you the cost of hiring him because of his knowledge of what is deductible and what isn't. And the time you save is better spent working at your profession. If you do go to an accountant, you should take with you written records of all your expenses including car expenses, purchases at yard sales, magazine subscriptions, and books that you bought for your work. The accountant can also probably tell you what licenses, if any, you need for your business.

If you are computer literate, you could try using one of the computerized tax-preparation programs. You need only enter the data and the program does the calculations for you.

CLOTHING FOR THE HANDYMAN

Belt	243	T-Shirt	246
Blue Jeans	244	Tool Belt	246
Cold-Weather Wear	244	Visor	246
Hot-Weather Wear	245	Work Gloves	247
Kneepads	246	Work Shoes	247
The Layered Look	246		

You should look neat and workmanlike, especially when you first show up to bid on a job. People will judge you and their expectations of your work by your appearance. Be clean shaven or have a neatly trimmed beard. It is a good idea to have a separate set of clothes, including shoes, for use when painting. Otherwise, all your clothes will soon have spatters. Because most paint jobs will use white or light paint, white overalls are a good choice. After you have worked for someone for a while, they will judge you by your work and your clothing becomes less important.

I like 100 percent cotton clothes; they are more comfortable, especially when the humidity is high. I like a shirt that has at least one front pocket, preferably two. I can keep a pencil and my pocket paper (where I make notes as I work) in one pocket and screws, nails, or whatever I need for the job at hand in the other pocket.

BELT

You want a sturdy leather or cloth belt, at least $1^1/2$ inches wide. A canvas or nylon belt is better than leather in hot weather because perspiration can cause a leather belt to harden and crack. If your belt is narrow and you use the belt clip on your measuring tape to hold the tape onto the belt, the clip may become snagged on a narrow belt and be very hard to remove.

BLUE JEANS

Jeans are ideal for work pants, but don't wear tight ones. You want to be able to get your hands into the pockets to grasp the tools and other items you have in there. Another reason to buy oversize jeans is that in winter you may want to wear long underwear. If you are working outdoors and it is not too hot, it is a good idea to wear long pants. You are less likely to have unfortunate encounters with bees, ticks, wasps, biting flies, mosquitoes, poison ivy, thorny bushes, and stinging nettle.

I like pants that have two back pockets. I can keep more tools (pliers, screwdrivers) in them or use one for tools and one for a rag when I am painting.

I always carry a pocketknife and my car keys in my right pants pocket. This tends to wear a hole in the bottom of the pocket. To prevent this, I turn the pocket inside out and put a piece of duct tape over the end of the pocket. Then I push the pocket back in. The duct tape takes the wear and prevents holes in the pocket. After a few washings, the duct tape may come loose, so I replace it when necessary.

COLD-WEATHER WEAR

Here are some suggestions to help you cope with the cold.

Body   To keep my body warm, I like a cotton undershirt, and over that, one or two long-sleeved cotton shirts, and over that as many increasingly large fiber-filled jackets as necessary. Insulated vests are excellent; they keep your body warm while allowing complete freedom of arm movement.

Hands and Wrists   Keeping your hands warm is not as easy. If I am doing work that cannot be done while wearing gloves, I wear "wristlets" that I make from old pairs of high socks with the feet removed. I put two of these socks, bunched up, on each wrist. These wristlets give much warmth to your wrists, and to your hands up to the last joint of the fingers. You can also buy gloves with the finger ends open.

Head and Ears   A large proportion of the heat lost in cold weather is from the head. A knit ski cap and/or earmuffs will keep your head and ears warm. Be sure your head wear is not too tight or it will be uncomfortable.

Legs and Feet   Long underwear, especially the quilted insulated kind, will keep your legs warm. In extreme cold, you can wear insulated overpants. These are light and loose and have zippers up the sides so you can put them on or off without removing your shoes. You can buy them from places like L. L. Bean. You can keep your feet warm by wearing insulated boots or by buying oversized shoes and wearing two or three pairs of heavy high socks.

HOT-WEATHER WEAR

Here are some suggestions to help you keep going in the heat of summer and still get the job done.

Shirt   In very hot weather, you might wear just shorts and sandals and a mesh-type sleeveless shirt (sometimes called a tank top). If you don't have such a shirt, you can make a good substitute by following these suggestions.

Take an old cotton shirt and cut off the sleeves. Make further cuts to extend the armholes downward by several inches. Cut off the collar and make two more cuts to cut off the material where the top button and the top button-hole had been. Now cut off the bottom of the shirt just below the navel (Fig. 53-1). There isn't much left of this shirt, and you won't win any fashion contests while wearing it, but you can wear it in places where shirts are required and it is the next best thing to no shirt at all, especially in hot humid weather. In extreme heat, I sometimes soak this shirt in cold water and put it back on.

Hat   If you will be working in the sun, perhaps doing fence work, you could get a broad-brimmed straw hat. It does a good job of shading your upper body. Make sure it has a string or band to hold it on so the wind doesn't blow it away. Keep some sun blocker in your car and use it before you get a sunburn.

Sweatband   A very helpful item in hot weather is a sweatband. This keeps sweat out of your eyes where it will sting and burn. I find that the cheap sweatbands sold in packs of three are not very good. They do not absorb enough sweat and they lose their stretch after a few uses. I buy some good-quality elastic about an inch wide and sew the ends to make a headband. Then I wrap a terry cloth washcloth around one part of the band and sew that on. This sweatband does the job.

Electric Fan   Some attics can be literally unbearable to work in because of the heat. In such cases, I take an electric fan into the attic and aim it at myself.

KNEEPADS

You should have a pair of kneepads to protect your knees if you will be kneeling on hard surfaces. Keep them in your car.

THE LAYERED LOOK

You might have to work in a cold environment and a hot environment on the same day. Example: You might arrive at the job site at 8 A.M. on a cold morning and have to work in deep shade on the north side of a house with a strong wind blowing. The windchill factor might be 10 degrees or less. As the day wears on and the temperature rises, you will gradually shed the outer layers of clothing. Late in the afternoon, you might have to be in the attic, which has been heated by the sun for several hours. There is no wind to cool you, and the attic temperature could be over 100 degrees. Now you are down to your T-shirt, or no shirt.

So, for the well-dressed handyman, the layered look is in. You don't want to wear a heavy parka, which is either on or off, leaving you either too hot or too cold. You want several light layers, so you can peel them off one at a time as the temperature rises, and put them back on again as it gets cooler in the evening. All the layers should be loose fitting; any tightness will restrict blood flow.

T-SHIRT

I know a handyman who always wears a bright orange T-shirt with HANDY-MAN JOHN and his phone number on it. Thus, he is always advertising himself wherever he goes and he says it does get him new customers.

TOOL BELT

A tool belt is a belt with a leather pouch that holds many tools. They are sometimes helpful if you have to do several different tasks while standing on a ladder. I don't like them because they seem to get in the way when I have to kneel down. I prefer to keep my tools (screwdrivers, pliers, etc.) in my various pockets and have a loop on my jeans for holding a hammer. But many tradesmen like the tool belts, so try one and decide for yourself.

VISOR

I wear a black visor to shade my eyes from sunlight or bright overhead lights. When I moved to a new area, I found that there was an advantage to wearing this visor. I was quickly recognized by store clerks as a repeat customer and they tried harder to be helpful to me. The visor is also good for keeping light rain off your glasses and out of your eyes.

WORK GLOVES

You will need some heavy-duty work gloves to protect your hands when handling objects such as rough cinder blocks, splintery boards, thorny branches, and sheet metal with sharp edges. These gloves should be loose enough so that you can get them on and off easily even if your skin is wet with perspiration.

WORK SHOES

If you are working with cinder blocks, or heavy boards, it's a good idea to have sturdy work shoes. High shoes are best, especially if you have to work in loose dirt or muddy areas.

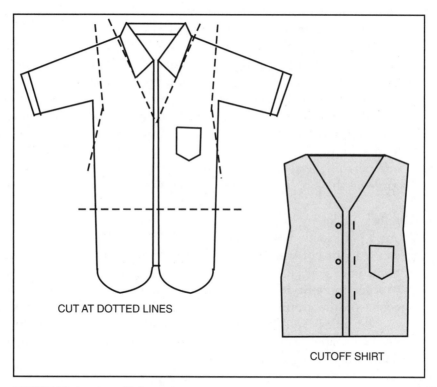

CUT AT DOTTED LINES

CUTOFF SHIRT

FIGURE 53-1   Cutoff shirt.

FOOD AND EXERCISE

FOOD

Handyman work is often quite physical. The more energy you have, the more you can get done each day and of course that means you earn more money each day. No two people are the same, but here's what I find works best for me (feel free to ignore it): Eat lots of raw fresh fruits and vegetables, whole grain cereals, whole grain bread, brown rice, and fish; no junk food, nothing made with white flour, no sugar or other sweeteners, no partially hydrogenated anything. Drink mainly water or fruit juice. Take the usual vitamins and minerals, no megadoses of anything. If there is a health food store near you, get acquainted with the people there. There is usually one person there who really knows about nutrition. Don't drink alcohol while on the job. If you like your beer, wait until you get home to indulge.

I always take my lunch with me when I work away from home. It saves time and I get exactly what I like. In cool weather, you can leave your lunch in your car. In hot weather, you should do something to keep the food cool. Sometimes you can put your food in the family's refrigerator. If not, carry your food in a Styrofoam cooler, use canned ice if convenient, and put your cooler on the ground in a shady spot. Be sure your cooler has a tightly fitting lid unless you like ants in your sandwiches. Be sure to have plenty of drinking water available in hot weather. I once drank 5 quarts of water in 4 hours when doing fence work in full sun on a hot day.

EXERCISE

If you are in good physical condition, you will be able to do more and earn more. You want good cardiovascular fitness (stepper, ski machine, jogging, stationary bike) and some upper body strength (dumbbells, pull-ups, push-ups) so that you can handle sledge hammers and heavy ladders. There is no need to handle very heavy weights, but you want to do many repetitions (reps) of each movement to develop endurance. If you have not worked out for years, start with very light weights. One of the most tiring tasks I sometimes have to do is to scrape paint on an overhead surface, such as a porch ceiling. That will make your arm, shoulder, and neck muscles scream if you have not exercised them regularly.

Rotate your muscle groups and you can work longer before fatigue sets in. On one occasion I had to move a pile of cinder blocks, cut some cordwood by hand, and dig some holes for planting bushes. I found that if I did each job for 30 minutes and then rotated to the next one, I could keep going much longer. Similarly, when I paint a house that requires some work while standing on a ladder, some work standing on the ground, and some work (basement windows) sitting on the ground, I do each type of work for half an hour and then rotate to the next.

If you smoke, try to quit.

HANDYMAN MYSTERIES

The Case of the Creeping Clock 250   The Case of the Inoperative Opener 251
The Case of the Failing Fan 251   The Case of the Leaking Light 252

As a handyman, you will occasionally come across baffling and mysterious situations. Here are four of the strangest.

THE CASE OF THE CREEPING CLOCK

My friend Charley told me that his electric clock was gaining a few minutes every day. Being rather young, and a bit overconfident, I told Charley that this was impossible. I explained that electric clocks have synchronous motors, which means that the motor rotation is tied tightly to the line frequency of the power that the electric company sends to you. And the electric company holds the line frequency constant to within a second or so per day. It is possible for a synchronous motor to *lose* time if there is an intermittent bad electrical connection or excessive friction somewhere in the clock. But *gain* time, no way. I even offered to bet Charley $100 if he could prove that the clock gained time.

Fortunately for me, Charley declined the bet. He just told me, "Take it home, plug it in, and watch it for a few days," which is what I did. And every day, that clock gained 2 or 3 minutes. I felt as though someone had told me they had invented a perpetual motion machine and then proceeded to show me one that worked.

So I watched and I watched and finally I saw what was happening. The concentric shafts that turned the hands of the clock were bent slightly; perhaps the clock had been dropped. And, when the minute hand was near 10, and the sweep second hand passed over the minute hand, it scraped against the minute hand and nudged it forward a tiny bit. In 24 hours, those little nudges added up to 2 or 3 minutes. I bent the second hand upward a millimeter or so, and the problem was solved. The moral of the story is: Listen to your customers and don't be sure you know it all, because sometimes you don't.

THE CASE OF THE FAILING FAN

On another occasion, I was given an almost new window fan. The person was discarding it because it had stopped working. When I got home and removed the blade guard the fan did not turn easily, it had to be pushed to make it move. The motor did not have a burned smell and seemed to be OK. Aha, I thought, a few drops of oil and I have a good fan. And I did, for a few days. Then it stiffened up and needed to be oiled again. That didn't make much sense.

I felt the motor when the fan was running. It was very hot, too hot to keep my hand on. That was a partial explanation; the oil was oxidizing and gumming up from the heat. So, thinking I was smart, I got out my high-temperature silicone oil and reoiled that motor. I was sure I had solved the problem. This time, the fan worked well for about a week; then even the silicone oil failed and the fan wouldn't turn.

Finally it dawned upon me that I was looking at a design flaw. The motor simply could not turn that big a fan without overheating. Fortunately, the fan was made of lightweight plastic. I took a pair of heavy scissors and, using a template to make them all the same, I cut the blades down to about two-thirds their original size. Now the motor stays cool, the fan works perfectly, and I oil it only once a year.

Does it make sense to put this much time and effort into fixing an inexpensive window fan? No. But it was a challenge and there is a certain feeling of accomplishment when you figure something out and your solution is proven to be correct.

THE CASE OF THE INOPERATIVE OPENER

A homeowner heard a loud bang in his garage. When he opened the door from the basement to the garage, he saw one of the big coil springs for his overhead door hanging by its pulley and cables. The other end of the spring had broken. He installed a new spring but the garage door opener would not work. Baffled, he called me. I checked and found power where the power cord for the opener was plugged in, but there was no power at the opener itself. I told him that, by the most bizarre and improbable of circumstances, the spring, when it broke, must have shot across the garage and struck the cord where it ran up the front wall of the garage and cut the cord even though it appeared untouched. The customer refused to believe me and I was puzzled myself. But I remembered Sherlock Holmes telling someone that when you have exhausted all possible explanations but one, that one, however unlikely, has to be the answer.

Upon very careful inspection of the power cord, we found a small, almost invisible cut in the heavy rubber jacket. The spring had hit that cord so hard that it completely cut one of the wires inside the cord. Then the heavy rubber jacket sprang back, leaving only a tiny telltale cut. After a repair to the power cord, the door resumed working.

THE CASE OF THE LEAKING LIGHT

A friend for whom I had done a lot of work called to tell me about a problem with her kitchen light.

"My kitchen light drips when I turn it on."

"Say what?"

"The light on my kitchen ceiling drips water when I turn it on."

"Does it drip all the time?"

"No, only when the light is on."

"What have you been drinking?"

"Nothing, can you come over and fix it?"

"I don't know if I can fix it, but it's worth coming over just to see it."

So I went there and we turned on the kitchen light.

Nothing happened.

"Aha."

"Wait a few minutes."

Three minutes went by, then, drip, drip, drip.

That ceiling fixture consisted of a chrome-plated metal cylinder with a bulb inside the cylinder and a glass lens at the bottom. Investigation revealed that the shower in the upstairs bathroom was leaking slightly and the water was working its way through the ceiling directly above the light fixture and accumulating inside it. You couldn't see the water because the lens had a patterned surface. Normally, the fit between the lens and the cylinder was so tight that no water could leak out. But, when the light was on for a while, the cylinder heated up and expanded and water could leak out slowly and drip onto the kitchen floor. Mystery solved.

FINAL WORDS

This book represents the experience of one person. Thomas Edison once said, "The biggest room in the world is the room for improvement." So keep an open mind, and if you think of a better way to do any of the tasks discussed in this book, try it, and if it works for you, do it your way.

I hope this book will help many people become happily and profitably employed or self-employed as handypersons. Good luck!

Many thanks to Janice Myers and Maria Rosdolsky for their editing assistance. Thanks also to my agent, Judy Buckner, for many extremely valuable suggestions.

INDEX

Adjustable end wrenches, 46, 51
Administration (*see* Business administration)
Aerators, 116
Allen wrenches, 46
Aluminum angles, 125
Aluminum-base bulbs, 219–220
Aluminum sheet, 38
Angle irons, 125
Answering machine, 175
Apprenticeship, 20–21
Approval tour, 191–192
Asbestos, 220
Assembly required, 9
Attach a screw, 205
Attics (old house), 216
Auger, 74
Auger bits, 85
Automobile repair, 10–11
Axe, 59

Baby food jars, 162
Ball peen hammer, 84, 90
Ball valve, 120
Bamboo water pipe, 205
Barrel bolts, 125–126, 130
Basement flooding, 14–15
Basin wrench, 74, 77
Batteries, 97–98
Battery charger, 155
Before you go to the job, 188–190
Before you leave the job, 191–193
Bench grinder, 82
Bicycle parts, 126
Bicycle repair, 9–10
Big paint jobs, 210–215
    brush/roller, 212
    cleaning brushes, 213–214
    cleaning roller covers, 214–215
    cleaning your skin, 215
    closing the can, 213
    paint can lids, 212–213
    paint left-handed, 211–212
    timesaving ideas, 210–211
    what color?, 212

Big wash jobs, 220
Billing the homeowner, 192–193
    (*See also* Fees)
Binder-head screw, 108
Block plane, 46
Boards, 145
Boats, 10
Bolt cutter, 84–85, 90
Bolts, 37, 104–106
Books, 21–23
Bow saws, 59–60, 63
Box wrenches, 45, 51, 85
Boxes, 159–164
Brace/auger bits, 85
Breakables, 180–181
Brick chisel, 53
Brushes, 70
Bucket dividers, 168, 171
Buckets, 155–156, 168, 171
Bulb receptacles, 98
Bundling branches, 220–221, 233
Burglar alarm, 12–13
Business administration, 194–200
    buy list, 194
    checks, 198–199
    hours file, 194–195
    maps, 195
    notetaking, 198
    phone books, 195, 199
    pocket paper, 198
    scheduling, 196–197
    time management, 194
    wall calendar, 195–196, 200
    (*See also* Operating the business)
Business cards, 172–174, 176
Business promotion (*see* Finding customers)
Butterfly bolt, 111
Butyl caulk, 132
Buy list, 194
Buying:
    fasteners, 104
    hardware, 93
    new products, 221
    paint (flea market), 236–237

Buying (*Cont.*):
   replacement parts, 221
   telephone hardware, 124
   tools, 43–44
   used tools, 237–239
   wood, 145
   work clothing, 239
BX staples, 129

C-clamps, 85, 90
Cabinet latches, 126
Cable ties, 126, 130
Calipers, 67, 68
Cannibalization, 205
Car-related items, 155
Car repair, 10–11
Carbide hacksaw blade, 85
Cardboard boxes, 160–163
Carpenters pencil, 46
Carriage bolt, 105–106
Casters, 127
Catalogs, 24
Caulk backing, 205
Caulk cartridge, 73
Caulking, 131–133
   (*See also* Painting and caulking tools)
Caulking gun, 70–71, 73
Ceiling installations, 228
Cement mix, 147–148
Cement-work tools, 53–55
   brick chisel, 53
   cold chisel, 53
   edge-rounding trowel, 53
   line-making trowel, 53
   plastic mixing tub, 54
   pointing trowel, 54
   small triangular trowel, 68, 70
   smoothing trowel, 68–69
   spray bottle, 69
   syringe, 69, 70
   wire brush, 69, 70
Center punch, 46
Chain saw, 78, 81
Chalk, 47
Chalk line, 45
Channel-lock pliers, 46
Charity work, 230
Checks, 198–199
China-marking pencil, 47
Cigar boxes, 160
Circuit breaker panels, 15
Circuit breakers, 98
Circular saw, 78, 81
Clamping device, 206
Cleaning paintbrushes, 213–214

Closet auger, 74
Clothing (*see* Work clothing)
Cold chisel, 45, 53
Cold-weather wear, 244–245
Come-along, 86
Compass, 47, 66
Compression valve, 119, 120
Computers, 222
Concrete patch, 147–148
Construction adhesive, 138
Contact-bond cement, 138
Containers, 162
Copper tubing, 117, 121
Cord and reel, 42
Cordless drill, 79, 81
Cordwood saws, 59
Correspondence courses, 25
Corrugated-cardboard boxes, 160–163
Countersink, 47
Coupler, 123
Crazy glue, 138–139
CRC, 141
Creeping clock, 250–251
Cube tap, 47
Customer information, 222–223
Customer personalities, 179–180
Customer satisfaction, 177–184
   approval tour, 191–192
   breakables, 180–181
   consideration, 177–178
   customer personalities, 179–180
   declining a job, 182–183
   difficult customers, 179–180
   friendliness, 178
   latest gadgets, 181
   politeness, 178
   recommendations, 181
   reliability, 177
   when you don't know how to fix it, 183, 226
   written estimate, 181–182, 184
Cuts (injuries), 202
Cutting plastic, 223

Deck screws, 107
Declining a job, 182–183
Dies, 88
Difficult customers, 179–180
Digging bar, 60, 63
Dimmers, 98–99
Dirt rake, 60, 64
Dividers, 66, 168, 171
Door hardware, 94–96
   door scope, 94
   doorbell, 95
   doorstops, 94–95

Door hardware (*Cont.*):
   garage door hardware, 95
   jimmy-proof lock, 95, 96
   knockers, 95
   lock cylinders, 95
   locksets, 95
   rollers, 95
   safety chains, 96
   storm door closers, 96
   storm door latches, 96
   turnbuckles, 96
Door scope, 94
Doorbell, 95
Doorbell/push button, 99
Doors that stick, 223
Doorstops, 94–95
Downspouts, 128
Drain augers, 74
Drainpipe, 206
Drill bits:
   electric drill, 79–80
   electrical work, 56–57
   toolbox, 47
Drill gauge, 67, 69
Drill press, 82
Drinking water, 39
Drive bits, 86, 90
Driving instructions, 188
Drop cloths, 71
Drop light, 36
Drywall, 148
Drywall-screw gun, 79
Drywall screws, 37, 107–108
Drywall square, 67, 69
Drywall tools, 86–87
Duct seal, 47, 148
Duct tape, 143
Dumpster devices, 224–225

Edge-rounding trowel, 53
Electric drill, 45, 79–81
Electric wire, 206
Electrical boxes, 99–100
Electrical cable, 100
Electrical outlets, 100
Electrical system (old house), 216–217
Electrical tape, 143
Electrical tester, 47, 56, 58
Electrical-work hardware, 97–103
   batteries, 97–98
   bulb receptacles, 98
   circuit breakers, 98
   dimmers, 98–99
   doorbell/push button, 99
   electrical boxes, 99–100

Electrical-work hardware (*Cont.*):
   electrical cable, 100
   electrical outlets, 100
   extension cords, 100–101
   fluorescent tubes, 101
   fuses, 98
   light bulbs, 101–102
   outdoor electrical fixtures, 102
   power strips, 102
   six-way outlets, 103
   surface-mount wiring, 103
   switches, 103
   wire nuts, 103
Electrical-work tools, 56–58
   electrical tester, 56, 58
   fish wire, 56, 58
   long drill bits, 56–57
   multitester, 57, 58
   outlet tester, 57, 58
   stud finder, 57, 58
   wire stripper, 57, 58
Electricity, 201
Electronic stud finder, 58
Epoxy, 139
Epoxy paste, 139
Epoxy putty, 136, 139
Estimate, 181–182, 184
Evening courses, 25
Exercise equipment, 11
Extension cords, 36, 100–101
Extension handles, 71
Extension ladders, 151
Eyebolts, 127
Eyeglasses, 12
Eyeglasses band, 36

Failing fan, 251
Fasteners, 104–109
   bolts, 104–106
   buying, 104
   nails, 106–107
   nuts, 106
   rivets, 107, 109
   screws, 107–108
   tacks, 109
   washers, 106
Faucet washers, 117
Fees (remuneration), 185–187
Fence hardware, 127
Fence posts, 231
Fence puller, 86
Fence staples, 129
Fiberglass fabric, 148
Fiberglass tape, 143
Files, 87

Fill valves, 118
Finding customers, 172–176
  answering machine, 175
  business cards, 172–174, 176
  car sign, 175
  friendliness, 174
  lawn sign, 175
  make an offer, 175
  newspaper advertising, 175
  realtors, 175
  storekeepers, 176
  T-shirts, 176
First aid, 202–203
Fish wire, 56, 58
5-gallon buckets, 155–156
Flammable liquids, 201
Flashlight, 36, 227
Flat-weave fiberglass fabrics, 148
Flea markets, 239–240
  (*See also* Yard sales/flea markets)
Float rods/floats, 119
Flooding, 14–15
Fluidmaster valve, 118
Fluorescent tubes, 101
Flush handles, 118–119
Flush valve, 119
Food/exercise, 248–249
45-degree cut, 204–205
Framing square, 67, 69, 87
Fuses, 98

Galvanized steel strapping, 148
Garage door hardware, 95
Gardening tools, 59–65
  axe, 59
  bow saws, 59–60, 63
  digging bar, 60–63
  dirt rake, 60, 64
  grass rake, 60, 64
  hand trowel, 60
  hatchet, 60
  hedge shears, 60
  hedge trimmer, 60
  hoe, 61
  hole digger, 61, 63
  lopping shears, 61, 63
  paint tools white, 62
  pick, 61, 65
  pole pruner, 61, 65
  pruning shears, 62
  shovel, 62, 64
  sickle, 62, 65
  spading fork, 62, 64
Gas appliances, 201
Glass cutter, 87

Glazier's putty, 136
Glazing compound, 136
Glue, 138–140
Glue gun, 139–140
Goop, 139
Grass rake, 60, 64
Guarantee, 227
Gutter-cleaning tool, 87, 91
Gutter seal caulk, 132
Gutters, 128

Hacksaw, 46
Half-round file, 46
Halogen work light, 156
Hammer drill, 80, 81
Hammer handle, 206
Hand trowel, 60
Hand truck, 156–158
Handle puller, 75, 77
Handles, 127
Handset cord, 123
Handy, 26
Handy box, 99
Handyman:
  food/exercise, 248–249
  frequently requested jobs, 4–19
  getting started, 4
  pros/cons, 2–3
  what one does, 1
  who should be one, 1
  why needed, 2
  (*See also* Operating the business)
Handyman Club of America, 25
Handyman mysteries, 250–253
  creeping clock, 250–251
  failing fan, 251
  inoperative opener, 251–252
  leaking light, 252–253
Handyman's vehicle, 31–42
Hanging objects on walls, 110–113
Hardware:
  angle iron/aluminum angles, 125
  barrel bolts, 125–126, 130
  bicycle parts, 126
  buying, 93
  cabinet latches, 126
  cable ties, 126, 130
  casters, 127
  door, 94–96
    (*See also* Door hardware)
  electrical work, 97–103
    (*See also* Electrical-work hardware)
  eyebolts, 127
  fasteners, 104–109
    (*See also* Fasteners)

Hardware (*Cont.*):
  fence, 127
  handles, 127
  hanging objects on walls, 110–113
  hasps, 127, 130
  hinges, 127
  hose clamps, 127, 130
  hose-repair, 114–115
  knobs, 127
  lamp parts, 128
  magnetic latches, 128
  padlocks, 128
  plumbing, 116–121
    (*See also* Plumbing hardware)
  pulleys, 128
  sink, 117–118
  springs, 128–129
  standards/brackets for shelving, 129
  staples, 129
  telephone, 122–124
    (*See also* Telephone hardware)
  toilet, 118–119
  turnbuckles, 129, 130
  window locks, 129
Hasps, 127, 130
Hatchet, 60
Heat-proof grease, 48
Hedge shears, 60
Hedge trimmer, 60
Hex key wrenches, 46
Hinge pin, 206
Hinges, 127
Hoe, 61
Hole digger, 61, 63
Home centers, 25
Home office, organizing, 17
Home security, 12–13
Hooks, 167
Hose clamps, 127, 130
Hose hanger, 114
Hose washers, 48, 114
Hot-melt glue gun, 139–140
Hot-weather wear, 245
Hours file, 194–195
House for sale, 18
House numbers, 206, 227–228
How-to books, 22–24
How-to video cassettes/CDs, 29
Hurricane, 13

Ice pick, 48
Improvising, 204–209
  attach a screw, 205
  bamboo water pipe, 205
  cannibalization, 205

Improvising (*Cont.*):
  caulk backing, 205
  clamping device, 206
  drainpipe, 206
  electric wire, 206
  final words, 254
  45-degree cut, 204–205
  hammer handle, 206
  hinge pin, 206
  house numbers, 206
  Madison bars, 207
  missing shingle, 207
  O ring that leaks, 207
  oil, 207
  paintbrush, 207
  Phillips screwdriver, 208
  pilot light, 208
  sawhorses, 208
  small hole, 208
  tub drain leak, 208–209
  washers, 209
  water valve, 209
Inaccurate customer information, 222–223
Inadequate knowledge of project, 225
Information sources, 20–30
Inoperative opener, 251–252
Insulated staples, 129
Insulating pipes, 17–18
Internet, 26

Jack, 122
Jewelry repair, 14
Jimmy-proof lock, 95, 96
Jumper cables, 155

Knee pads, 38
Knobs, 127
Knockers, 95

Ladder mitts, 152, 153
Ladder safety, 203
Ladder stabilizers, 152, 153
Ladders, 151–153, 203
Lag bolts, 108
Lag screws, 108
Lamp parts, 128
Latches, 126, 128, 172, 174
Latest gadgets, 181
Latex caulk, 131
Layout and measuring tools, 66–69
  compass, 66
  dividers, 66
  drill gauge, 67, 69
  drywall square, 67, 69
  framing square, 67, 69

Layout and measuring tools (*Cont.*):
    level gauge, 66, 68
    outside calipers, 67, 68
    protractor, 67, 69
    speed square, 67, 69
    steel measuring tape, 67
    straightedge, 67
    triangles, 67
Leaking light, 252–253
Left-handed painting, 211–212
Letterhead, 192
Level, 48, 89
Level gauge, 66, 68
Light bulbs, 101–102
Light household oil, 141
Line cord, 123
Line level, 48
Line-making trowel, 53
Line tester, 123
Lock cylinders, 95
Locksets, 95
Long drill bits, 56–57
Lopping shears, 38, 61, 63
Lubricants, 141–142
Lubricating household devices, 16
Lubricating oil, 48

Machine screws, 37, 105
Madison bars, 207
Magazines, 26
Magnet, 38
Magnetic latches, 128
Maps, 188, 195
Masking tape, 143
Mathematical symbols, 163
Measuring tape, 48
Measuring tools (*see* Layout and measuring tools)
Metal punch, 87, 91
Metal-sash putty, 136
Metal strapping, 148
Metric bolts, 106
Missing shingle, 207
Modular handset cord, 123
Moly bolts, 111, 113
Mortar mix, 147–148
Moving-day assistance, 16
Multimeter, 57
Multiple ways to do a job, 228
Multitester, 57, 58
Murphy's law jobs, 228–229
Mysteries (*see* Handyman mysteries)

Nail set, 48
Nails, 106–107
New installations, 229–230

Newspaper advertising, 175
Newspapers, 27
Noise reduction, 16
Notetaking, 198
Nuts, 106

O ring that leaks, 207
Octagon box, 99
Oil, 207
Old house vs. new house, 216–218
    attics, 216
    doors, 216
    electrical system, 216–217
    paint, 217
    plumbing system, 217–218
    walls, 218
One-piece phone, 124
Operating the business:
    approval tour, 191–192
    billing the homeowner, 192–193
    charity work, 230
    clothing, 239, 243–247
    customer satisfaction, 177–184
      (*See also* Customer satisfaction)
    declining a job, 182–183
    fees, 185–187
    finding customers, 172–176
    food/exercise, 248–249
    guarantee, 227
    hardware (*see* Hardware)
    improvising, 204–209
      (*See also* Improvising)
    knowledge acquisition, 20–30
    receipts, 242
    record keeping, 241–242
    safety, 201–203
    storage, 159–164
    taxes, 242
    tools (*see* Tools)
    vehicle, 31–42
    when business is slow, 232
    written estimate, 181–182, 184
    before you go to the job, 188–190
    before you leave the job, 191–193
    (*See also* Handyman)
Outdoor electrical fixtures, 102
Outdoor play equipment, 17
Outdoor table, 157
Outlet tester, 48, 57, 58
Outside calipers, 67, 68
Overlay map, 235

Packaging tape, 144
Padlocks, 128
Paint, 134–137

Paint brush extender, 71, 72
Paint can lids, 212–213
Paint can openers, 49, 71
Paint jobs (see Big paint jobs)
Paint stirrers, 39
Paint tray, 72
Paintbrush, 207
Painting and caulking tools,
        70–73
    brushes, 70
    caulking gun, 70–71, 73
    drop cloths, 71
    extension handles, 71
    paint brush extender, 71, 72
    paint can opener, 71
    paint tray, 72
    roller, 72
    roller covers, 72
    scraper, 72, 73
    wire brush, 73
Pamphlets, 27
Pancake box, 99
Paraffin wax, 141
Patching cement, 148
Patching plaster, 149–150
Patio furniture springs, 128
Pest control, 17–18
Phenoseal, 132
Phillips bits, 49
Phillips screwdriver, 208
Phone books, 195, 199
Phone jack, 122
Pick, 61, 65
Picture hangers, 112, 113
Pilot light, 208
Pipe clamps, 157, 158
Pipe-threading tools, 75
Pipe wrenches, 46, 75, 77
Plane, 46
Plastic compartment boxes, 160
Plastic containers, 162
Plastic mixing tub, 54
Pliers, 46
Plumber's heat-proof grease, 142
Plumber's putty, 136
Plumbing hardware, 116–121
    aerators, 116
    copper tubing, 117, 121
    faucet washers, 117
    flexible supply hoses, 117
    showerheads, 117
    sink hardware, 117–118
    toilet hardware, 118–119
    valve seats, 120–121
    valves, 119–120

Plumbing system (old house), 217–218
Plumbing tools, 74–77
    basin wrench, 74, 77
    closet auger, 74
    drain augers, 74
    handle puller, 75, 77
    pipe-threading tools, 75
    pipe wrenches, 75, 77
    plunger, 75
    propane torch, 75–76
    seat wrenches, 76, 77
    spud wrenches, 76, 77
    stem wrenches, 76, 77
    tubing cutter, 76, 77
Plunger, 75
Plywood, 145–146
Pocket paper, 198
Pocketknife, 230
Pointing, 54
Pointing trowel, 54
Pole pruner, 61, 65
Polyseamseal, 132
Polyurethane, 132
Pop-riveting tool, 107, 109
Pop rivets, 107, 109
Popular Mechanics, 26
Popular Science, 26
Popular Woodworking, 26
Portable folding worktable, 157
Portable power tools, 78–81
    chain saw, 78, 81
    circular saw, 78, 81
    cordless drill, 79, 81
    drywall-screw gun, 79
    electric drill, 79–81
    hammer drill, 80, 81
    reciprocating saw, 80, 81
    router, 80
    saber saw, 81
Power drop, 17
Power strips, 102
Power tools, 78–83
    (See also Portable power tools; Stationary
        power tools)
Practical business tips (see Operating the business)
Pressure-treated wood, 146
Pro bono, 230
Propane torch, 75–76
Protractor, 67, 69
Pruning shears, 62
Pry bar, 88, 91
Pulleys, 128
Purchases (see Buying)
Putty, 136
Putty knife, 49

Racks, 167–168
Radial-arm saw, 83
Rafter angle square, 69
Rags, 39
Rat-tail file, 49
Realtors, 175
Reassembly, 231
Receipts, 242
Reciprocating saw, 80, 81
Recommendations, 181
Record keeping, 241–242
Refill valves, 118
Reliability, 177
Remuneration (fees), 185–187
Rental center, 27
Replacement parts, 221
Rivets, 107, 109
Roller, 72
Roller covers, 72
Rollers, 95
Romex staples, 129
Roof repair, 11–12
Rope, 157
Round file, 49
Router, 80
Rugs, 40–41

Saber saw, 81
Safety, 201–203
Safety chains, 96
Safety goggles, 41
Sales clerks, 27–28
Sandpaper, 39, 149
Sash chain, 149
Saw:
    bow, 59–60, 63
    chain, 78, 81
    circular, 78, 81
    hacksaw, 46
    radial-arm, 83
    reciprocating, 80, 81
    saber, 81
    table, 83
Sawhorses, 158, 208
Scavenging, 224
Scheduling, 196–197
Scissors, 49
SCORE, 28
Scraper, 72, 73
Screw eyes, 112, 113
Screw-in hooks, 112, 113
Screw-in outlet, 49
Screwdriver, 49
Screws, 107–108
Screws, not nails or glue, 230–231

Seat wrenches, 76, 77
Sharpening stone, 50
Sharpening tools, 18
Sheds, 19
Sheet metal, 149
Sheet metal screws, 108
Shelf brackets, 129
Shelf-support bracket, 170
Shelves, 165–167, 169, 170
Shoe boxes, 160
Shovel, 62, 64
Showerheads, 117
Sickle, 62, 65
Silicone caulk, 131–132
Silicone grease, 48
Silicone lubricant, 39, 142
Sink hardware, 117–118
6-volt lantern, 227
Six-way outlets, 103
Sledge hammer, 88
Small hole, 208
Small triangular trowel, 53, 54
Smoothing trowel, 68–69
Snakes, 74
Socket wrenches, 41
Solderless connectors, 103
Sources of information, 20–30
Spackling compound, 149–150
Spading fork, 62, 64
Speed square, 67, 69
Splinters, 203
Splitting wedge, 88
Spray bottle, 69
Spray paints, 135–136
Springs, 128–129
Spud wrench, 76, 77
Square, 46
Stainless steel strapping, 148
Standard-and-bracket shelf system, 129
Staple gun, 88, 92
Staples, 129
Stationary power tools, 82–83
Steel measuring tape, 67
Stem wrenches, 76, 77
Stepladders, 151
Stop and waste valves, 120
Storage:
    boxes, 159–164
    buckets, 168, 171
    hooks, 167
    racks, 167–168
    shelves, 165–167, 169, 170
Storage systems, 19
Storekeepers, 176
Storm door closers, 96

Storm door latches, 96
Storm door springs, 128
Straightedge, 67
Stud finder, 50, 57, 58
Studs, 146
Sunscreen, 202
Superglue, 138–139
Surface-mount wiring, 103
Switch box, 99
Switches, 103
Syringe, 54, 55

T-shirts, 176
Table saw, 83
Tacks, 109
Taking things apart, 231
Tape, 143–144
Taps, 88
Taxes, 242
Teflon tape, 50
Telephone cable staples, 129
Telephone hardware, 165–169
    adapter, 123
    buying, 124
    coupler, 123
    final test, 124
    handset cord, 123
    line cord, 123
    line tester, 123
    one-piece phone, 124
    phone jack, 122
    telephone wire, 122
    wire stripper, 123
    wiring diagram, 124
Telephone wire, 122
Telephones, 19
Television shows, 29
Three-corner scraper, 72, 73
3-foot level, 89
Three-ring notebook, 241
3-way switch, 103
Tile cutter, 89
Time management, 194
Tin snips, 46
Tips (see Operating the business)
Toggle bolt, 111
Toggle switch, 103
Toilet hardware, 118–119
Toilet-seat bolts, 119
Toolbox, 45–51
Tools:
    ball peen hammer, 84, 90
    bolt cutter, 84–85, 90
    box wrenches, 85
    brace/auger bits, 85

Tools (Cont.):
    buying, 43–44
    C-clamps, 85, 90
    carbide hacksaw blade, 85
    cement-work, 53–55
    come-along, 86
    drive bits, 86, 90
    drywall, 86, 90
    electrical-work, 56–58
    files, 87
    framing square, 87
    gardening, 59–65
    glass cutter, 87
    gutter-cleaning, 87, 91
    layout/measuring, 66–69
    marking the, 89
    metal punch, 87, 91
    organizing, 52
    painting/caulking, 70–73
    plumbing, 74–77
    power, 78–83
    pry bar, 88, 91
    sledge hammer, 88
    splitting wedge, 88
    staple gun, 88, 92
    taps/dies, 88
    3-foot level, 89
    tile cutter, 89
    toolbox, 45–51
    vise grips, 89
    wood rasp, 89
    wrecking bar, 89, 92
    (See also specific tools)
Tornadoes, 13
Torpedo level, 48
Trash, 190, 224
Trash and dumpsters, 28
Trees (see Gardening tools)
Triangles, 67
Trouble light, 36
Trowel, 53–55, 60
Try square, 69
Tub drain leak, 208–209
Tubing cutter, 76, 77
Turkey baster, 54
Turnbuckles, 96, 129, 130
TV shows, 29
12-volt tester, 155
Two-faced foam tape, 144

Used tools, 237–239
Utility knives, 50, 51

Valve seats, 120–121
Valves, 118–120

Vinyl sheet, 39
Vinyl siding, 150
Vise, 154, 158
Vise grips, 89
Volt-ohm-milliammeter (VOM), 57

Wall calendar, 195–196, 200
Walls (old house), 218
Washers, 106, 209
Water valve, 209
WD40, 141
Wedge, 42
When you don't know it works, 183, 226
Window balance springs, 129
Window locks, 129
Wire, 150
Wire brush, 55, 73
Wire nuts, 50, 103
Wire stripper, 50, 57, 58, 123
Wood, 40, 145–146
Wood chisel, 50
Wood rasp, 89
Wood screws, 108
Work clothing, 239, 243–247
    belt, 243
    blue jeans, 244
    buying, 239
    cold-weather wear, 244–245
    hot-weather wear, 245
    kneepads, 246

Work clothing (*Cont.*):
    layered look, 246
    T-shirt, 246
    tool belt, 246
    visor, 246
    work gloves, 247
    work shoes, 247
Workbench, 26
Workbench with vise, 154
Workmate, 157
Wrecking bar, 89, 92
Wrench:
    Allen, 46
    box, 45, 85
    end, 46
    pipe, 46
    plumbing, 74–77
    socket, 41
Written estimate, 181–182, 184

Yard sales/flea markets, 234–240
    antiques/collectibles, 240
    bargaining, 236
    items to take with you, 234–236
    paint, 236–237
    people you meet, 239–240
    used tools, 237–239
    work clothing, 239
Yellow carpenter's glue, 140